SPINOZA
Dictionary

Edited by
Dagobert D. Runes

With a Foreword by
ALBERT EINSTEIN

PHILOSOPHICAL LIBRARY
New York

ISBN: 978-0-8065-2964-6

PRINTED IN THE UNITED STATES OF AMERICA

FOREWORD

I HAVE READ THE SPINOZA DICTIONARY with great care. It is, in my opinion, a valuable contribution to philosophical literature. Spinoza is, among the great classical thinkers, one of the least accessible because of his rigid adherence to the geometric form of argumentation, in which form he obviously saw somewhat of an insurance against fallacies. In fact, Spinoza thereby made it difficult for the reader who all too quickly loses patience and breath before he reaches the heart of the philosopher's ideas.

Many have attempted to present Spinoza's thoughts in modern language—a daring as well as irreverent enterprise which offers no guarantee against misinterpretation. Yet throughout Spinoza's writings one will find sharp and clear propositions which are masterpieces of concise formulation.

In the book before us no one has the word but Spinoza himself. In alphabetical order one will find definitions, propositions and explanations in Spinoza's own words which interpret essential issues in a manner comparatively easy to comprehend, avoiding forbidding formalism.

It certainly is not the purpose of the editor to make, through this book, the study of the original works superfluous. If however the reader despairs of the business of finding his way through Spinoza's works, here he will find a reliable guide. Where there is still lack of clarity this is caused only by the fact that Spinoza himself in his struggle for clarity did not reach full perfection.

Here one will find, for instance, detailed statements about "substance" and "modes" where one can notice the hard struggle. Here one finds the majestic concept that thinking (soul) and extension (naturalistically conceived world) are only different forms of appearance resp. conceptual interpretations of the same "substance". (In expressing it this way, however, I have committed the very sin I mentioned above.) Well, everyone may interpret Spinoza's text in his own way. It is certain that our philosopher had fully recognized the senselessness of the question of an interaction of soul and body, as well as the problem which of both be the "primary".

The grand ideas of the *Ethics* are brought out clearly in the book, not less than the heroic illusions of this great and passionate man.

ALBERT EINSTEIN

Princeton, 1951

By Way of Introduction

It is with a certain amount of hesitance that I bring this small book before the general public. I had planned and prepared it, originally, for some of my friends who were desirous of becoming acquainted with the philosophy of our most well-known but least-read thinker. They, like many others, felt the spark that blinked through the massive, rigid structure of Spinoza's writings, but in spite of the serious efforts of many of them, they did not feel that they had succeeded in breaking through the terminological walls of the philosopher.

As a writer, Spinoza is a difficult man to comprehend. He set down his sentences cagily, in a circumscribed manner, and hintfully, sometimes allegorically, sometimes mockingly, often with tongue in cheek, and where permissible, with majestic grace and finality. Unlike other cardinal thinkers, he had no gift for word creation. There are so many new concepts in his metaphysical web, but hardly a single new term or word. He borrowed his words from the Atomists of ancient Greece, the Stoics, the scholastic theologians, as well as from his Hebrew predecessors: Maimonides, Averroes, Crescas, and of course, the Frenchman Descartes.

This policy of word borrowing is quite confounding to the novice in the study of Spinoza, and it has confused even experienced students of philosophy, so much more so as our author felt obliged to adopt for his dissertations the then modish manner of writing *more geometrico*. One must bear in mind when reading Spinoza that he was a much watched man in a very watchful time. Some of his close friends were put to severe physical torture by the Dutch authorities. Our author had only one of his works published during his lifetime, although a number of them were ready for publication for many years. In some manner, however, Spinoza and the other thoughtful men of his time managed to put ideas and hand-copied manuscripts into circulation by way of a considerable underground machinery. Many important books of that time were known to hundreds of men before they received the public impress of printer's ink.

It is obvious that since such conditions prevailed even in comparatively enlightened seventeenth century Holland, Spinoza put down many of his ideas *sub rosa*.

As if these obstacles were not enough, we face, in the study of Spinoza, another, his quarrels with the Jewish community.

Spinoza, who died at the early age of forty-five, was a descendant of rather poor Portuguese exiles, who had escaped the zealots of the Catholic Iberian Peninsula gone berserk with pillaging, expulsion, torture and *auto da fé*. Some of those who escaped the most ungracious interpreters of Christian grace found asylum in Holland, which was then seething with Socinians, Mennonites, Puritans and other seekers of a Christian life that would no longer make a cruel mockery of the tenets of the Lord.

The Jews in Holland and the other countries of Western Europe lived in daily terror of their unfathomable Christian neighbors who, at the drop of some vile man's ugly word, would throw them [the Jews] into torturous dungeons or tie them to a spit and burn alive whimpering humans as you might roast a pig. And from the East of Europe came equally horrifying news of hordes of Cossack troops invading the defenseless ghettos of Poland, massacring the "pagan" Jews—men, women and children—upon the open invitation and with the fatherly blessings of the Russian Czar, the devout head of the Orthodox Church of the Christian Slavs.

BY WAY OF INTRODUCTION

In those fearful days we find Baruch Spinoza, a Talmudic student in Amsterdam. There is actually little known as to how and why and when young Spinoza became involved in the activities of Socinians and other church groups of that city. But involved he became, and, after he had deserted his Jewish school (later, after the death of his father, even the Synagogue) it became known around town that the youth was doing considerable preaching of some peculiar text. The Jews of seventeenth century Amsterdam, as well as all the Jews of the *Diaspora,* had become accustomed to men and women who preferred the comparative safety of a superficially adopted dominant faith to living dangerously as a Jew in a Christian world. The Jews would cross those persons off their books, interpreting such reneging as purification of their community from the weaklings and opportunists.

But Spinoza, following in some way in the footsteps of that renegade, Uriel da Costa, was not and did not become a convert in the usual sense. Had he done so, the Jewish community would have treated him as it had all other runaways—with indifference. But Spinoza remained a Jew, although he walked about propagating a threatening gospel, namely, that the Jewish Torah, the Book of Law, was written merely as a state law and was to be regarded only as such and nothing else, and inasmuch as the Jewish state had ceased to exist, the Jews of the world were no longer bound by the laws of the Torah. The Torah, in his opinion, was written, designed and meant for the physical comfort and security of the State of Israel, while, on the other hand, the New Testament bears witness to God's revelation to Jesus Christ, Whose voice, therefore, was to be regarded as no more and no less than the voice of God Himself. *Vox Christi est vox Dei.*

What made Spinoza yearn for such distinction between the Old and New Testaments we do not know—a distinction which would have been utterly alien to Jesus, who said: "I did not come to destroy the Torah, but to fulfill it."

However, Spinoza did not see eye-to-eye with either Christ or Paul on the meaning and origin of the Old Testament. Spinoza's dissension from fundamental Judaism would have meant nothing to the Jews of Amsterdam had not Spinoza gone about town buttonholing, with a strong and Talmudically trained mind, bewildered Jewish adolescents, trying to persuade them to disregard the laws of the Torah as being obsolete; this without thinking that thus he would leave the widely dispersed and cruelly suppressed tribes of Israel without their great inner refuge. To the Jews of Israel, then as now and ever before and ever after, the Torah meant the binding (*religio*) between man and man, family and family, tribe and tribe, over all continents. To the Jews in the mansions of England, in the ghettos of New York, in the dust of the market place of Yemen, in the native quarters of Morocco, in the universities of Italy, the Torah is the one book in their blood-spattered history that holds them together.

This ancient heritage, as first revealed to the bewildered people of the desert, chosen by Him as the instrument with which to destroy the polytheistic temples of a pagan world—this immeasurable heritage is symbolized in the Torah, the Books of Wisdom, the Admonitions of the Prophets, and the rest of the God-inspired literature which, for want of a better name, we still call the Bible [*biblion*, which is Greek for *book*], and the Jews, wherefrom the Lord chose a son, are still the People of the Book. From this people, his own people, Spinoza wanted to take the Book.

Perhaps the Jews of Amsterdam should have let the young man go about his fantastic preaching, which surely would have been in vain. But the Jews were terrified at the mere thought that one of their own would want to steal that Book from them, that Book for which so many of their tribe had perished at the stake. They offered the irreverent a bribe. They even tried to assassinate him. And finally, they placed over him the ban by which no Jew could either speak with him or approach him. For he was driven from the tribe of Israel, a renegade and dangerous traitor. Spinoza was only twenty-six when the Jews cast him out of their ranks. He wrote an irate *Apologia*, defending his rather untenable position. Unfortunately this essay, written in Spanish, the language of the Inquisitors, has not been found. Spinoza never forgot his accusers and in his *Tractatus Theologico-Politicus*, a much, much later book, he still deals most negatively with orthodox Jewry. It is significant that Spinoza posits in this work the only condition under which the Torah, in his opinion, might become valid again, namely, through the re-creation of a Jewish state which, he meditates, is quite a possibility, considering the changing fortunes of world history. Well, the Jewish state has been re-created, and the Torah is valid again, even according to doubting Baruch, and all is well that ends well. The Jews have long forgiven Spinoza his juvenile paradoxisms and at the three hundredth anniversary of his birth, in 1932, he was publicly taken back into the Jewish fold by a duly representative assembly at the Hebrew University in Jerusalem.

*   *   *

I have mentioned these semi-tragic events in Spinoza's life because they have direct bearing upon some of his writings. We must take many of Spinoza's theological propositions with a grain of salt, as they were written by an outwardly cold and collected person, in whose heart burned a volcano of fire, love, devotion and pride. It was Nietzsche who first pointed out that Spinoza never forgave his people the excommunication.

I should also like to state at this time that there is as little true evidence to be found of Spinoza having been a lonely recluse, as there is truth in statements of some ill-wishing contemporaries that he was a sinner and scoundrel. Spinoza was not a lonely man; he had many, many friends, —personal friends and social acquaintances, undoubtedly more than you and I can call our own. The wardrobe found at the time of his death indicates that he was neither impoverished nor dressed like a hermit.

I hope that a perusal of this small dictionary will indicate to the reader that only a man troubled by great desires and deep emotions would give so much of his mental efforts to clarifying his inner life and desires; only a man plagued by the devil could find the path that angels tread.

D. D. R.

Acknowledgments

The following translations were used as a basis for this edition:

The Chief Works of Benedict de Spinoza, translated from the Latin, with an introduction by R. H. M. Elwes; London: George Bell & Sons. Volume I: Introduction, Tractatus Theologico-Politicus, Tractatus Politicus. Second edition, revised. 1887; Volume II: De Intellectus Emendatione — Ethica. (Select Letters). Third edition. 1889. *Spinoza's Short Treatise on God, Man, & His Well-Being,* translated and edited, with an introduction and commentary and a life of Spinoza by A. Wolf; London: Adam and Charles Black. 1910.

Only unavoidable changes were made by the editor. Those changes are based on the C. H. Bruder edition, *Opera quae supersunt omnia,* 3 volumes, Leipzig, 1843-46.

KEY TO REFERENCES

C-PB—*Correspondence with Peter Balling.*

C-B—*Correspondence with Blyenbergh.*

C-HB—*Correspondence with Hugo Boxel.*

C-IB—*I. B. has been identified by some with John Bredenburg, a citizen of Rotterdam, who translated into Latin (1675) a Dutch attack on the Tractatus Theologico-Politicus, but the tone of the letter renders this improbable. Murr and Van Vloten think that I. B. may be the physician, John Bresser, who prefixed some verses to the "Principles of Cartesian Philosophy."*

C-F—*Correspondence with Fabritius.*

C-CH—*Correspondence with Christian Huyghens.*

C-JJ—*Correspondence with Jarig Jellis.*

C-LM—*Correspondence with Lewis Meyer.*

C-O—*Correspondence with Oldenburg.*

C-GHS—*Correspondence with G. H. Schaller.*

C-T—*Correspondence with Tschirnhausen.*

C-S DE V—*Correspondence with Simon de Vries.*

E-I—*The Ethics. (Part I)*

E-II—*Of the Nature and Origin of the Mind. (Part II)*

E-III—*On the Origin and Nature of the Emotions. (Part III)*

E-IV—*Of Human Bondage, or the Strength of the Emotions. (Part IV)*

E-V—*Of Human Freedom. (Part V)*

G-1—*God, Book 1.*

G-2—*God, Book 2.*

P-T—*A Political Treatise.*

T-P—*Theologico-Political Treatise.*

U—*On the Improvement of the Understanding.*

A

ADEQUATE CAUSE

By an *adequate* cause, I mean a cause through which its effect can be clearly and distinctly perceived. By an *inadequate* or partial cause, I mean a cause through which, by itself, its effect cannot be understood.   —E-III

ADEQUATE IDEAS

Between a true and an adequate idea, I recognize no difference, except that the epithet true only has regard to the agreement between the idea and its object, whereas the epithet adequate has regard to the nature of the idea in itself; so that in reality there is no difference between a true and an adequate idea beyond this extrinsic relation. However, in order that I may know, from which idea out of many all the properties of its object may be deduced, I pay attention to one point only, namely, that the idea or definition should express the efficient cause of its object. For instance, in inquiring into the properties of a circle, I ask, whether from the idea of a circle, that it consists of infinite right angles, I can deduce all its properties. I ask, I repeat, whether this idea involves the efficient cause of a circle. If it does not, I look for another, namely, that a circle is the space described by a line, of which one point is fixed, and the other movable. As this definition explains the efficient cause, I know that I can deduce from it all the properties of a circle. So, also, when I define God as a supremely perfect Being, then, since that definition does not express the efficient cause (I mean the efficient cause internal as well as external) I shall not be able to infer therefrom all the properties of God; as I can, when I define God as a Being.

I assert, that from certain properties of any particular thing (whatever idea be given) some things may be discovered more readily, others with more difficulty, though all are concerned with the nature of the thing. I think it need only be observed, that an idea should be sought for of such a kind, that all properties may be inferred, as has been said above. He, who is about to deduce all the properties of a particular thing, knows that the ultimate properties will necessarily be the most difficult to discover.   —C-LXIV T

The activities of the mind arise solely from adequate ideas; the passive states of the mind depend solely on inadequate ideas.   —E-III

There is no modification of the body, whereof we cannot form some clear and distinct conception.

Hence it follows that there is no emotion, whereof we cannot form some clear and distinct conception. For an emotion is the idea of a modification of the body, and must therefore involve some clear and distinct conception.

Seeing that there is nothing which is not followed by an effect, and that we clearly and distinctly understand whatever follows from an idea, which in us is adequate, it follows that everyone has the power of clearly and distinctly understanding himself and his emotions, if not absolutely, at any rate in part, and consequently of bringing it about, that he should become less subject to them. To attain this result, therefore, we must chiefly direct our efforts to acquiring, as far as possible, a clear and distinct knowledge of every emotion, in order that the mind may thus, through emotion, be determined to think of those things which it clearly and distinctly perceives, and wherein it fully acquiesces: and thus that the emotion itself may be separated from the thought of an external cause, and may be associated with true thoughts; whence it will come to pass, not only that love, hatred, &c. will be destroyed, but also that the appetites or desires, which are wont to arise from such emotion, will become incapable of being excessive. For it must be especially remarked, that the appetite through which a man is said to be active, and that through which he is said to be passive is one and the same. For instance, we have shown that human nature is so constituted, that everyone desires his fellow-men to live after his own fashion; in a man, who is not guided by reason, this appetite is a passion which is called ambition, and does not greatly differ from pride; whereas in a man, who lives by the dictates of reason, it is an activity or virtue which is called piety. In like manner all appetites or desires are only passions, in so far as they spring from inadequate ideas; the same results are accredited to virtue, when they are aroused or created by adequate ideas. For all desires, whereby we are determined to any given action, may arise as much from adequate as from inadequate ideas. Than this remedy for the emotions (to return to the point from which I started), which consists in a true knowledge thereof, nothing more excellent, being within our power, can be devised. For the mind has no other power save that of thinking and of forming adequate ideas. —E-V

ADMIRATION
See Rational Life

AFFECTIONS
Different men may be differently affected by the same object, and the same man may be differently affected at different times by the same object.

We thus see that it is possible, that what one man loves another may hate, and that what one man fears another may not fear; or, again, that one and the same man may love what he once hated, or may be bold where he once was timid, and so on. Again, as everyone judges according to his emotions what is good, what bad, what better, and what worse, it follows that men's judgments may vary no less than their emotions, hence when we compare some with others, we distinguish them solely by the diversity of their emotions, and style some intrepid, others timid, others by some other epithet. —E-III

AFFECTS

Whatsoever disposes the human body, so as to render it capable of being affected in an increased number of ways, is useful to man; and is so, in proportion as the body is thereby rendered more capable of being affected or affecting other bodies in an increased number of ways; contrariwise, whatsoever renders the body less capable in this respect is hurtful to man. —E-IV

Towards something future, which we conceive as close at hand, we are affected more intensely, than if we conceive that its time for existence is separated from the present by a longer interval; so too by the remembrance of what we conceive to have not long passed away we are affected more intensely, than if we conceive that it has long passed away. —E-IV

AFFIRMATION
See Ideas; Will

ALLIES
See Democracy

AMAZONS
See Women

AMBITION

Ambition is the immoderate desire for power.

Ambition is the desire, whereby all the emotions are fostered and strengthened; therefore this emotion can with difficulty be overcome. For, so long as a man is bound by any desire, he is at the same time necessarily bound by this. "The best men," says Cicero, "are especially led by honor.

SPINOZA DICTIONARY

Even philosophers, when they write a book condemning
honor, sign their names thereto," and so on.　　　—E-III

We endeavor to do whatsoever we conceive others to
regard with pleasure, and contrariwise we shrink from doing that which we conceive men to shrink from.

This endeavor to do a thing or leave it undone, solely
in order to please men, we call *ambition*, especially when
we so eagerly endeavor to please the vulgar, that we do or
omit certain things to our own or another's hurt: in other
cases it is generally called *kindliness*.　　　—E-III

See Adequate Ideas; Emotions; Love; Lust

AMOS

See Words

ANGER

The endeavor to injure one whom we hate is called
Anger; the endeavor to repay in kind injury done to ourselves is called *Revenge*.　　　—E-III

Anger is the desire, whereby through hatred we are induced to injure one whom we hate.　　　—E-III

See Enmity; Hate

ANTIPATHY

Simply from the fact that we conceive, that a given object has some point of resemblance with another object
which is wont to affect the mind pleasurably or painfully,
although the point of resemblance be not the efficient cause
of the said emotions, we shall still regard the first-named
object with love or hate.　　　—E-III

It may happen, that we love or hate a thing without any
cause for our emotion being known to us; merely, as the
phrase is, from *sympathy* or *antipathy*. We should refer to
the same category those objects, which affect us pleasurably
or painfully, simply because they resemble other objects

[5]

which affect us in the same way. I am aware that certain authors, who were the first to introduce these terms "sympathy" and "antipathy," wished to signify thereby some occult qualities in things; nevertheless I think we may be permitted to use the same terms to indicate known or manifest qualities. —E-III

APPETITE

Endeavor, when referred solely to the mind, is called *will*, when referred to the mind and body in conjunction it is called *appetite*; it is, in fact, nothing else but man's essence, from the nature of which necessarily follow all those results which tend to its preservation; and which man has thus been determined to perform.

Further, between appetite and desire there is no difference, except that the term desire is generally applied to men, in so far as they are conscious of their appetite, and may accordingly be thus defined: *Desire is appetite with consciousness thereof.* It is thus plain from what has been said, that in no case do we strive for, wish for, long for, or desire anything, because we deem it to be good, but on the other hand we deem a thing to be good, because we strive for it, wish for it, long for it, or desire it. —E-III

See Desire

APPROVAL

If we conceive that anything pleasurably affects some object of our love, we shall be affected with love towards that thing. Contrariwise, if we conceive that it affects an object of our love painfully, we shall be affected with hatred towards it.

We will call the *love towards him who confers a benefit on another, Approval*; and the *hatred towards him who injures another*, we will call *Indignation*. We must further remark, that we not only feel pity for a thing which we have loved, but also for a thing which we have hitherto regarded without emotion, provided that we deem that it resembles ourselves. Thus, we bestow approval on one who has benefited anything resembling ourselves, and, contrariwise, are indignant with him who has done it an injury.

—E-III

Approval is love towards one who has done good to another. —E-III

A PRIORI
See Persuasion

ARISTOTLE
See Bible

ARISTOTELIANS
See Superstition

ARTS
See Education

ATHEISM
See Miracles; Prophecy

ATTRIBUTE
By *attribute*, I mean that which the intellect perceives as constituting the essence of substance. —E-I

See Definitions; Existence; God; Substance

AVARICE
Avarice is the excessive desire and love of riches. —E-III

See Emotions; Love; Lust

AVERSION
Aversion is pain, accompanied by the idea of something which is accidentally the cause of pain. —E-III

See Hate

AXIOM
See Definition

B

BAD
See Bondage; God, Nature and Properties of; Good and Bad; Natural Right

BASE
See Natural Right

BASHFULNESS
See Timidity

BEASTS
See Natural Right; Social Life

BEAUTY
I do not attribute to nature either beauty or deformity, order or confusion. Only in relation to our imagination can things be called beautiful or deformed, ordered or confused.

By the association of parts, then, I merely mean that the laws or nature of one part adapt themselves to the laws or nature of another part, so as to cause the least possible inconsistency. As to the whole and the parts, I mean that a given number of things are parts of a whole, in so far as the nature of each of them is adapted to the nature of the rest, so that they all, as far as possible, agree together. On the other hand, in so far as they do not agree, each of them forms, in our mind, a separate idea, and is to that extent considered as a whole, not as a part. For instance, when the parts of lymph, chyle, &c., combine, according to the proportion of the figure and size of each, so as to evidently unite, and form one fluid, the chyle, lymph, &c., considered under this aspect, are part of the blood; but, in so far as we consider the particles of lymph as differing in figure and size from the particles of chyle, we shall consider each of the two as a whole, not as a part.

Let us imagine, a little worm, living in the blood, able to distinguish by sight the particles of blood, lymph, &c., and to reflect on the manner in which each particle, on meeting with another particle, either is repulsed, or communicates a portion of its own motion. This little worm would live in the blood, in the same way as we live in a part of the universe, and would consider each particle of blood, not as part, but as a whole. He would be unable to determine, how all the parts are modified by the general nature of blood, and are compelled by it to adapt themselves, so as to stand in a fixed relation to one another. For, if we imagine that there are no causes external to the blood, which could communicate fresh movements to it, nor any space beyond the blood, nor any bodies whereto the particles of blood could communicate their motion, it is certain that the blood would always remain in the same state, and its particles would undergo no modifications, save those which may be conceived as arising from the relations of motion existing between the lymph, the chyle, &c. The blood would then always have to be considered as a whole, not as a part. But, as there exist, as a matter of fact, very many causes which modify, in a given manner, the nature of the blood, and are, in turn, modified thereby, it follows that other motions and other relations arise in the blood, springing not from the mutual relations of its parts only, but from the mutual relations between the blood as a whole and external causes. Thus the blood comes to be regarded as a part, not as a whole. So much for the whole and the part.

All natural bodies can and ought to be considered in the same way as we have here considered the blood, for all bodies are surrounded by others, and are mutually determined to exist and operate in a fixed and definite proportion, while the relations between motion and rest in the sum total of them, that is, in the whole universe, remain unchanged. Hence it follows that each body, in so far as it exists as modified in a particular manner, must be considered as a part of the whole universe, as agreeing with the whole, and associated with the remaining parts. As the nature of the universe is not limited, like the nature of blood, but is absolutely infinite, its parts are by this nature of infinite power infinitely modified, and compelled to undergo infinite variations. But, in respect to substance, I conceive that each part has a more close union with its whole. For substance being infinite in its nature, it follows that each part belongs to the nature of substance, and, without it, can neither be nor be conceived.

One sees, therefore, how and why I think that the human body is a part of nature. As regards the human mind, I believe that it also is a part of nature; for I maintain that there exists in nature an infinite power of thinking, which, in so far as it is infinite, contains subjectively the whole of nature, and its thoughts proceed in the same manner as nature—that is, in the sphere of ideas. Further, I take the human mind to be identical with this said power, not in so far as it is infinite, and perceives the whole of nature, but in so far as it is finite, and perceives only the human body; in this manner, I maintain that the human mind is a part of an infinite understanding.   —C-XV-O

See God, Nature and Properties of

BEING
See Bondage; Definition; Ideas

BELIEF
Everyone must recognize that knowledge of God is not equal among all good men. Moreover, a man cannot be ordered to be wise any more than he can be ordered to live and exist. Men, women, and children are all alike able to

obey by commandment, but not to be wise. If any tell us
that it is not necessary to understand the Divine attributes,
but that we must believe them simply without proof, he is
plainly trifling. For what is invisible and can only be perceived by the mind, cannot be apprehended by any other
means than proofs; if these are absent the object remains
ungrasped; the repetition of what has been heard on such
subjects no more indicates or attains to their meaning than
the words of a parrot or a puppet speaking without sense
or signification.   —T P-XIII

BENEVOLENCE

Benevolence is the desire of benefiting one whom we
pity.   —E-III

We seek to free from misery, as far as we can, a thing
which we pity.

This will for doing good, which arises from pity of the
thing whereon we would confer a benefit, is called *benevolence,* and is nothing else but *desire arising from compassion.*   —E-III

BIBLE

Scriptural doctrine contains no lofty speculations nor
philosophic reasoning, but only very simple matters, such
as could be understood by the slowest intelligence.

I am consequently lost in wonder at the ingenuity of
those who detect in the Bible mysteries so profound that
they cannot be explained in human language, and who have
introduced so many philosophical speculations into religion
that the church seems like an academy, and religion like a
science, or rather a dispute.

It is not to be wondered at that men, who boast of possessing supernatural intelligence, should be unwilling to
yield the palm of knowledge to philosophers who have only
their ordinary faculties; still I should be surprised if I

found them teaching any new speculative doctrine, which was not a commonplace to those Gentile philosophers whom, in spite of all, they stigmatize as blind; for, if one inquires what these mysteries lurking in Scriptures may be, one is confronted with nothing but the reflections of Plato or Aristotle, or the like, which it would often be easier for an ignorant man to dream than for the most accomplished scholar to wrest out of the Bible. —T P-XIII

See Superstition

BLESSEDNESS

Blessedness is not the reward of virtue, but virtue itself; neither do we rejoice therein, because we control our lusts, but, contrariwise, because we rejoice therein, we are able to control our lusts.

It appears, how potent the wise man is, and how much he surpasses the ignorant man, who is driven only by his lusts. For the ignorant man is not only distracted in various ways by external causes without ever gaining the true acquiescence of his spirit, but moreover lives, as it were unwitting of himself, and of God, and of things, and as soon as he ceases to suffer, ceases also to be.

Whereas the wise man, in so far as he is regarded as such, is scarcely at all disturbed in spirit, but, being conscious of himself, and of God, and of things, by a certain eternal necessity, never ceases to be, but always possesses true acquiescence of his spirit.

If the way which I am pointing out as leading to this result seems exceedingly hard, it may nevertheless be discovered. Needs must it be hard, since it is so seldom found. How would it be possible, if salvation were ready to our hand, and could without great labor be found, that it should be by almost all men neglected? But all things majestic are as difficult as they are rare. —E-V

In respect of blessedness—God was equally gracious to all. —T P-III

Every man's true happiness and blessedness consist solely in the enjoyment of what is good, not in the pride that he alone is enjoying it, to the exclusion of others. He who thinks himself the more blessed because he is enjoying benefits which others are not, or because he is more blessed or more fortunate than his fellows, is ignorant of true happiness and blessedness, and the joy which he feels is either childish or envious and malicious. For instance, a man's true happiness consists only in wisdom, and the knowledge of the truth, not at all in the fact that he is wiser than others, or that others lack such knowledge: such considerations do not increase his wisdom or true happiness.

Whoever, therefore, rejoices for such reasons, rejoices in another's misfortune, and is, so far, malicious and bad, knowing neither true happiness nor the peace of the true life.   —T P-III

See Ideas; Intellect; Intellectual Love; Knowledge; Rational Life; Well-Being

BODY

Desire arising from a pleasure or pain, that is not attributable to the whole body, but only to one or certain parts thereof, is without utility in respect to a man as a whole.

As pleasure is generally attributed to one part of the body, we generally desire to preserve our being without taking into consideration our health as a whole: to which it may be added, that all desires which have most hold over us take account of the present and not of the future. —E-IV

Whatsoever brings out the preservation of the proportion of motion and rest, which the parts of the human body mutually possess, is good; contrariwise, whatsoever causes a change in such proportion is bad.

I consider that a body undergoes death, when the proportion of motion and rest which obtained mutually among its several parts is changed. For I do not venture to deny that a human body, while keeping the circulation of the blood and other properties, wherein the life of a body is thought to consist, may none the less be changed into another nature totally different from its own. There is no reason, which compels me to maintain that a body does not die, unless it becomes a corpse; nay, experience would seem to point to the opposite conclusion. It sometimes happens, that a man undergoes such changes, that I should hardly call him the same. As I have heard tell of a certain Spanish poet, who had been seized with sickness, and though he recovered therefrom yet remained so oblivious of his past life, that he would not believe the plays and tragedies he had written to be his own: indeed, he might have been taken for a grown-up child, if he had also forgotten his native tongue. If this instance seems incredible, what shall we say of infants? A man of ripe age deems their nature so unlike his own, that he can only be persuaded that he too has been an infant by the analogy of other men. However, I prefer to leave such questions undiscussed, lest I should give ground to the superstitious for raising new issues.   —E-IV

The endeavor, whereby a thing continues to persist in its being, involves no finite time, but an indefinite time.
                                                      —E-III

If the human body has once been affected by two or more bodies at the same time, when the mind afterwards imagines any of them, it will straightway remember the others also.   —E-II

The idea of each modification of the human body does not involve an adequate knowledge of the human body in toto.   —E-II

The idea of each modification of the human body does not involve an adequate knowledge of the external body.
                                                      —E-II

SPINOZA DICTIONARY

The human mind is capable of perceiving a great number of things, and is so in proportion as its body is capable of receiving a great number of impressions.   —E-II

The human mind has no knowledge of the body, and does not know it to exist, save through the ideas of the modifications whereby the body is affected.   —E-II

The human mind perceives not only the modifications of the body, but also the ideas of such modifications.   —E-II

We can only have a very inadequate knowledge of the duration of our body.   —E-II

The idea of every mode, in which the human body is affected by external bodies, must involve the nature of the human body, and also the nature of the external body.
Hence it follows, first, that the human mind perceives the nature of a variety of bodies, together with the nature of its own.
It follows, secondly, that the ideas, which we have of external bodies, indicate rather the constitution of our own body than the nature of external bodies.   —E-II

The object of the idea constituting the human mind is the body, in other words a certain mode of extension which actually exists, and nothing else.   —E-II

If the human body is affected in a manner which involves the nature of any external body, the human mind will regard the said external body as actually existing, or as present to itself, until the human body be affected in such a way, as to exclude the existence or the presence of the said external body.   —E-II

The idea of the idea of each modification of the human body does not involve an adequate knowledge of the human mind.
Hence it follows that the human mind, when it perceives things after the common order of nature, has not an ade-

quate but only a confused and fragmentary knowledge of itself, of its own body, and of external bodies. For the mind does not know itself, except in so far as it perceives the ideas of the modifications of body. It only perceives its own body through the ideas of the modifications, and only perceives external bodies through the same means; thus, in so far as it has such ideas of modification, it has not an adequate knowledge of itself, nor of its body, nor of external bodies, but only fragmentary and confused knowledge thereof.

I say expressly, that the mind has not an adequate but only a confused knowledge of itself, its own body, and of external bodies, whenever it perceives things after the common order of nature; that is, whenever it is determined from without, namely, by the fortuitous play of circumstances, to regard this or that; not at such times as it is determined from within, that is, by the fact of regarding several things at once, to understand their points of agreement, difference, and contrast. Whenever it is determined in anywise from within, it regards things clearly and distinctly.   —E-II

The ideas of the modifications of the human body, in so far as they have reference only to the human mind, are not clear and distinct, but confused.   —E-II

The idea or knowledge of the human mind is also in God, following in God in the same manner, and being referred to God in the same manner, as the idea or knowledge of the human body.   —E-II

The individual preserves its nature, whether it be, as a whole, in motion or at rest, whether it be moved in this or that direction; so long as each part retains its motion, and preserves its communication with other parts as before.

We thus see, how a composite individual may be affected in many different ways, and preserve its nature notwithstanding. Thus far we have conceived an individual as com-

[17]

posed of bodies only distinguished one from the other in respect of motion and rest, speed and slowness; that is, of bodies of the most simple character. If, however, we now conceive another individual composed of several individuals of diverse natures, we shall find that the number of ways in which it can be affected, without losing its nature, will be greatly multiplied. Each of its parts would consist of several bodies, and therefore each part would admit, without change to its nature, of quicker or slower motion, and would consequently be able to transmit its motions more quickly or more slowly to the remaining parts. If we further conceive a third kind of individuals composed of individuals of this second kind, we shall find that they may be affected in a still greater number of ways without changing their actuality. We may easily proceed thus to infinity, and conceive the whole of nature as one individual, whose parts, that is, all bodies, vary in infinite ways, without any change in the individual as a whole. I should feel bound to explain and demonstrate this point at more length, if I were writing a special treatise on body. But I have already said that such is not my object, I have only touched on the question, because it enables me to prove easily that which I have in view.

I. The human body is composed of a number of individual parts, of diverse nature, each one of which is in itself extremely complex.

II. Of the individual parts composing the human body some are fluid, some soft, some hard.

III. The individual parts composing the human body, and consequently the human body itself, are affected in a variety of ways by external bodies.

IV. The human body stands in need for its preservation of a number of other bodies, by which it is continually, so to speak, regenerated.

[18]

V. When the fluid part of the human body is determined by an external body to impinge often on another soft part, it changes the surface of the latter, and, as it were, leaves the impression thereupon of the external body which impels it.

VI. The human body can move external bodies, and arrange them in a variety of ways.   —E-II

We comprehend, not only that the human mind is united to the body, but also the nature of the union between mind and body. However, no one will be able to grasp this adequately or distinctly, unless he first has adequate knowledge of the nature of our body. The propositions we have advanced hitherto have been entirely general, applying not more to men than to other individual things, all of which, though in different degrees, are animated. For of everything there is necessarily an idea in God, of which God is the cause, in the same way as there is an idea of the human body; thus whatever we have asserted of the idea of the human body must necessarily also be asserted of the idea of everything else. Still, on the other hand, we cannot deny that ideas, like objects, differ one from the other, one being more excellent than another and containing more reality, just as the object of one idea is more excellent than the object of another idea, and contains more reality.

Wherefore, in order to determine, wherein the human mind differs from other things, and wherein it surpasses them, it is necessary for us to know the nature of its object, that is, of the human body. What this nature is, I am not able here to explain, nor is it necessary for the proof of what I advance, that I should do so. I will only say generally, that in proportion as any given body is more fitted than others for doing many actions or receiving many impressions at once, so also is the mind, of which it is the object, more fitted than others for forming many simultaneous perceptions; and the more the actions of one body depend on itself alone, and the fewer other bodies concur with it in action, the more fitted is the mind of which it is the object for distinct comprehension. We may thus recognize the superiority of one mind over others, and may further see the cause, why we have only a very confused knowledge of our body. —E-II

Bodies are distinguished from one another in respect of motion and rest, quickness and slowness, and not in respect of substance. —E-II

All bodies agree in certain respects. —E-II

If the parts composing become greater or less, but in such proportion, that they all preserve the same mutual relations of motion and rest, the individual will still preserve its original nature, and its actuality will not be changed. —E-II

If from a body or individual, compounded of several bodies, certain bodies be separated, and if, at the same time, an equal number of other bodies of the same nature take their place, the individual will preserve its nature as before, without any change in its actuality. —E-II

Every body is moved sometimes more slowly, sometimes more quickly. —E-II

By *body* I mean a mode which expresses in a certain determinate manner the essence of God, in so far as He is considered as an extended thing. —E-II

See Communion with God; Immortality of the Soul; Mind

BODY AND MIND

Body cannot determine mind to think, neither can mind determine body to motion or rest or any state different from these, if such there be. —E-III

The mind can only imagine anything, or remember what is past, while the body endures. —E-V

[20]

BONDAGE

Human infirmity in moderating and checking the emotions I name bondage: for, when a man is a prey to his emotions, he is not his own master, but lies at the mercy of fortune: so much so, that he is often compelled, while seeing that which is better for him, to follow that which is worse.

When a man has purposed to make a given thing, and has brought it to perfection, his work will be pronounced perfect, not only by himself, but by everyone who rightly knows, or thinks that he knows, the intention and aim of its author. For instance, suppose anyone sees a work (which I assume to be not yet completed), and knows that the aim of the author of that work is to build a house, he will call the work imperfect; he will, on the other hand, call it perfect, as soon as he sees that it is carried through to the end, which its author had purposed for it. But if a man sees a work, the like whereof he has never seen before, and if he knows not the intention of the artificer, he plainly cannot know, whether that work be perfect or imperfect. Such seems to be the primary meaning of these terms.

But, after men began to form general ideas, to think out types of houses, buildings, towers, &c., and to prefer certain types to others, it came about, that each man called perfect that which he saw agree with the general idea he had formed of the thing in question, and called imperfect that which he saw agree less with his own preconceived type, even though it had evidently been completed in accordance with the idea of its artificer. This seems to be the only reason for calling natural phenomena, which, indeed, are not made with human hands, perfect or imperfect: for men are wont to form general ideas of things natural, no less than of things artificial, and such ideas they hold as types, believing that Nature (who they think does nothing without an object) has them in view, and has set them as types before herself. Therefore, when they behold something in

Nature, which does not wholly conform to the preconceived type which they have formed of the thing in question, they say that Nature has fallen short or has blundered, and has left her work incomplete. Thus we see that men are wont to style natural phenomena perfect or imperfect rather from their own prejudices, than from true knowledge of what they pronounce upon.

Now we showed that Nature does not work with an end in view. For the eternal and infinite Being, which we call God or Nature, acts by the same necessity as that whereby it exists. For we have shown, that by the same necessity of its nature, whereby it exists, it likewise works. The reason or cause why God or Nature exists, and the reason why He acts, are one and the same. Therefore, as He does not exist for the sake of an end, so neither does He act for the sake of an end; of His existence and of His action there is neither origin nor end. Wherefore, a cause which is called final is nothing else but human desire, in so far as it is considered as the origin or cause of anything. For example, when we say that to be inhabited is the final cause of this or that house, we mean nothing more than that a man, conceiving the conveniences of household life, had a desire to build a house. Wherefore, the being inhabited, in so far as it is re-garded as a final cause, is nothing else but this particular desire, which is really the efficient cause; it is regarded as the primary cause, because men are generally ignorant of the causes of their desires. They are, as I have often said already, conscious of their own actions and appetites, but ignorant of the causes whereby they are determined to any particular desire. Perfection and imperfection, then, are in reality merely modes of thinking or notions which we form from a comparison among one another of individuals of the same species; hence I said that by reality and perfection I mean the same thing. For we are wont to refer all the individual things in nature to one genus, which is called the highest genus, namely, to the category of Being, whereto absolutely all individuals in nature belong. Thus, in so far as we refer the individuals in nature to this category, and comparing them one with another, find that some possess more of being or reality than others, we, to this extent, say that some are more perfect than others. Again, in so far as we attribute to them anything implying nega-tion—as term, end, infirmity, etc.,—we, to this extent, call them imperfect, because they do not affect our mind so much as the things which we call perfect, not because they have any intrinsic deficiency, or because Nature has blundered. For nothing lies within the scope of a thing's nature, save that which follows from the necessity of the nature of its efficient cause, and whatsoever follows from the necessity of the nature of its efficient cause necessarily comes to pass.

As for the terms *good* and *bad*, they indicate no positive quality in things regarded in themselves, but are merely modes of thinking, or notions which we form from the comparison of things one with another. Thus one and the same thing can be at the same time good, bad, and indif-ferent. For instance, music is good for him that is melan-choly, bad for him that mourns; for him that is deaf, it is neither good nor bad.

Nevertheless, though this be so, the terms should still be retained. For, inasmuch as we desire to form an idea of man as a type of human nature which we may hold in view, it will be useful for us to retain the terms in question, in the sense I have indicated.

In what follows, then, I shall mean by "good" that which we certainly know to be a means of approaching more nearly to the type of human nature, which we have set be-fore ourselves; by "bad," that which we certainly know to be a hindrance to us in approaching the said type. Again, we shall say that men are more perfect, or more imperfect, in proportion as they approach more or less nearly to the said type. For it must be specially remarked that, when I say that a man passes from a lesser to a greater perfection, or *vice versâ*, I do not mean that he is changed from one essence or reality to another; for instance, a horse would be as completely destroyed by being changed into a man, as by being changed into an insect. What I mean is, that we conceive the thing's power of action, in so far as this is understood by its nature, to be increased or diminished. Lastly, by perfection in general I shall, as I have said, mean reality—in other words, each thing's essence, in so far as it exists, and operates in a particular manner, and without paying any regard to its duration. For no given thing can be said to be more perfect, because it has passed a longer time in existence. The duration of things cannot be determined by their essence, for the essence of things involves no fixed and definite period of existence; but everything, whether it be more perfect or less perfect, will always be able to persist in existence with the same force wherewith it began to exist; wherefore, in this respect, all things are equal.

—E-IV

BOOKS

If we read a book which contains incredible or impossible narratives, or is written in a very obscure style, and if we know nothing of its author, nor of the time or occasion of its being written, we shall vainly endeavor to gain any certain knowledge of its true meaning. For being in ignorance of these points we cannot possibly know the aim or intended aim of the author; if we are fully informed, we so order our thoughts as not to be in any way prejudiced either in ascribing to the author or him for whom the author wrote either more or less than his meaning, and we only take into consideration what the author may have had in his mind, or what the time and occasion demanded. I think this must be tolerably evident to all.

It often happens that in different books we read histories in themselves similar, but which we judge very differently, according to the opinions we have formed of the authors. I remember once to have read in some book that a man named Orlando Furioso used to drive a kind of winged monster through the air, fly over any countries he liked, kill unaided vast numbers of men and giants, and such like fancies, which from the point of view of reason are obviously absurd. A very similar story I read in Ovid of Perseus, and also in the books of Judges and Kings of Samson, who alone and unarmed killed thousands of men, and of Elijah, who flew through the air, and at last went up to heaven in a chariot of fire, with horses of fire. All these stories are obviously alike, but we judge them very differently. The first only sought to amuse, the second had a political object, the third a religious object. We gather this simply from the opinions we had previously formed of the authors. Thus it is evidently necessary to know something of the authors of writings which are obscure or unintelligible, if we would interpret their meaning; and for the same reason, in order to choose the proper reading from among a great variety, we ought to have information as to the versions in which the differences are found, and as to the possibility of other readings having been discovered by persons of greater authority.

A further difficulty attends this method in the case of some of the books of Scripture, namely, that they are no longer extant in their original language. The Gospel according to Matthew, and certainly the Epistle to the Hebrews, were written, it is thought, in Hebrew, though they no longer exist in that form. Aben Ezra affirms in his commentaries that the book of Job was translated into Hebrew out of another language, and that its obscurity arises from this fact. I say nothing of the apocryphal books, for their authority stands on very inferior ground.

The foregoing difficulties in this method of interpreting Scripture from its own history, I conceive to be so great that I do not hesitate to say that the true meaning of Scripture is in many places inexplicable, or at best mere subject for guesswork; but I must again point out, on the other hand, that such difficulties only arise when we endeavor to follow the meaning of a prophet in matters which cannot be perceived, but only imagined, not in things, whereof the understanding can give a clear and distinct idea, and which are conceivable through themselves: matters which by their nature are easily perceived cannot be expressed so obscurely as to be unintelligible; as the proverb says, "a word is enough to the wise." Euclid, who only wrote of matters very simple and easily understood, can easily be comprehended by anyone in any language; we can follow his intention perfectly, and be certain of his true meaning, without having a thorough knowledge of the language in which he wrote; in fact, a quite rudimentary acquaintance is sufficient. We need make no researches concerning the life, the pursuits, or the habits of the author; nor need we inquire in what language, nor when he wrote, nor the vicissitudes of his book, nor its various readings, nor how, nor by whose advice it has been received.

What we here say of Euclid might equally be said of any book which treats of things by their nature perceptible: thus we conclude that we can easily follow the intention of Scripture in moral questions, from the history we possess of it, and we can be sure of its true meaning.   —T P-VII

BOREL
See Definition

BRAVERY
See Courage

C

CAUSE AND EFFECT
There is no cause from whose nature some effect does
not follow.   —E-I

Nothing can be destroyed, except by a cause external to
itself.   —E-III

CAUSE OF ALL THINGS
See Essence; Intellect

CAUSE, IMMANENT
See God

CEREMONIES
Natural Divine law does not demand the performance
of ceremonies.   —T P-IV

CERTAINTY
See Ideas

CHARITY
See Faith; Liberty; Worship

CHARACTER
See Emotions

CHASTITY
See Emotions; Lust

CHILDREN
See Democracy; Imagination

CHRISTIANS
The most ignorant are ever the most audacious and the
most ready to rush into print. The Christians seem to me to

expose their wares for sale like hucksters, who always show
first that which is worst. The devil is said to be very cunning, but to my thinking the tricks of these people are in
cunning far beyond his.   —C-I-JJ
See Hate, Religion

CHRISTIANITY
See Superstition

CITIZENS
See Natural Right

CIVIL RIGHT
See Democracy

CLASS HATRED
If a man has been affected pleasurably or painfully by
anyone, of a class or nation different from his own, and if
the pleasure or pain has been accompanied by the idea of
the said stranger as cause, under the general category of the
class or nation: the man will feel love or hatred, not only
to the individual stranger, but also to the whole class or
nation whereto he belongs.   —E-III

CLEMENCY
See Cruelty

COMMONWEALTH
See Government; Ideas

COMMUNION WITH GOD
The influences of the body on the soul: The most important of these, we maintain, is that it causes the soul to become aware of it, and through it also of other bodies. This
is effected by Motion and Rest conjointly, and by nothing
else: for the body has nothing else than these wherewith to
operate; so that whatever else comes to the soul, besides
this awareness, cannot be caused through the body. And as
the first thing which the soul gets to know is the body, the

result is that the soul loves it so, and becomes united with it. But since, as we have already said before, the cause of Love, Hatred, and Sorrow must not be sought for in the body but only in the soul (because all the activities of the body must proceed from motion and rest), and since we see clearly and distinctly that one love comes to an end as soon as we come to know something else that is better, it follows clearly from all this that, *If we get to know God, at least with a knowledge as clear as that with which we also know our body, then we must become united with Him even more closely than we are with our body, and be, as it were, released from the body.* I say *more closely*, because we have already proved before that without Him we can neither be, nor be known; and this is so because we know and must know Him, not through something else, as is the case with all other things, but only through Himself, as we have already said before. Indeed, we know Him better even than we know ourselves, because without Him we could not know ourselves at all. —G 2-XIX

COMPASSION

By the very fact that we conceive a thing (which is like ourselves, and which we have not regarded with any emotion) to be affected with any emotion, we are ourselves affected with a like emotion.

This imitation of emotions, when it is referred to pain, is called *compassion*; when it is referred to desire, it is called *emulation*, which is nothing else but *the desire of anything, engendered in us by the fact that we conceive that others have the like desire.*

If we conceive that anyone, whom we have hitherto regarded with no emotion, pleasurably affects something similar to ourselves, we shall be affected with love towards him. If, on the other hand, we conceive that he painfully affects the same, we shall be affected with hatred towards him. —E-III

See Benevolence; Fame; Rational Life

COMPLACENCY

The greater the emotion with which we conceive a loved object to be affected towards us, the greater will be our complacency.　　　　　　　　　　　　　　—E-III

CONCEIT

Conceit is this, when some one attributes to himself a perfection which is not to be found in him.　　—G 2-VIII

See Inferiority, Feeling of

CONCEPTION

See Ideas

CONDITIONING

Nothing in the universe is contingent, but all things are conditioned to exist and operate in a particular manner by the necessity of the Divine nature.　　　　　　—E-I

A thing, which has been conditioned by God to act in a particular way, cannot render itself unconditioned.　—E-I

Every individual thing, or everything which is finite and has a conditioned existence, cannot exist or be conditioned to act, unless it be conditioned for existence and action by a cause other than itself, which also is finite, and has a conditioned existence; and likewise this cause cannot in its turn exist, or be conditioned to act, unless it be conditioned for existence and action by another cause, which also is finite, and has a conditioned existence, and so on to infinity.　　　　　　　　　　　　　　—E-I

CONFIDENCE

If a thing is regarded by us as good, and, at the same time, as something that necessarily must come, then there comes into the soul that repose which we call *confidence*; which is a certain joy not mingled with sorrow, as hope is.
　　　　　　　　　　　　　　　　　—G 2-IX

Confidence is pleasure arising from the idea of something, wherefrom all cause of doubt has been removed.

—E-III

See Despair; Fear

CONSCIENCE
See Hate

CONSTERNATION
Consternation is attributed to one, whose desire of avoiding evil is checked by amazement at the evil which he fears.
Consternation is, therefore, a species of cowardice. But, inasmuch as consternation arises from a double fear, it may be more conveniently defined as a fear which keeps a man so bewildered and wavering, that he is not able to remove the evil. I say bewildered, in so far as we understand his desire of removing the evil to be constrained by his amazement. I say wavering, in so far as we understand the said desire to be constrained by the fear of another evil, which equally torments him: whence it comes to pass that he knows not, which he may avert of the two.   —E-III
See Timidity; Wonder

CONTEMPT
Contempt is the conception of anything which touches the mind so little, that its presence leads the mind to imagine those qualities which are not in it, rather than such as are in it.   —E-III

To admire is opposed *contempt,* which generally arises from the fact that, because we see someone wondering at, loving, or fearing something, or because something, at first sight, appears to be like things, which we ourselves wonder at, love, fear, &c., we are, in consequence, determined to wonder at, love, or fear that thing. But if from the presence, or more accurate contemplation of the said things, we are compelled to deny concerning it all that can be the cause of admiration, love, fear, &c., the mind then, by the presence

[31]

of the thing, remains determined to think rather of those qualities which are not in it, than of those which are in it; whereas, on the other hand, the presence of the object would cause it more particularly to regard that which is therein. —E-III

See Esteem

CONTINGENT

Particular things I call *contingent* in so far as, while regarding their essence only, we find nothing therein, which necessarily asserts their existence or excludes it. —E-IV

See Mind

CONTRARY

Things are naturally *contrary*, that is, cannot exist in the same object, in so far as one is capable of destroying the other. —E-III

CONTROVERSIES

See Ideas; Meaning

CORRECTNESS OF CONDUCT

See Rational Life

COURAGE

If something must be done in order to bring a thing about, and we come to no decision concerning it, then the mind receives that form which we call *vacillation*. But when it makes a manly resolve to produce the thing, and this can be brought about, then that is called *courage*; and if the thing is difficult to effect, then that is called *intrepidity* or *bravery*. —G 2-IX

See Emotions; Freedom; Human

COURTESY

Courtesy is the desire of acting in a way that should please men, and refraining from that which should displease them. —E-III

See Emotions

COWARDICE

Cowardice is attributed to one, whose desire is checked by the fear of some danger which his equals dare to encounter.

Cowardice is, therefore, nothing else but the fear of some evil, which most men are wont to fear; hence I do not reckon it among the emotions springing from desire. Nevertheless, I have chosen to explain it here, because, in so far as we look to the desire, it is truly opposed to the emotion of daring. —E-III

A man will appear *timid* to me, if he fears an evil which I am accustomed to despise; and if I further take into consideration that his desire is restrained by the fear of an evil, which is not sufficient to restrain me, I shall say that he is *cowardly*; and in like manner will everyone pass judgment. —E-III

See Consternation

CRIME
See Essence

CRUELTY

Cruelty is the desire, whereby a man is impelled to injure one whom we love or pity.

To cruelty is opposed clemency, which is not a passive state of the mind, but a power whereby man restrains his anger and revenge. —E-III

See Gratitude

CULTURE

Without mutual help men can hardly support life and cultivate the mind. —P T-II

D

DARING
Daring is the desire, whereby a man is set on to do something dangerous which his equals fear to attempt.
—E-III

See Intrepid

DEATH
A free man thinks of death least of all things; and his wisdom is a meditation not of death but of life.   —E-IV

See Body, Fear, Knowledge, Passive and Active, Religion

DEBAUCHERY
See Lust

DEFINITION
Difficulties arise from not distinguishing between kinds of definition: that is, between a definition serving to explain a thing, of which the essence only is sought and in question, and a definition which is put forward only for purposes of inquiry. The former having a definite object ought to be true, the latter need not. For instance, if someone asks me for a description of Solomon's temple, I am bound to give him a true description, unless I want to talk nonsense with him. But if I have constructed, in my mind, a temple which I desire to build, and infer from the description of it that I must buy such and such a site and so many thousand stones and other materials, will any sane person tell me that I have drawn a wrong conclusion because my definition is possibly untrue? or will anyone ask me to prove my definition? Such a person would simply be telling me, that I had not conceived that which I had conceived, or be requiring me to

[35]

prove, that I had conceived that which I had conceived; in fact, evidently trifling. Hence a definition either explains a thing, in so far as it is external to the intellect, in which case it ought to be true and only to differ from a proposition or an axiom in being concerned merely with the essences of things, or the modifications of things, whereas the latter has a wider scope and extends also to eternal truths. Or else it explains a thing, as it is conceived or can be conceived by us; and then it differs from an axiom or proposition, inasmuch as it only requires to be conceived absolutely, and not like an axiom as true. Hence a bad definition is one which is not conceived. To explain my meaning, I will take Borel's example—a man saying that two straight lines enclosing a space shall be called "figurals." If the man means by a straight line the same as the rest of the world means by a curved line, his definition is good (for by the definition would be meant some such figure as ( ), or the like); so long as he does not afterwards mean a square or other kind of figure. But, if he attaches the ordinary meaning to the words straight line, the thing is evidently inconceivable, and therefore there is no definition. These considerations are plainly confused by Borel, to whose opinion you incline. I give another example. If I say that each substance has only one attribute, this is an unsupported statement and needs proof. But, if I say that I mean by substance that which consists in only one attribute, the definition will be good, so long as entities consisting of several attributes are afterwards styled by some name other than substance. When you say that I do not prove, that substance (or being) may have several attributes, you do not perhaps pay attention to the proofs given. I adduced two:—First, "that nothing is plainer to us, than that every being may be conceived by us under some attribute, and that the more reality or essence a given being has, the more attributes may be attributed to it. Hence a being absolutely infinite must be defined, &c." Secondly, and I think this is the stronger proof of the two, "the more attributes I assign to any being, the more am I compelled to assign to its existence;" in other words, the more I conceive it as true. The contrary would evidently result, if I were feigning a chimera or some such thing.　　　　　　　　　—C-XXVII S DE V

See Existence

DEJECTION
See Pride

DEMOCRACY
By the right and ordinance of nature, I merely mean those natural laws wherewith we conceive every individual to be conditioned by nature, so as to live and act in a given way. For instance, fishes are naturally conditioned for swimming, and the greater for devouring the less; therefore fishes enjoy the water, and the greater devour the less by sovereign natural right. For it is certain that nature, taken in the abstract, has sovereign right to do anything she can; in other words, her right is co-extensive with her power. The power of nature is the power of God, which has sovereign right over all things; and, inasmuch as the power of nature is simply the aggregate of the powers of all her individual components, it follows that every individual has sovereign right to do all that he can; in other words, the rights of an individual extend to the utmost limits of his power as it has been conditioned. Now it is the sovereign law and right of nature that each individual should endeavor to preserve itself as it is, without regard to anything but itself; therefore this sovereign law and right belongs to every individual, namely, to exist and act according to its natural conditions. We do not here acknowledge any difference between mankind and other individual natural entities, nor between men endowed with reason and those to whom reason is unknown; nor between fools, madmen, and sane men. Whatsoever an individual does by the laws of its nature it has a sovereign right to do, inasmuch

as it acts as it was conditioned by nature, and cannot act otherwise. Wherefore among men, so long as they are considered as living under the sway of nature, he who does not yet know reason, or who has not yet acquired the habit of virtue, acts solely according to the laws of his desire with as sovereign a right as he who orders his life entirely by the laws of reason.

That is, as the wise man has sovereign right to do all that reason dictates, or to live according to the laws of reason, so also the ignorant and foolish man has sovereign right to do all that desire dictates, or to live according to the laws of desire. This is identical with the teaching of Paul, who acknowledges that previous to the law—that is, so long as men are considered of as living under the sway of nature, there is no sin.

The natural right of the individual man is thus determined, not by sound reason, but by desire and power. All are not naturally conditioned so as to act according to the laws and rules of reason; nay, on the contrary, all men are born ignorant, and before they can learn the right way of life and acquire the habit of virtue, the greater part of their life, even if they have been well brought up, has passed away. Nevertheless, they are in the meanwhile bound to live and preserve themselves as far as they can by the unaided impulses of desire. Nature has given them no other guide, and has denied them the present power of living according to sound reason; so that they are no more bound to live by the dictates of an enlightened mind, than a cat is bound to live by the laws of the nature of a lion.

Whatsoever, therefore, an individual (considered as under the sway of nature) thinks useful for himself, whether led by sound reason or impelled by the passions, that he has a sovereign right to seek and to take for himself as he best can, whether by force, cunning, entreaty, or any other means; consequently he may regard as an enemy anyone who hinders the accomplishment of his purpose.

It follows from what we have said that the right and ordinance of nature, under which all men are born, and under which they mostly live, only prohibits such things as no one desires, and no one can attain: it does not forbid strife, nor hatred, nor anger, nor deceit, nor, indeed, any of the means suggested by desire.

This we need not wonder at, for nature is not bounded by the laws of human reason, which aims only at man's true benefit and preservation; her limits are infinitely wider, and have reference to the eternal order of nature, wherein man is but a speck; it is by the necessity of this alone that all individuals are conditioned for living and acting in a particular way. If anything, therefore, in nature seems to us ridiculous, absurd, or evil, it is because we only know in part, and are almost entirely ignorant of the order and interdependence of nature as a whole, and also because we want everything to be arranged according to the dictates of our human reason; in reality that which reason considers evil, is not evil in respect to the order and laws of nature as a whole, but only in respect to the laws of our reason.

Nevertheless, no one can doubt that it is much better for us to live according to the laws and assured dictates of reason, for, as we said, they have men's true good for their object. Moreover, everyone wishes to live as far as possible securely beyond the reach of fear, and this would be quite impossible so long as everyone did everything he liked, and reason's claim was lowered to a par with those of hatred and anger; there is no one who is not ill at ease in the midst of enmity, hatred, anger, and deceit, and who does not seek to avoid them as much as he can. When we reflect that men without mutual help, or the aid of reason, must needs live most miserably, we shall plainly see that men must necessarily come to an agreement to live together as securely and well as possible if they are to enjoy as a whole the rights which naturally belong to them as individuals, and their life should be no more conditioned by the force and desire of individuals, but by the power and will of the whole body. This end they will be unable to attain if desire be their only guide (for by the laws of desire each man is drawn in a different direction); they must, therefore, most firmly decree and establish that they will be guided in everything by reason (which nobody will dare openly to repudiate lest he should be taken for a madman), and will restrain any desire which is injurious to a man's fellows, that they will do to all as they would be done by, and that they will defend their neighbor's rights as their own.

How such a compact as this should be entered into, how ratified and established, we will now inquire.

Now it is a universal law of human nature that no one ever neglects anything which he judges to be good, except with the hope of gaining a greater good, or from the fear of a greater evil; nor does anyone endure an evil except for the sake of avoiding a greater evil, or gaining a greater good. That is, everyone will, of two goods, choose that which he thinks the greatest; and, of two evils, that which he thinks the least. I say advisedly that which he thinks the greatest or the least, for it does not necessarily follow that he judges right. This law is so deeply implanted in the human mind that it ought to be counted among eternal truths and axioms.

As a necessary consequence of the principle just enunciated, no one can honestly promise to forego the right which he has over all things, and in general no one will abide by his promises, unless under the fear of a greater evil, or the hope of a greater good. An example will make the matter clearer. Suppose that a robber forces me to promise that I will give him my goods at his will and pleasure. It is plain (inasmuch as my natural right is, as I have shown, co-extensive with my power) that if I can free myself from this robber by stratagem, by assenting to his demands, I have the natural right to do so, and to pretend to accept his conditions. Or again, suppose I have genuinely promised someone that for the space of twenty days I will not taste food or any nourishment; and suppose I afterwards find that my promise was foolish, and cannot be kept without very great injury to myself; as I am bound by natural law and right to choose the least of two evils, I have complete right to break my compact, and act as if my promise had never been uttered. I say that I should have perfect natural right to do so, whether I was actuated by true and evident reason, or whether I was actuated by mere opinion in thinking I had promised rashly; whether my reasons were true or false, I should be in fear of a greater evil, which, by the ordinance of nature, I should strive to avoid by every means in my power.

We may, therefore, conclude that a compact is only made valid by its utility, without which it becomes null and void. It is, therefore, foolish to ask a man to keep his faith with us for ever, unless we also endeavor that the violation of the compact we enter into shall involve for the violator more harm than good. This consideration should have very great weight in forming a state. However, if all men could be easily led by reason alone, and could recognize what is best and most useful for a state, there would be no one who would not forswear deceit, for everyone would keep most religiously to their compact in their desire for the chief good, namely, the preservation of the state, and would cherish good faith above all things as the shield and buckler of the commonwealth. However, it is far from being the case that all men can always be easily led by reason alone; everyone is drawn away by his pleasure, while avarice, ambition, envy, hatred, and the like so engross the mind that reason has no place therein. Hence, though men make promises with all the appearances of good faith, and agree that they will keep to their engagement, no one can absolutely rely on another man's promise unless there is something behind it. Everyone has by nature a right to act deceitfully, and to break his compacts, unless he be restrained by the hope of some greater good, or the fear of some greater evil.

However, as we have shown that the natural right of the individual is only limited by his power, it is clear that by transferring, either willingly or under compulsion, this power into the hands of another, he in so doing necessarily cedes also a part of his right; and further, that the sovereign right over all men belongs to him who has sovereign power, wherewith he can compel men by force, or restrain them by threats of the universally feared punishment of death; such sovereign right he will retain only so long as he can maintain his power of enforcing his will; otherwise he will totter on his throne, and no one who is stronger than he will be bound unwillingly to obey him.

In this manner a society can be formed without any violation of natural right, and the covenant can always be strictly kept—that is, if each individual hands over the whole of his power to the body politic, the latter will then possess sovereign natural right over all things; that is, it will have sole and unquestioned dominion, and everyone will be bound to obey, under pain of the severest punishment. A body politic of this kind is called a Democracy, which may be defined as a society which wields all its power as a whole. The sovereign power is not restrained by any laws, but everyone is bound to obey it in all things; such is the state of things implied when men either tacitly or expressly handed over to it all their power of self-defense, or in other words, all their right. For if they had wished to retain any right for themselves, they ought to have taken precautions for its defense and preservation; as they have not done so, and indeed could not have done so without dividing and consequently ruining the state, they placed themselves absolutely at the mercy of the sovereign power; and, therefore, having acted (as we have shown) as reason and necessity demanded, they are obliged to fulfill the commands of the sovereign power, however absurd these may be, else they will be public enemies, and will act against reason, which urges the preservation of the state as a primary duty. For reason bids us choose the least of two evils.

Furthermore, this danger of submitting absolutely to the dominion and will of another, is one which may be incurred with a light heart: for we have shown that sovereigns only possess this right of imposing their will, so long as they have the full power to enforce it: if such power be lost their right to command is lost also, or lapses to those who have assumed it and can keep it. Thus it is very rare for sovereigns to impose thoroughly irrational commands, for they are bound to consult their own interests, and retain their power by consulting the public good and acting according to the dictates of reason, as Seneca says, "No one can long retain a tyrant's sway."

In a democracy, irrational commands are still less to be feared: for it is almost impossible that the majority of a people, especially if it be a large one, should agree in an irrational design: and, moreover, the basis and aim of a democracy is to avoid the desires as irrational, and to bring men as far as possible under the control of reason, so that they may live in peace and harmony: if this basis be removed the whole fabric falls to ruin.

Such being the ends in view for the sovereign power, the duty of subjects is, as I have said, to obey its commands, and to recognize no right save that which it sanctions.

It will, perhaps, be thought that we are turning subjects into slaves: for slaves obey commands and free men live as they like; but this idea is based on a misconception, for the true slave is he who is led away by his pleasures and can neither see what is good for him nor act accordingly: he alone is free who lives with free consent under the entire guidance of reason.

Action in obedience to orders does take away freedom in a certain sense, but it does not, therefore, make a man a slave, all depends on the object of the action. If the object of the action be the good of the state, and not the good of the agent, the latter is a slave and does himself no good: but in a state or kingdom where the will of the whole people, and not that of the ruler, is the supreme law, obedience to the sovereign power does not make a man a slave, of no use to himself, but a subject. Therefore, that state is the freest whose laws are founded on sound reason, so that every member of it may, if he will, be free; that is, live with full consent under the entire guidance of reason.

Children, though they are bound to obey all the commands of their parents, are yet not slaves: for the commands of parents look generally to the children's benefit.

We must, therefore, acknowledge a great difference between a slave, a son, and a subject; their positions may be thus defined. A slave is one who is bound to obey his master's orders, though they are given solely in the master's interest: a son is one who obeys his father's orders, given in his own interest; a subject obeys the orders of the sovereign power, given for the common interest, wherein he is included.

I think I have now shown sufficiently clearly the basis of a democracy: I have especially desired to do so, for I believe it to be of all forms of government the most natural, and the most consonant with individual liberty. In it no one transfers his natural right so absolutely that he has no further voice in affairs, he only hands it over to the majority of a society, whereof he is a unit. Thus all men remain, as they were in the state of nature, equals.

This is the only form of government which I have treated of at length, for it is the one most akin to my purpose of showing the benefits of freedom in a state.

I may pass over the fundamental principles of other forms of government, for we may gather from what has been said whence their right arises without going into its origin. The possessor of sovereign power, whether he be one, or many, or the whole body politic, has the sovereign right of imposing any commands he pleases: and he who has either voluntarily, or under compulsion, transferred the right to defend him to another, has, in so doing, renounced his natural right and is therefore bound to obey, in all things, the commands to the sovereign power; and will be bound so to do so long as the king, or nobles, or the people preserve the sovereign power which formed the basis of the original transfer. I need add no more.

The bases and rights of dominion being thus displayed, we shall readily be able to define private civil right, wrong, justice, and injustice, with their relations to the state; and also to determine what constitutes an ally, or an enemy, or the crime of treason.

By private civil right we can only mean the liberty every man possesses to preserve his existence, a liberty limited by the edicts of the sovereign power, and preserved only by its authority: for when a man has transferred to another his right of living as he likes, which was only limited by his power, that is, has transferred his liberty and power of self-defense, he is bound to live as that other dictates, and to trust to him entirely for his defense. Wrong takes place when a citizen, or subject, is forced by another to undergo some loss or pain in contradiction to the authority of the law, or the edict of the sovereign power.

Wrong is conceivable only in an organized community: nor can it ever accrue to subjects from any act of the sovereign, who has the right to do what he likes. It can only arise, therefore, between private persons, who are bound by law and right not to injure one another. Justice consists in the habitual rendering to every man his lawful due: injustice consists in depriving a man, under the pretence of legality, of what the laws, rightly interpreted, would allow him. These last are also called equity and iniquity, because those who administer the laws are bound to show no respect of persons, but to account all men equal, and to defend every man's right equally, neither envying the rich nor despising the poor.

The men of two states become allies, when for the sake of avoiding war, or for some other advantage, they covenant to do each other no hurt, but on the contrary, to assist each other if necessity arises, each retaining his independence. Such a covenant is valid so long as its basis of danger or advantage is in force: no one enters into an engagement, or is bound to stand by his compacts unless there be a hope of some accruing good, or the fear of some evil: if this basis be removed the compact thereby becomes void: this has been abundantly shown by experience. For although different states make treaties not to harm one another, they always take every possible precaution against such treaties being broken by the stronger party, and do not rely on the compact, unless there is a sufficiently obvious object and advantage to both parties in observing it. Otherwise they would fear a breach of faith, nor would there be any wrong done thereby: for who in his proper senses, and aware of the right of the sovereign power, would trust in the promises of one who has the will and the power to do what he likes, and who aims solely at the safety and advantage of his dominion? Moreover, if we consult loyalty and religion, we shall see that no one in possession of power ought to abide by his promises to the injury of his dominion; for he cannot keep such promises without breaking the engagement he made with his subjects, by which both he and they are most solemnly bound.

An enemy is one who lives apart from the state, and does not recognize its authority either as a subject or as an ally. It is not hatred which makes a man an enemy, but the rights of the state. The rights of the state are the same in regard to him who does not recognize by any compact the state authority, as they are against him who has done the state an injury: it has the right to force him as best it can, either to submit, or to contract an alliance.   —T P-XVI

See Tyranny

DEMOCRITUS
See Occult

DENIAL
See Privation; Will

DERISION
Derision is pleasure arising from our conceiving the presence of a quality, which we despise, in an object which we hate.

In so far as we despise a thing which we hate, we deny existence thereof, and to that extent rejoice. But since we assume that man hates that which he derides, it follows that the pleasure in question is not without alloy.   —E-III

As devotion springs from wonder at a thing which we love, so does *Derision* spring from contempt of a thing which we hate or fear, and *Scorn* from contempt of folly, as veneration from wonder at prudence.   —E-III
See Hate, Ridicule

DESCARTES
See Emotions, Free Will, Human Conduct

DESIRE
By an *end*, for the sake of which we do something, I mean a desire.   —E-IV

Desire arising from the knowledge of good and bad can be quenched or checked by many of the other desires arising from the emotions whereby we are assailed.   —E-IV

Desire which springs from reason cannot be excessive.   —E-IV

Desire arising from the true knowledge of good and evil, in so far as such knowledge is concerned with what is contingent, can be controlled far more easily still, than desire for things that are present.

I think I have now shown the reason, why men are moved

[47]

by opinion more readily than by true reason, why it is that the true knowledge of good and evil stirs up conflicts in the soul, and often yields to every kind of passion. This state of things gave rise to the exclamation of the poet:

*"The better path I gaze at and approve,
The worse—I follow."*

Ecclesiastes seems to have had the same thought in mind, when saying, "He who increaseth knowledge increaseth sorrow." I have not written the above with the object of drawing the conclusion, that ignorance is more excellent than knowledge, or that a wise man is on a par with a fool in controlling his emotions, but because it is necessary to know the power and the infirmity of our nature, before we can determine what reason can do in restraining the emotions, and what is beyond her power.   —E-IV

Desire arising from pleasure is, other conditions being equal, stronger than desire arising from pain.

As reason makes no demands contrary to nature, it demands, that every man should love himself, should seek that which is useful to him—I mean, that which is really useful to him, should desire everything which really brings man to greater perfection, and should, each for himself, endeavor as far as he can to preserve his own being. This is as necessarily true, as that a whole is greater than its part.

Again, as virtue is nothing else but action in accordance with the laws of one's own nature, and as no one endeavors to preserve his own being, except in accordance with the laws of his own nature, it follows, *first*, that the foundation of virtue is the endeavor to preserve one's own being, and that happiness consists in man's power of preserving his own being; *secondly*, that virtue is to be desired for its own sake, and that there is nothing more excellent or more useful to us, for the sake of which we should desire it; *thirdly* and lastly, that suicides are weak-minded, and are overcome by external causes repugnant to their nature. Further, that we can never arrive at doing without all external things for the preservation of our being or living, so as to have no relations with things which are outside ourselves. Again, if we consider our mind, we see that our intellect would be more imperfect, if mind were alone, and could understand nothing besides itself. There are, then, many things outside ourselves, which are useful to us, and are, therefore, to be desired. Of such none can be discerned more excellent, than those which are in entire agreement with our nature. For if, for example, two individuals of entirely the same nature are united, they form a combination twice as powerful as either of them singly.

Therefore, to man there is nothing more useful than man—nothing, I repeat, more excellent for preserving their being can be wished for by men, than that all should so in all points agree, that the minds and bodies of all should form, as it were, one single mind and one single body, and that all should, with one consent, as far as they are able, endeavor to preserve their being, and all with one consent seek what is useful to them all. Hence, men who are governed by reason—that is, who seek what is useful to them in accordance with reason,—desire for themselves nothing, which they do not also desire for the rest of mankind, and, consequently, are just, faithful, and honorable in their conduct.   —E-IV

Desire arising from the knowledge of good and evil, in so far as such knowledge regards what is future, may be more easily controlled or quenched, than the desire for what is agreeable at the present moment.   —E-IV

Desire is the actual essence of man, in so far as it is conceived, as determined to a particular activity by some given modification of itself.

Desire is appetite, with consciousness thereof; further, that appetite is the essence of man, in so far as it is determined to act in a way tending to promote its own persistence. But, in the same note, I also remarked that, strictly speaking, I recognize no distinction between appetite and desire. For whether a man be conscious of his appetite or not, it remains one and the same appetite. Thus, in order to avoid the appearance of tautology, I have refrained from explaining desire by appetite; but I have taken care to define it in such a manner, as to comprehend, under one head, all those endeavors of human nature, which we distinguish by the terms appetite, will, desire, or impulse. I might, indeed, have said, that desire is the essence of man, in so far as it is conceived as determined to a particular activity; but from such a definition it would not follow that the mind can be conscious of its desire or appetite. Therefore, in order to imply the cause of such consciousness, it was necessary to add, *in so far as it is determined by some given modification,* &c. For, by a modification of man's essence, we understand every disposition of the said essence, whether such disposition be innate, or whether it be conceived solely under the attribute of thought, or solely under the attribute of extension, or whether, lastly, it be referred simultaneously to both these attributes. By the term desire, then, I here mean all man's endeavors, impulses, appetites, and volitions, which vary according to each man's disposition, and are, therefore, not seldom opposed one to another, according as a man is drawn in different directions, and knows not where to turn.   —E-III

Desire arising through pain or pleasure, hatred or love, is greater in proportion as the emotion is greater.

Lastly, since hatred and love are themselves emotions of pain and pleasure, it follows in like manner that the endeavor, appetite, or desire, which arises through hatred or love, will be greater in proportion to the hatred or love.

—E-III

Desire. Whether (as some will have it) it consists only in a longing or inclination to obtain what is wanting, or (as

SPINOZA DICTIONARY

others will have it) to retain the things which we already enjoy, it is certain that it cannot be found to have come upon any one except for an apparent good. It is therefore clear that Desire, is the outcome of the first superficial kind of knowledge. For if any one has heard that a certain thing is good, he feels a longing and inclination for the same, as may be seen in the case of an invalid who, through hearing the doctor say that such or such a remedy is good for his ailment, at once longs for the same, and feels a desire for it.

—G 2-III

See Adequate Ideas, Body, Emotion, Knowledge, Will, Wrongdoing

DESPAIR

Despair is pain arising from the idea of something past or future, wherefore all cause of doubt has been removed.

Thus confidence springs from hope, and despair from fear, when all cause for doubt as to the issue of an event has been removed: this comes to pass, because man conceives something past or future as present and regards it as such, or else because he conceives other things, which exclude the existence of the causes of his doubt. For, although we can never be absolutely certain of the issue of any particular event, it may nevertheless happen that we feel no doubt concerning it. For we have shown, that to feel no doubt concerning a thing is not the same as to be quite certain of it. Thus it may happen that we are affected by the same emotion of pleasure or pain concerning a thing past or future, as concerning the conception of a thing present.

—E-III

When we think that a thing is bad, and that it necessarily must come, then *despair* enters into the soul; which is nothing else than a certain kind of sorrow.   —G 2-IX

See Fear

DEVIL

If the *Devil* is a thing that is once for all opposed to God, and has absolutely nothing from God, then he is precisely identical with Nothing, which we have already discussed before.

If, with some, we represent him as a thinking thing that absolutely neither wills nor does any good, and so sets himself, once for all, in opposition to God, then surely he is very wretched, and, if prayers could help, then one ought to pray for his conversion.

As, however, there is no necessity whatever why we should posit the existence of Devils, why then should they be posited? For we need not, like others, posit Devils in order to find [in them] the cause of Hatred, Envy, Wrath, and such-like passions, since we have found this sufficiently, without such fictions.   —G 2-XXV

DEVOTION

Devotion is love towards one whom we admire.

Wonder arises from the novelty of a thing. If, therefore, it happens that the object of our wonder is often conceived by us, we shall cease to wonder at it; thus we see, that the emotion of devotion readily degenerates into simple love.
                                                                —E-III

If it be the prudence, industry, or what not, of a man we love, that we wonder at, our love will on this account be the greater, and when joined to wonder or veneration is called *Devotion*.   —E-III

DICTATORS

Those who administer or possess governing power, always try to surround their high-handed actions with a cloak of legality, and to persuade the people that they act from good motives; this they are easily able to effect when they are the sole interpreters of the law.   —T P-XVII

SPINOZA DICTIONARY

DISAPPOINTMENT
Disappointment is pain accompanied by the idea of something past, which has had an issue contrary to our hope.   —E-III

Disappointment is the *Pain opposed to Joy.*   —E-III

DISDAIN
The pleasure which arises from thinking too little of a man is called *disdain.*   —E-III

DISPARAGEMENT
Disparagement is thinking too meanly of anyone, because we hate him.

Thus partiality is an effect of love, and disparagement an effect of hatred: so that *partiality* may also be defined as *love, in so far as it induces a man to think too highly of a beloved object.* Contrariwise, *disparagement* may be defined as *hatred, in so far as it induces a man to think too meanly of a hated object.*   —E-III

The emotions of over-esteem and disparagement are always bad.   —E-IV

DIVINE COMMANDMENTS
See Religion

DIVINE LAW
We see that the highest reward of the Divine law is the law itself, namely, to know God and to love Him of our free choice, and with an undivided and fruitful spirit; while its penalty is the absence of these things, and being in bondage to the flesh—that is, having an inconstant and wavering spirit.   —T P-IV
See Intellectual Love, Law

DIVISION OF LABOR
See Society

DOGMATISTS
See Philosophy

DOGMAS
See Religion

DOING GOOD
See State

DREAM
See Mind

DRUNKENNESS
See Emotions, Lust

DURATION
Duration is the indefinite continuance of existing.

I say *indefinite*, because it cannot be determined through the existence itself of the existing thing, or by its efficient cause, which necessarily gives the existence of the thing, but does not take it away.　　　　　　　—E-II

See Immortality of the Soul, Mode, Reason

DUTY
See Public Welfare, Rational Life

E

ECCLESIASTES
See Desire

EDUCATION
Academies, that are founded at the public expense, are instituted not so much to cultivate men's natural abilities as to restrain them. But in a free commonwealth arts and sciences will be best cultivated to the full, if everyone that asks leave is allowed to teach publicly, and that at his own cost and risk.   —P T-VIII
See Envy, Hate, Liberty, Repentance

ELIJAH
See Books

EMOTIONS
By *conflicting emotions* I mean those which draw a man in different directions, though they are of the same kind, such as luxury and avarice, which are both species of love, and are contraries, not by nature, but by accident.   —E-IV

Any emotion of a given individual differs from the emotion of another individual, only in so far as the essence of the one individual differs from the essence of the other.
Hence it follows, that the emotions of the animals which are called irrational (for after learning the origin of mind we cannot doubt that brutes feel) only differ from man's emotions, to the extent that brute nature differs from human nature. Horse and man are alike carried away by the desire of procreation; but the desire of the former is equine, the desire of the latter is human. So also the lusts and appetites of insects, fishes, and birds must needs vary according

SPINOZA DICTIONARY

to the several natures. Thus, although each individual lives content and rejoices in that nature belonging to him wherein he has his being, yet the life, wherein each is content and rejoices, is nothing else but the idea, or soul, of the said individual, and hence the joy of one only differs in nature from the joy of another, to the extent that the essence of one differs from the essence of another. Lastly, it follows from the foregoing proposition, that there is no small difference between the joy which actuates, say, a drunkard, and the joy possessed by a philosopher, as I just mention here by the way.   —E-III

An emotion towards a thing, which we know not to exist at the present time, and which we conceive as possible, is more intense, other conditions being equal, than an emotion towards a thing contingent.

An emotion towards a thing, which we know not to exist in the present, and which we conceive as contingent, is far fainter, than if we conceive the thing to be present with us.
                                        —E-IV

Emotion towards a thing contingent, which we know not to exist in the present, is other conditions being equal, fainter than an emotion towards a thing past.   —E-IV

Emotion, which is called a passivity of the soul, is a confused idea, whereby the mind affirms concerning its body, or any part thereof, a force for existence greater or less than before, and by the presence of which the mind is determined to think of one thing rather than another.

I say, first, that emotion or passion of the soul is a *confused idea.* For we have shown that the mind is only passive, in so far as it has inadequate or confused ideas. I say, further, *whereby the mind affirms concerning its body or part thereof a force for existence greater than before.* For all the ideas of bodies, which we possess, denote rather the actual disposition of our own body than the nature of an external body. But the idea which constitutes the reality of

[56]

an emotion must denote or express the disposition of the body, or of some part thereof, which is possessed by the body, or some part thereof, because its power of action or force for existence is increased or diminished, helped or hindered. But it must be noted that, when I say *a greater or less force for existence* than before, I do not mean that the mind compares the present with the past disposition of the body, but that the idea which constitutes the reality of an emotion affirms something of the body, which, in fact, involves more or less of reality than before.

And inasmuch as the essence of mind consists in the fact that it affirms the actual existence of its own body, and inasmuch as we understand by perfection the very essence of a thing, it follows that the mind passes to greater or less perfection, when it happens to affirm concerning its own body, or any part thereof, something involving more or less reality than before.

When, therefore, I said above that the power of the mind is increased or diminished, I merely meant that the mind had formed of its own body, or of some part thereof, an idea involving more or less of reality, than it had already affirmed concerning its own body. For the excellence of ideas, and the actual power of thinking are measured by the excellence of the object. Lastly, I have added *by the presence of which the mind is determined to think of one thing rather than another*, so that, besides the nature of pleasure and pain, which the first part of the definition explains, I might also express the nature of desire. —E-III

An emotion, whereof we conceive the cause to be with us at the present time, is stronger than if we did not conceive the cause to be with us.

I said that we are affected by the image of what is past or future with the same emotion as if the thing conceived were present, I expressly stated, that this is only true in so far as we look solely to the image of the thing in question

[57]

itself; for the thing's nature is unchanged, whether we have conceived it or not; I did not deny that the image becomes weaker, when we regard as present to us other things which exclude the present existence of the future object: I did not expressly call attention to the fact, because I purposed to treat of the strength of the emotions in this part of my work.

The image of something past or future, that is, of a thing which we regard as in relation to time past or time future, to the exclusion of time present, is, when other conditions are equal, weaker than the image of something present; consequently an emotion felt towards what is past or future is less intense, other conditions being equal, than an emotion felt towards something present.　　　—E-IV

An emotion can only be controlled or destroyed by another emotion contrary thereto, and with more power for controlling emotion.

An emotion, in so far as it is referred to the mind, can only be controlled or destroyed through an idea of a modification of the body contrary to, and stronger than, that which we are undergoing. For the emotion which we undergo can only be checked or destroyed by an emotion contrary to, and stronger than, itself, in other words (by the general Definition of the Emotions) only by an idea of a modification of the body contrary to, and stronger than, the modification which we undergo.　　　—E-IV

An emotion towards a thing, which we conceive simply, and not as necessary, or as contingent, or as possible, is, other conditions being equal, greater than any other emotion.　　　—E-V

That we do not possess absolute dominion over emotions, I have shown. Yet the Stoics have thought, that the emotions, depended absolutely on our will, and that we could absolutely govern them. But these philosophers were compelled, by the protest of experience, not from their own principles, to confess, that no slight practice and zeal is needed to control and moderate them: and this someone endeavored to illustrate by the example (if I remember rightly) of two dogs, the one a house-dog and the other a hunting-dog. For by long training it could be brought about, that the house-dog should become accustomed to hunt, and the hunting-dog to cease from running after hares.

To this opinion Descartes not a little inclines. For he maintained, that the soul or mind is specially united to a particular part of the brain, namely, to that part called the pineal gland, by the aid of which the mind is enabled to feel all the movements which are set going in the body, and also external objects, and which the mind by a simple act of volition can put in motion in various ways. He asserted, that this gland is so suspended in the midst of the brain, that it could be moved by the slightest motion of the animal spirits: further, that this gland is suspended in the midst of the brain in as many different manners, as the animal spirits can impinge thereon; and, again, that as many different marks are impressed on the said gland, as there are different external objects which impel the animal spirits towards it; whence it follows, that if the will of the soul suspends the gland in a position, wherein it has already been suspended once before by the animal spirits driven in one way or another, the gland in its turn reacts on the said spirits, driving and determining them to the condition wherein they were, when repulsed before by a similar position of the gland. He further asserted, that every act of mental volition is united in nature to a certain given motion of the gland. For instance, whenever anyone desires to look at a remote object, the act of volition causes the pupil of the eye to dilate, whereas, if the person in question had only thought of the dilatation of the pupil, the mere wish to dilate it would not have brought about the result, inasmuch as the motion of the gland, which serves to impel the animal spirits towards the optic nerve in a way which would dilate or contract the pupil, is not associated in nature with the wish to dilate or contract the pupil, but with the wish to look at remote or very near objects. Lastly, he maintained that, although every motion of the aforesaid gland seems to have been united by nature to one particular thought out of the whole number of our thoughts from the very beginning of our life, yet it can nevertheless become through habituation associated with other thoughts; this he endeavors to prove in the *Passions de l'âme*, I. 50. He thence concludes, that there is no soul so weak, that it cannot, under proper direction, acquire absolute power over its passions. For passions as defined by him are "perceptions, or feelings, or disturbances of the soul, which are referred to the soul as species, and which (mark the expression) are produced, preserved, and strengthened through some movement of the spirits." (*Passions de l'âme*, I. 27.) But, seeing that we can join any motion of the gland, or consequently of the spirits, to any volition, the determination of the will depends entirely on our own powers; if, therefore, we determine our will with sure and firm decisions in the direction to which we wish our actions to tend, and associate the motions of the passions which we wish to acquire with the said decisions, we shall acquire an absolute dominion over our passions.

Such is the doctrine of this illustrious philosopher (in so far as I gather it from his own words); it is one which, had it been less ingenious, I could hardly believe to have proceeded from so great a man. Indeed, I am lost in wonder, that a philosopher, who had stoutly asserted, that he would draw no conclusions which do not follow from self-evident premises, and would affirm nothing which he did not clearly and distinctly perceive, and who had so often taken to task the Scholastics for wishing to explain obscurities through occult qualities, could maintain a hypothesis, beside which occult qualities are commonplace.

What does he understand, I ask, by the union of the mind and the body? What clear and distinct conception has he got of thought in most intimate union with a certain particle of extended matter? Truly I should like him to explain this union through its proximate cause. But he had so distinct a conception of mind being distinct from body, that he could not assign any particular cause of the union between the two, or of the mind itself, but was obliged to have recourse to the cause of the whole universe, that is to God. Further, I should much like to know, what degree of motion the mind can impart to this pineal gland, and with what force can it hold it suspended? For I am in ignorance, whether this gland can be agitated more slowly or more quickly by the mind than by the animal spirits, and whether the motions of the passions, which we have closely united with firm decisions, cannot be again disjoined therefrom by physical causes; in which case it would follow that, although the mind firmly intended to face a given danger, and had united to this decision the motions of boldness, yet at the sight of danger the gland might become suspended in a way, which would preclude the mind thinking of anything except running away. In truth, as there is no common standard of volition and motion, so is there no comparison possible between the powers of the mind and the power or strength of the body; consequently the strength of one cannot in any wise be determined by the strength of the other. We may add, that there is no gland discoverable in the midst of the brain, so placed that it can thus easily be set in motion in so many ways, and also that all the nerves are not prolonged so far as the cavities of the brain. Lastly, I omit all the assertions which he makes concerning the will and its freedom, inasmuch as I have abundantly proved that his premises are false. Therefore, since the power of the mind, as I have shown above, is defined by the understanding only, we shall determine solely by the knowledge of the mind the remedies against the emotions, which I believe all have had experience of, but do not accurately observe or distinctly see, and from the same basis we shall deduce all those conclusions, which have regard to the mind's blessedness. —E-V

An emotion, which is attributable to many and diverse causes which the mind regards as simultaneous with the emotion itself, is less hurtful, and we are less subject thereto and less affected towards each of its causes, than if it were a different and equally powerful emotion attributable to fewer causes or to single cause. —E-V

An emotion is stronger in proportion to the number of simultaneous concurrent causes whereby it is aroused. —E-V

If the mind has once been affected by two emotions at the same time, it will, whenever it is afterwards affected by one of the two, be also affected by the other. —E-III

Emotions which are aroused or spring from reason, if we take account of time, are stronger than those, which are attributable to particular objects that we regard as absent. —E-V

Among the kinds of emotions, the chief are *luxury, drunkenness, lust, avarice,* and *ambition,* being merely species of love or desire, displaying the nature of those emotions in a manner varying according to the object, with which they are concerned. For by luxury, drunkenness, lust, avarice, ambition, &c., we simply mean the immoderate love of feasting, drinking, venery, riches, and fame. Furthermore, these emotions, in so far as we distinguish them from others merely by the objects wherewith they are concerned, have no contraries. For *temperance, sobriety,* and *chastity,* which we are wont to oppose to luxury, drunkenness, and lust, are not emotions or passive states, but indicate a power of the mind which moderates the last-named emotions. However, I cannot here explain the remaining kinds of emotions (seeing that they are as numerous as the kinds of objects), nor, if I could, would it be necessary. It is sufficient for our purpose, namely, to determine the strength of the emotions, and the mind's power over them, to have a general definition of each emotion. It is sufficient, I repeat, to understand the general properties of the emotions and the mind, to enable us to determine the quality and extent of the mind's power in moderating and checking the emotions. Thus, though there is a great difference between various emotions of love, hatred, or desire, for instance between love felt towards children, and love felt towards a wife, there is no need for us to take cognizance of such differences, or to track out further the nature and origin of the emotions. —E-III

Anything can, accidentally, be the cause of pleasure, pain, or desire. —E-III

Among all the emotions attributable to the mind as active, there are none which cannot be referred to pleasure or pain.

All actions following from emotion, which are attributable to the mind in virtue of its understanding, I set down to *strength of character*, which I divide into *courage* and *high-mindedness*. By *courage* I mean *the desire whereby every man strives to preserve his own being in accordance solely with the dictates of reason*. By *high-mindedness* I mean *the desire whereby every man endeavors, solely under the dictates of reason, to aid other men and to unite them to himself in friendship*. Those actions, therefore, which have regard solely to the good of the agent I set down to courage, those which aim at the good of others I set down to high-mindedness. Thus temperance, sobriety, and presence of mind in danger, &c., are varieties of courage; courtesy, mercy, &c., are varieties of high-mindedness.

I think I have thus explained, and displayed through their primary causes the principal emotions and vacillations of spirit, which arise from the combination of the three primary emotions, to wit, desire, pleasure, and pain. It is evident from what I have said, that we are in many ways driven about by external causes, and that like waves of the sea driven by contrary winds we toss to and fro unwitting of the issue and of our fate. But I have said, that I have only set forth the chief conflicting emotions, not all that might be given. For, by proceeding in the same way as above, we can easily show that love is united to repentance, scorn, shame, &c. I think everyone will agree that the emotions may be compounded one with another in so many ways, and so many variations may arise therefrom, as to exceed all possibility of computation. However, for my purpose, it is enough to have enumerated the most important; to reckon up the rest which I have omitted would be more curious than profitable. It remains to remark concerning love, that it very often happens that while we are enjoying a thing which we longed for, the body, from the act of enjoyment, acquires a new disposition, whereby it is determined in another way, other images of things are aroused in it, and the mind begins to conceive and desire something fresh. For example, when we conceive something which generally delights us with its flavor, we desire to enjoy, that is, to eat it. But whilst we are thus enjoying it, the stomach is filled and the body is otherwise disposed. If, therefore, when the body is thus otherwise disposed, the image of the food which is present be stimulated, and consequently the endeavor or desire to eat it be stimulated also, the new disposition of the body will feel repugnance to the desire or attempt, and consequently the presence of the food which we formerly longed for will become odious. This revulsion of feeling is called *satiety* or weariness. For the rest, I have neglected the outward modifications of the body observable in emotions, such, for instance, as trembling, pallor, sobbing, laughter, &c., for these are attributable to the body only, without any reference to the mind.

—E-III

See Adequate Ideas, Bondage, Compassion, Intellectual
Love, Love, Lust, Nature, Passions, Passive and Active,
Reason, Vacillation of the Soul

EMOTIONS, PRIMARY

I recognize only three primitive or primary emotions,
namely, pleasure, pain, and desire. I have spoken of wonder, simply because it is customary to speak of certain emotions springing from the three primitive ones by different
names, when they are referred to the objects of our wonder.

—E-III

The mind can undergo many changes, and can pass sometimes to a state of greater perfection, sometimes to a state
of lesser perfection. These passive states of transition explain to us the emotions of pleasure and pain. By *pleasure*
therefore I signify *a passive state wherein the mind passes
to a greater perfection*. By *pain* I signify *a passive state
wherein the mind passes to a lesser perfection*. Further, the
emotion of pleasure in reference to the body and mind together I call *stimulation* or *merriment,* the emotion of pain
in the same relation I call *suffering* or *melancholy*. But we
must bear in mind, that stimulation and suffering are attributed to man, when one part of his nature is more affected than the rest, merriment and melancholy, when all
parts are alike affected. What I mean by desire I have
explained; beyond these three I recognize no other primary
emotion. All other emotions arise from these three. —E-III

EMULATION

When some one decides to do a thing because another
(who had done it first) has met with success, then we call
it *emulation*.   —G 2-IX

Emulation is the desire of something, engendered in us
by our conception that others have the same desire.

He who runs away, because he sees others running away,

or he who fears, because he sees others in fear; or again, he who, on seeing that another man has burnt his hand, draws towards him his own hand, and moves his body as though his own hand were burnt; such an one can be said to imitate another's emotion, but not to emulate him; not because the causes of emulation and imitation are different, but because it has become customary to speak of emulation only in him, who imitates that which we deem to be honorable, useful, or pleasant. —E-III

See Compassion

ENEMY

See Democracy

ENMITY

In so far as men are tormented by anger, envy, or any passion implying hatred, they are drawn asunder and made contrary one to another, and therefore are so much the more to be feared, as they are more powerful, crafty, and cunning than the other animals. And because men are in the highest degree liable to these passions, therefore men are naturally enemies. For he is my greatest enemy, whom I most fear and be on my guard against. —P T-II

ENVY

If we conceive that anyone pleasurably affects an object of our hate, we shall feel hatred towards him also. If we conceive that he painfully affects the said object, we shall feel love towards him.

These and similar emotions of hatred are attributable to *envy*, which, accordingly, is nothing else but *hatred, in so far as it is regarded as disposing a man to rejoice in another's hurt, and to grieve at another's advantage.* —E-III

If we conceive that anyone takes delight in something, which only one person can possess, we shall endeavor to bring it about that the man in question shall not gain possession thereof.

SPINOZA DICTIONARY

We thus see that man's nature is generally so constituted, that he takes pity on those who fare ill and envies those who fare well with an amount of hatred proportioned to his own love for the goods in their possession. Further, we see that from the same property of human nature, whence it follows that men are merciful, it follows also that they are envious and ambitious. Lastly, if we make appeal to Experience, we shall find that she entirely confirms what we have said; more especially if we turn our attention to the first years of our life. We find that children, whose body is continually, as it were, in equilibrium, laugh or cry simply because they see others laughing or crying; moreover, they desire forthwith to imitate whatever they see others doing, and to possess themselves whatever they conceive as delighting others: inasmuch as the images of things are, as we have said, modifications of the human body, or modes wherein the human body is affected and disposed by external causes to act in this or that manner.   —E-III

Men are naturally envious, rejoicing in the shortcomings of their equals, and feeling pain at their virtues. For whenever a man conceives his own actions, he is affected with pleasure, in proportion as his actions display more perfection, and he conceives them more distinctly—that is, in proportion as he can distinguish them from others, and regard them as something special. Therefore, a man will take most pleasure in contemplating himself, when he contemplates some quality which he denies to others. But, if that which he affirms of himself be attributable to the idea of man or animals in general, he will not be so greatly pleased: he will, on the contrary, feel pain, if he conceives that his own actions fall short when compared with those of others. This pain he will endeavor to remove, by putting a wrong construction on the actions of his equals, or by, as far as he can, embellishing his own.

It is thus apparent that men are naturally prone to hatred

and envy, which latter is fostered by their education. For parents are accustomed to incite their children to virtue solely by the spur of honor and envy. But, perhaps, some will scruple to assent to what I have said, because we not seldom admire men's virtues, and venerate their possessors. In order to remove ..uch doubts, I append the following corollary.

No one envies the virtue of anyone who is not his equal.

As we venerate a man, through wonder at his prudence, fortitude, &c., we do so, because we conceive those qualities to be peculiar to him, and not as common to our nature; we, therefore, no more envy their possessor, than we envy trees for being tall, or lions for being courageous.

—E-III

See Enmity, Jealousy, Pride, Rational Life, Sympathy, Timidity, Utopia

EQUALITY
See Virtue

EQUITY
See Democracy, Rational Life

ERROR
See Falsity, Meaning
ESSENCE
The endeavor, wherewith everything endeavors to persist in its own being, is nothing else but the actual essence of the thing in question.   —E-III

I maintain, in the first place, that God is absolutely and really the cause of all things which have essence, whatsoever they may be. If you can demonstrate that evil, error, crime, &c., have any positive existence, which expresses essence, I will fully grant you that God is the cause of crime, evil, error, &c. I believe myself to have sufficiently shown, that that which constitutes the reality of evil, error,

[68]

crime, &c., does not consist in anything, which expresses essence, and therefore we cannot say that God is the cause. For instance, Nero's matricide, in so far as it comprehended anything positive, was not a crime; the same outward act was perpetrated, and the same matricidal intention was entertained by Orestes; who, nevertheless, is not blamed— at any rate, not so much as Nero. Wherein, then, did Nero's crime consist? In nothing else, but that by his deed he showed himself to be ungrateful, unmerciful, and disobedient. Certainly none of these qualities express aught of essence, therefore God was not the cause of them, though He was the cause of Nero's act and intention.

Further, that, while we speak philosophically, we ought not to employ theological phrases. For, since theology frequently, and not unwisely, represents God as a perfect man, it is often expedient in theology to say, that God desires a given thing, that He is angry at the actions of the wicked, and delights in those of the good. But in philosophy, when we clearly perceive that the attributes which make men perfect can as ill be ascribed and assigned to God, as the attributes which go to make perfect the elephant and the ass can be ascribed to man; here I say these and similar phrases have no place, nor can we employ them without causing extreme confusion in our conceptions. Hence, in the language of philosophy, it cannot be said that God desires anything of any man, or that anything is displeasing or pleasing to Him: all these are human qualities and have no place in God.

I would have it observed, that although the actions of the good (that is of those who have a clear idea of God, whereby all their actions and their thoughts are determined) and of the wicked (that is of those who do not possess the idea of God, but only the ideas of earthly things, whereby their actions and thoughts are determined), and, in fact, of all things that are, necessarily flow from God's eternal laws and decrees; yet they do not differ from one another in degree only, but also in essence. A mouse no less than an angel, and sorrow no less than joy depend on God; yet a mouse is not a kind of angel, neither is sorrow a kind of joy.

However, this will appear more clearly, if I answer the questions some propose on these principles. First, Whether murder is as acceptable to God as alms-giving? Secondly, Whether stealing is as good in relation to God as honesty? Thirdly and lastly, Whether if there be a mind so framed, that it would agree with, rather than be repugnant to its proper nature, to give way to lust, and to commit crimes, whether, I repeat, there can be any reason given, why such a mind should do good and eschew evil?

To the first question, I answer, that I do not know, speaking as a philosopher, what they mean by the words "acceptable to God." If they ask, whether God does not hate the wicked, and love the good? whether God does not regard the former with dislike, and the latter with favor? I answer, No. If the meaning of their question is: Are murderers and almsgivers equally good and perfect? my answer is again in the negative. To their second question, I reply: If, by "good in relation to God," they mean that the honest man confers a favor on God, and the thief does Him an injury, I answer that neither the honest man nor the thief can cause God any pleasure or displeasure. If they mean to ask, whether the actions of each, in so far as they possess reality, and are caused by God, are equally perfect? I reply that, if we merely regard the actions and the manner of their execution, both may be equally perfect. If they, therefore, inquire whether the thief and the honest man are equally perfect and blessed? I answer, No. For, by an honest man, I mean one who always desires, that everyone should possess that which is his. This desire necessarily derives its origin in the pious from the clear knowledge which they possess, of God and of themselves. As a thief has no desire of the kind, he is necessarily without the knowledge of God and of himself—in other words, without the chief element of our blessedness. If you further ask, What causes you to perform a given action, which I call virtuous, rather than another? I reply, that I cannot know which method, out of the infinite methods at His disposal, God employs to determine you to the said action. It may be, that God has impressed you with a clear idea of Himself, so that you forget the world for love of Him, and love your fellow-men as yourself; it is plain that such a disposition is at variance with those dispositions which are called bad, and, therefore, could not co-exist with them in the same man.

Lastly, as to your third question, it assumes a contradiction, and seems to me to be, as though one asked: If it agreed better with a man's nature that he should hang himself, could any reason be given for his not hanging himself? Can such a nature possibly exist? If so, I maintain (whether I do or do not grant free will), that such an one, if he sees that he can live more conveniently on the gallows than sitting at his own table, would act most foolishly, if he did not commit suicide. So anyone who clearly saw that, by committing crimes, he would enjoy a really more perfect and better life and existence, than he could attain by the practice of virtue, would be foolish if he did not act on his convictions. For, with such a perverse human nature as his, crime would become virtue. —C-XXXVI-B

I consider as belonging to the essence of a thing that, which being given, the thing is necessarily given also, and, which being removed, the thing is necessarily removed also; in other words, that without which the thing, and which itself without the thing, can neither be nor be conceived.
—E-II

In God there is necessarily the idea not only of his essence, but also of all things which necessarily follow from his essence. —E-II

See Eternity; Freedom, Human; Ideas; Intellect; Love; Substance

ESSENTIALITY
See God

ESTEEM

Esteem and Contempt are felt in so far as we know a thing to be something great or small, be this great or little thing in us or outside us.   —G 2-VIII

The pleasure which arises from a man thinking too highly of another is called over-esteem.   —E-III

Over-esteem is apt to render its object proud.   —E-IV

Partiality is thinking too highly of anyone because of the love we bear him.   —E-III

ETERNAL AND INFINITE ESSENTIALITY
See Substance

ETERNAL LAWS
See Law of Nature

ETERNAL TRUTHS

As to whether things and their modifications are eternal truths, I answer: Certainly. If you ask me, why I do not call them eternal truths, I answer, in order to distinguish them, in accordance with general usage, from those propositions, which do not make manifest any particular thing or modification of a thing; for example, *nothing comes from nothing.* These and such like propositions are, I repeat, called eternal truths simply, the meaning merely being, that they have no standpoint external to the mind.   —C-XXVIII-S DE V

ETERNITY

By *eternity*, I mean existence itself, in so far as it is conceived necessarily to follow solely from the definition of that which is eternal.

Existence of this kind is conceived as an eternal truth, like the essence of a thing, and, therefore, cannot be explained by means of continuance or time, though continuance may be conceived without a beginning or end.   —E-I

Whatsoever the mind understands under the form of eternity, it does not understand by virtue of conceiving the present actual existence of the body, but by virtue of conceiving the essence of the body under the form of eternity.

Things are conceived by us as actual in two ways; either as existing in relation to a given time and place, or as contained in God and following from the necessity of the Divine nature. Whatsoever we conceive in this second way as true or real, we conceive under the form of eternity, and their ideas involve the eternal and infinite essence of God.
    —E-V

In God there is necessarily an idea, which expresses the essence of this or that human body under the form of eternity.   —E-V

See Immortality of the Soul, Mode, Passive and Active, Religion

ETHICS
    See Evil

EUCLID
    See Books

EVIL
    Philosophers conceive of the passions which harass us as vices into which men fall by their own fault, and, therefore, generally deride, bewail, or blame them, or execrate them, if they wish to seem unusually pious. And so they think they are doing something wonderful, and reaching the pinnacle of learning, when they are clever enough to bestow manifold praise on such human nature, as is nowhere to be found, and to make verbal attacks on that which, in fact, exists. For they conceive of men, not as they are, but as they themselves would like them to be. Whence it has come to pass that, instead of ethics, they have generally written

satire, and that they have never conceived a theory of politics, which could be turned to use, but such as might be taken for a chimera, or might have been formed in Utopia, or in that golden age of the poets when, to be sure, there was least need of it. Accordingly, as in all sciences, which have a useful application, so especially in that of politics, theory is supposed to be at variance with practice; and no men are esteemed less fit to direct public affairs than theorists or philosophers.

2. But statesmen, on the other hand, are suspected of plotting against mankind, rather than consulting their interests, and are esteemed more crafty than learned. No doubt nature has taught them, that vices will exist, while men do. And so, while they study to anticipate human wickedness, and that by arts, which experience and long practice have taught, and which men generally use under the guidance more of fear than of reason, they are thought to be enemies of religion, especially by divines, who believe that supreme authorities should handle public affairs in accordance with the same rules of piety, as bind a private individual. Yet there can be no doubt, that statesmen have written about politics far more happily than philosophers. For, as they had experience for their mistress, they taught nothing that was inconsistent with practice.

3. And, certainly, I am fully persuaded that experience has revealed all conceivable sorts of commonwealth, which are consistent with men's living in unity, and likewise the means by which the multitude may be guided or kept within fixed bounds. So that I do not believe that we can by meditation discover in this matter anything not yet tried and ascertained, which shall be consistent with experience or practice. For men are so situated, that they cannot live without some general law. But general laws and public affairs are ordained and managed by men of the utmost acuteness, or, if you like, of great cunning or craft. And so it is hardly credible, that we should be able to conceive of anything

serviceable to a general society, that occasion or chance has not offered, or that men, intent upon their common affairs, and seeking their own safety, have not seen for themselves.

—P T-I

By *evil* I mean that which we certainly know to be a hindrance to us in the attainment of any good.   —E-IV

The knowledge of evil is an inadequate knowledge.

Hence it follows that, if the human mind possessed only adequate ideas, it would form no conception of evil. —E-IV

See Good and Bad, Rational Life, Reason, Wisdom

EXCESS
See Lust

EXISTENCE
The force whereby a man persists in existing is limited, and is infinitely surpassed by the power of external causes.

—E-IV

No one can desire to be blessed, to act rightly, and to live rightly, without at the same time wishing to be, to act, and to live—in other words, to actually exist.   —E-IV

The true definition of anything includes nothing except the simple nature of the thing defined. From this it follows—

That no definition can involve or express a multitude or a given number of individuals, inasmuch as it involves and expresses nothing except the nature of the thing as it is in itself. For instance, the definition of a triangle includes nothing beyond the simple nature of a triangle; it does not include any given number of triangles. In like manner, the definition of the mind as a thinking thing, or the definition of God as a perfect Being, includes nothing beyond the natures of the mind and of God, not a given number of minds or gods.

For everything that exists there must necessarily be a positive cause, through which it exists.

This cause may be situate either in the nature and definition of the thing itself (to wit, because existence belongs to its nature or necessarily includes it), or externally to the thing.

From these premises it follows, that if any given number of individuals exists in nature, there must be one or more causes, which have been able to produce exactly that number of individuals, neither more nor less. If, for instance, there existed in nature twenty men (in order to avoid all confusion, I will assume that these all exist together as primary entities), it is not enough to investigate the cause of human nature in general, in order to account for the existence of these twenty; we must also inquire into the reason, why there exist exactly twenty men, neither more nor less. For for each man a reason and a cause must be forthcoming, why he should exist. But this cause cannot be contained in the nature of man himself; for the true definition of man does not involve the number of twenty men. Hence the cause for the existence of these twenty men, and consequently for the existence of each of them, must exist externally to them. We may thus absolutely conclude, that all things, which are conceived to exist in the plural number, must necessarily be produced by external causes and not by the force of their own nature. But since necessary existence appertains to the nature of God, His true definition must necessarily include necessary existence: therefore from His true definition His necessary existence must be inferred. But from His true definition the necessary existence of many gods cannot be inferred. Therefore there only follows the existence of a single God.   —C-XXXIX-C H

We never need experience, except in cases when the existence of the thing cannot be inferred from its definition, as, for instance, the existence of modes (which cannot be inferred from their definition); experience is not needed, when the existence of the things in question is not distinguished from their essence, and is therefore inferred from their definition. This can never be taught us by any experience, for experience does not teach us any essences of things; the utmost it can do is to set our mind thinking about definite essences only. Wherefore, when the existence of attributes does not differ from their essence, no experience is capable of attaining it for us. —C-XXVIII-S DE V

See Eternity, Substance

EXPERIENCE
See Persuasion

EXTENSION
Extension is an attribute of God, or God is an extended thing. —E-II

See Motion

EXTERNAL CAUSES
See Rational Life

F

FAITH

Faith allows the greatest latitude in philosophic speculation, allowing us without blame to think what we like about anything, and only condemning, as heretics and schismatics, those who teach opinions which tend to produce obstinacy, hatred, strife, and anger; while, on the other hand, only considering as faithful those who persuade us, as far as their reason and faculties will permit, to follow justice and charity.   —T P-XIV

But as to what God, or the Exemplar of the true life, may be, whether fire, or spirit, or light, or thought, or what not, this, I say, has nothing to do with faith any more than has the question how He comes to be the Exemplar of the true life, whether it be because He has a just and merciful mind, or because all things exist and act through Him, and consequently that we understand through Him, and through Him see what is truly just and good. Everyone may think on such questions as he likes.

Furthermore, faith is not affected, whether we hold that God is omnipresent essentially or potentially; that He directs all things by absolute fiat, or by the necessity of His nature; that He dictates laws like a prince, or that He sets them forth as eternal truths; that man obeys Him by virtue of free will, or by virtue of the necessity of the Divine decree; lastly, that the reward of the good and the punishment of the wicked is natural or supernatural: these and such like questions have no bearing on faith, except in so far as they are used as means to give us license to sin more, or to obey God less. I will go further, and maintain that every man is bound to adapt these dogmas to his own way of thinking, and to interpret them according as he feels that he can give them his fullest and most unhesitating assent, so that he may the more easily obey God with his whole heart.

Such was the manner, as we have already pointed out, in which the faith was in old time revealed and written, in accordance with the understanding and opinions of the prophets and people of the period; so, in like fashion, every man is bound to adapt it to his own opinions, so that he may accept it without any hesitation or mental repugnance. We have shown that faith does not so much require truth as piety, and that it is only quickening and pious through obedience, consequently no one is faithful save by obedience alone. The best faith is not necessarily possessed by him who displays the best reasons, but by him who displays the best fruits of justice and charity. How salutary and necessary this doctrine is for a state, in order that men may dwell together in peace and concord; and how many and how great causes of disturbance and crime are thereby cut off, I leave everyone to judge for himself!   —T P-XIV

See Liberty, Philosophy, Religion, Superstition

FALSITY

Falsity consists in the privation of knowledge, which inadequate, fragmentary, or confused ideas involve.

Error consists in the privation of knowledge, but in order to throw more light on the subject I will give an éxample. For instance, men are mistaken in thinking themselves free willed; their opinion is made up of consciousness of their own actions, and ignorance of the causes by which they are conditioned. Their idea of freedom, therefore, is simply their ignorance of any cause for their actions. As for their saying that human actions depend on the will, this is a mere phrase without any idea to correspond thereto. What the will is, and how it moves the body, they none of them know; those who boast of such knowledge, and feign dwellings and habitations for the soul, are wont to provoke either laughter or disgust. So, again, when we look at the sun, we imagine that it is distant from us about two hundred feet; this error does not lie solely in this fancy, but in the fact that, while we thus imagine, we do know the sun's true distance or the cause of the fancy. For although we afterwards learn, that the sun is distant from us more than six hundred of the earth's diameters, we none the less shall fancy it to be near; for we do not imagine the sun as near us, because we are ignorant of its true distance, but because the modification of our body involves the essence of the sun, in so far as our said body is affected thereby.   —E-II

No positive quality possessed by a false idea is removed by the presence of what is true, in virtue of its being true.
                                                          —E-IV

Falsity is an affirmation (or a denial) about a thing, which does not agree with the thing itself. But this being so, it may appear that there is no difference between the false and the true Idea, or, since the [affirmation or] denial of this or that are mere modes of thought, and [the true and the false Idea] differ in no other way except that the one agrees with the thing, and the other does not, that they are therefore, not really, but only logically different; and if this should be so, one may justly ask, what advantage has the one from his Truth, and what harm does the other incur through his falsity? and how shall the one know that his conception or Idea agrees with the thing more than the other does? lastly, whence does it come that the one errs, and the other does not?

To this it may, in the first place, serve as an answer that the clearest ideas of all make known both themselves and also what is false, in such a manner that it would be a great folly to ask how we are to become aware of them; for, since they are said to be the clearest of all, there can never be any other clearness through which they might be made clear; it follows, therefore, that truth at once reveals itself and also what is false, because truth is made clear through truth, that is through itself, and through it also is falsity made clear; but falsity is never revealed and made manifest through itself. So that any one who is in possession of the truth cannot doubt that he possesses it, while one who is sunk in falsity or in error can well suppose that he has got at the truth; just as someone who is dreaming can well think that he is awake, but one who is actually awake can never think that he is dreaming.

These remarks also explain to some extent what we said about God being the Truth, or that *the Truth is God Himself.*

Now the reason why the one is more conscious of his truth than the other is, is because the Idea of [his] affirmation (or denial) entirely agrees with the nature of the thing, and consequently has more essence. It may help some to grasp this better if it be observed that Understanding (although the word does not sound like it) is a mere or pure passivity; that is, that our soul is changed in such a way that it receives other modes of thought, which it did not have before. Now when some one, in consequence of the whole object having acted upon him, receives corresponding forms or modes of thought, then it is clear that he receives a totally different feeling of the form or character of the object than does another who has not had so many causes [acting upon him], and is therefore moved to make an affirmation or denial about that thing by a different and slighter action (because he becomes aware of it only through a few, or the less important, of its attributes). From this, then, we see the perfection of one who takes his stand upon Truth, as contrasted with one who does not take his stand upon it. Since the one changes easily, while the other does not change easily, it follows therefrom that the one has more stability and essence than the other has: likewise,

SPINOZA DICTIONARY

since the modes of thought which agree with the thing have had more causes [to produce them] they have also more stability and essence in them: and, since they entirely agree with the thing, it is impossible that they should after a time be made different or undergo some change, all the less so because we have already seen before that the essence of a thing is unchangeable. Such is not the case with falsity. And with these remarks all the above questions will be suf-ficiently answered.   —G 2-XV
See Ideas, Knowledge

FAME

Fame is a certain kind of joy which every one feels in himself whenever he becomes aware that his conduct is esteemed and praised by others, without regard to any other advantage or profit which they may have in view. —G 2-XII

Honor is not repugnant to reason, but may arise there-from.

Empty honor, as it is styled, is self-approval, fostered only by the good opinion of the populace; when this good opinion ceases there ceases also the self-approval, in other words, the highest object of each man's love; consequently, he whose honor is rooted in popular approval must, day by day, anxiously strive, act, and scheme in order to retain his reputation. For the populace is variable and inconstant, so that, if a reputation be not kept up, it quickly withers away. Everyone wishes to catch popular applause for himself, and readily represses the fame of others. The object of the strife being estimated as the greatest of all goods, each com-batant is seized with a fierce desire to put down his rivals in every possible way, till he who at last comes out vic-torious is more proud of having done harm to others than of having done good to himself. This sort of honor, then, is really empty, being nothing.

The points to note concerning shame may easily be in-ferred from what was said on the subject of mercy and re-

[83]

pentance. I will only add that shame, like compassion, though not a virtue, is yet good, in so far as it shows, that the feeler of shame is really imbued with the desire to live honorably; in the same way as suffering is good, as showing that the injured part is not mortified. Therefore, though a man who feels shame is sorrowful, he is yet more perfect than he, who is shameless, and has no desire to live honorably.

Such are the points which I undertook to remark upon concerning the emotions of pleasure and pain; as for the desires, they are good or bad according as they spring from good or evil emotions. But all, in so far as they are engendered in us by emotions wherein the mind is passive, are blind and would be useless, if men could easily be induced to live by the guidance of reason only, as I will now briefly show. —E-IV

If anyone has done something which he conceives as affecting other men pleasurably, he will be affected by pleasure, accompanied by the idea of himself as cause; in other words, he will regard himself with pleasure. On the other hand, if he has done anything which he conceives as affecting others painfully, he will regard himself with pain.

As love is pleasure accompanied by the idea of an external cause, and hatred is pain accompanied by the idea of an external cause; the pleasure and pain in question will be a species of love and hatred. But, as the terms love and hatred are used in reference to external objects, we will employ other names for the emotions now under discussion: pleasure accompanied by the idea of an external cause we will style *Honor*, and the emotion contrary thereto we will style *Shame*: I mean in such cases as where pleasure or pain arises from a man's belief, that he is being praised or blamed: otherwise pleasure accompanied by the idea of an external cause is called *self-complacency*, and its contrary pain is called *repentance*. Again, as it may happen that the pleasure, wherewith a man conceives that he affects others, may exist solely in his own imagination, and as everyone endeavors to conceive concerning himself that which he conceives will affect him with pleasure, it may easily come to pass that a man of vanity may proudly imagine that he is pleasing to all, when in reality he may be an annoyance to all.   —E-III

Honor is pleasure accompanied by the idea of some action of our own, which we believe to be praised by others.

See Happiness   —E-III

FAVORS

The free man, who lives among the ignorant, strives, as far as he can, to avoid receiving favors from them.

I say, *as far as he can.* For though men be ignorant, yet are they men, and in cases of necessity could afford us human aid, the most excellent of all things: therefore it is often necessary to accept favors from them, and consequently to repay such favors in kind; we must, therefore, exercise caution in declining favors, lest we should have the appearance of despising those who bestow them, or of being, from avaricious motives, unwilling to requite them, and so give ground for offense by the very fact of striving to avoid it. Thus, in declining favors, we must look to the requirements of utility and courtesy.   —E-IV

FEAR

If we judge that that which may be coming is bad, then that form enters into our soul which we call *fear.* —G 2-IX

Fear is an inconstant pain arising from the idea of something past or future, whereof we to a certain extent doubt the issue.

From these definitions it follows, that there is no hope unmingled with fear, and no fear unmingled with hope. For he, who depends on hope and doubts concerning the issue of anything, is assumed to conceive something, which ex-

cludes the existence of the said thing in the future; therefore he, to this extent, feels pain; consequently, while dependent on hope, he fears for the issue. Contrariwise he,
who fears, in other words doubts, concerning the issue of
something which he hates, also conceives something which
excludes the existence of the thing in question; to this extent he feels pleasure and consequently to this extent he
hopes that it will turn out as he desires.   —E-III

He who is led by fear, and does good in order to escape
evil, is not led by reason.

Superstitious persons, who know better how to rail at
vice than how to teach virtue, and who strive not to guide
men by reason, but so to restrain them that they would
rather escape evil than love virtue, have no other aim but
to make others as wretched as themselves; wherefore it is
nothing wonderful, if they be generally troublesome and
odious to their fellow-men.

Under desire which springs from reason, we seek good
odious to their fellowmen.

This may be illustrated by the example of a sick and a
healthy man. The sick man through fear of death eats what
he naturally shrinks from, but the healthy man takes pleasure in his food, and thus gets a better enjoyment out of life,
than if he were in fear of death, and desired directly to
avoid it. So a judge, who condemns a criminal to death,
not from hatred or anger but from love of the public well-
being, is guided solely by reason.   —E-IV

Anything whatever can be, accidentally, a cause of hope
or fear.

Things which are accidentally the causes of hope or fear
are called good or evil omens. Now, in so far as such omens
are the cause of hope or fear, they are the causes also of
pleasure and pain; consequently we, to this extent, regard
them with love or hatred, and endeavour either to invoke
them as means towards that which we hope for, or to re-

move them as obstacles, or causes of that which we fear. We are naturally so constituted as to believe readily in that which we hope for, and with difficulty in that which we fear; moreover, we are apt to estimate such objects above or below their true value. Hence there have arisen superstitions, whereby men are everywhere assailed. However, I do not think it worth while to point out here the vacillations springing from hope and fear; it follows from the definition of these emotions, that there can be no hope without fear, and no fear without hope, as I will duly explain in the proper place. Further, in so far as we hope for or fear anything, we regard it with love or hatred; thus everyone can apply by himself to hope and fear what we have said concerning love and hatred. —E-III

Fear is an inconstant pain arising from the image of something concerning which we are in doubt. If the element of doubt be removed from these emotions, hope becomes *Confidence* and fear becomes *Despair.* In other words, *Pleasure or Pain arising from the image of something concerning which we have hoped or feared.* —E-III

See Consternation, Democracy, Liberty, Lust, Rational Life

FELLOWSHIP
See Rational Life

FINAL CAUSE
See God, Nature and Properties of

FINITE
A thing is called *finite after its kind,* when it can be limited by another thing of the same nature; for instance, a body is called finite because we always conceive another greater body. So, also, a thought is limited by another thought, but a body is not limited by thought, nor a thought by body. —E-I

FIRST KIND OF KNOWLEDGE
See Knowledge

FLATTERY
See Pride, Rational Life

FORTUNE
By fortune, I mean the ordinance of God in so far as it directs human life through external and unexpected means.
—T P-III

FREE
That thing is called free, which exists solely by the necessity of its own nature, and of which the action is determined by itself alone. On the other hand, that thing is necessary, or rather constrained, which is determined by something external to itself to a fixed and definite method of existence or action.
—E-I

FREE CAUSE
See Love

FREE DECISION
See Mind

FREEDOM
If men were born free, they would, so long as they remained free, form no conception of good and evil.

This seems to have been signified by Moses in the history of the first man. For in that narrative no other power of God is conceived, save that whereby he created man, that is the power wherewith he provided solely for man's advantage; it is stated that God forbade man, being free, to eat of the tree of the knowledge of good and evil, and that, as soon as man should have eaten of it, he would straightway fear death rather than desire to live. Further, it is written that when man had found a wife, who was in entire harmony with his nature, he knew that there could be nothing in nature which could be more useful to him; but that after he believed the beasts to be like himself, he straightway began to imitate their emotions, and to lose his freedom; this freedom was afterwards recovered by the patriarchs, led by the idea of God, whereon alone it depends, that man may be free, and desire for others the good which he desires for himself, as we have shown above. —E-IV

See Democracy, Ideas, Intellectual Love, Liberty, Superstition, Tyranny

FREEDOM, HUMAN
The free man never acts fraudulently, but always in good faith. —E-IV

Inasmuch as human power is to be reckoned less by physical vigor than by mental strength, it follows that those men are most independent whose reason is strongest, and who are most guided thereby. And so I am altogether for calling a man so far free, as he is led by reason; because so far he is determined to action by such causes, as can be adequately understood by his unassisted nature, although by these causes he be necessarily determined to action. —P T-II

The virtue of a free man is seen to be as great, when it declines dangers, as when it overcomes them.
The free man is as courageous in timely retreat as in combat; or, a free man shows equal courage or presence of mind, whether he elect to give battle or to retreat. —E-IV

1. The more essence a thing has, so much more has it also of activity, and so much less of passivity. For it is certain that what is active acts through what it has, and that the thing which is passive is affected through what it has not.
2. All passivity that passes from non-being to being, or from being to non-being, must result from some external agent, and not from an inner one: because no thing, considered by itself, contains in itself the conditions that will enable it to annihilate itself when it exists, or to create itself when it does not exist.

3. Whatever is not produced by external causes can have
nothing in common with them, and can, consequently, be
neither changed nor transformed by them.

And from these last two [propositions] I infer the following fourth proposition:

4. The effect of an immanent or inner cause (which is
all one to me) cannot possibly pass away or change so long
as this cause of it remains. For such an effect, just as it is
not produced by external causes, so also it cannot be
changed [by them]; following the third proposition. And
since no thing whatever can come to naught except through
external causes, it is not possible that this effect should be
liable to perish so long as its cause endures; following the
second proposition.

5. The freest cause of all, and that which is most appropriate to God, is the immanent: for the effect of this cause
depends on it in such a way that it can neither be, nor be
understood without it, nor is it subjected to any other cause;
it is, moreover, united with it in such a way that together
they form one whole.

Now let us just see what we must conclude from the
above propositions. In the first place, then,

1. Since the essence of God is infinite, therefore it has
an infinite activity, and an infinite negation of passivity,
following the first proposition; and, in consequence of this,
the more that, through their greater essence, things are
united with God, so much the more also do they have of
activity, and the less of passivity; and so much the more
also are they free from change and corruption.

2. The true understanding can never perish; for in itself
it can have no cause to destroy itself, following the second
proposition. And as it did not emanate from external causes,
but from God, so it is not susceptible to any change
through them, following the third proposition. And since
God has produced it immediately and he is only an inner
cause, it follows necessarily that it cannot perish so long

[90]

as this cause of it remains, following the fourth proposition. Now this cause of it is eternal, therefore it is too.

3. All the effects of the true understanding, which are united with it, are the most excellent, and must be valued above all the others; for as they are inner effects, they must be the most excellent; following the fifth proposition; and, besides this, they are also necessarily eternal, because their cause is such.

4. All the effects which we produce outside ourselves are the more perfect, the more they are capable of becoming united with us, so as to constitute one and the same nature with us; for in this way they come nearest to inner effects. For example, if I teach my neighbors to love pleasure, glory, avarice, then whether I myself also love these or do not love them, whatever the case may be, I deserve to be punished, this is clear. Not so, however, when the only end that I endeavor to attain is, to be able to taste of union with God, and to bring forth true ideas, and to make these things known also to my neighbors; for we can all participate equally in this happiness, as happens when it creates in them the same desire that I have, thus causing their will and mine to be one and the same, constituting one and the same nature, agreeing always in all things.

From all that has been said it may now be very easily conceived what is human freedom, which I define to be this: it is, namely, a firm reality which our understanding acquires through direct union with God, so that it can bring forth ideas in itself, and effects outside itself, in complete harmony with its nature; without, however, its effects being subjected to any external causes, so as to be capable of being changed or transformed by them. Thus it is, at the same time, evident from what has been said, what things there are that are in our power, and are not subjected to any external causes; we have likewise also proved here, and that in a different way from before, the eternal and lasting duration of our understanding; and, lastly, which effects they are that we have to value above all others. —G 2-XXVI

FREEDOM OF JUDGMENT
See Tyranny

FREEDOM OF RELIGIOUS BELIEF
See Liberty

FREEDOM OF SPEECH
See Liberty

FREEDOM OF THE SOUL
See Rational Life

FREEDOM OF THOUGHT
See Liberty

FREE MAN
See Favors, Reason

FREE WILL
I say that a thing is free, which exists and acts solely by the necessity of its own nature. Thus also God understands Himself and all things freely, because it follows solely from the necessity of His nature, that He should understand all things. I do not place freedom in free decision, but in free necessity. However, let us descend to created things, which are all determined by external causes to exist and operate in a given determinate manner. In order that this may be clearly understood, let us conceive a very simple thing. For instance, a stone receives from the impulsion of an external cause, a certain quantity of motion, by virtue of which it continues to move after the impulsion given by the external cause has ceased. The permanence of the stone's motion is constrained, not necessary, because it must be defined by the impulsion of an external cause. What is true of the stone is true of any individual, however complicated its nature, or varied its functions inasmuch as every individual

thing is necessarily determined by some external cause to exist and operate in a fixed and determined manner.

Further conceive, I beg, that a stone, while continuing in motion, should be capable of thinking and knowing, that it is endeavoring, as far as it can, to continue to move. Such a stone, being conscious merely of its own endeavor and not at all indifferent, would believe itself to be completely free, and would think that it continued in motion solely because of its own wish. This is that human freedom, which all boast that they possess, and which consists solely in the fact, that men are conscious of their own desire, but are ignorant of the causes whereby that desire has been determined. Thus an infant believes that it desires milk freely; an angry child thinks he wishes freely for vengeance, a timid child thinks he wishes freely to run away. Again, a drunken man thinks, that from the free decision of his mind he speaks words, which afterwards, when sober, he would like to have left unsaid. So the delirious, the garrulous, and others of the same sort think that they act from the free decision of their mind, not that they are carried away by impulse. As this misconception is innate in all men, it is not easily conquered. For, although experience abundantly shows, that men can do anything rather than check their desires, and that very often, when a prey to conflicting emotions, they see the better course and follow the worse, they yet believe themselves to be free; because in some cases their desire for a thing is slight, and can easily be overruled by the recollection of something else, which is frequently present in the mind.

I have thus, if I mistake not, sufficiently explained my opinion regarding free and constrained necessity, and also regarding so-called human freedom: from what I have said you will easily be able to reply to your friend's objections. For when he says, with Descartes, that he who is constrained by no external cause is free, if by being constrained he means acting against one's will, I grant that we are in some cases quite unrestrained, and in this respect possess free will. But if by constrained he means acting necessarily, although not against one's will (as I have explained above), I deny that we are in any instance free. —C-LXII-G H S

In the mind there is no absolute or free will; but the mind is determined to wish this or that by a cause, which has also been determined by another cause, and this last by another cause, and so on to infinity.

In the same way it is proved, that there is in the mind no absolute faculty of understanding, desiring, loving, &c. Whence it follows, that these and similar faculties are either entirely fictitious, or are merely abstract or general terms, such as we are accustomed to put together from particular things. Thus the intellect and the will stand in the same relation to this or that idea, or this or that volition, as "lapidity" to this or that stone, or as "man" to Peter and Paul. —E-II

That man, like other beings, as far as in him lies, strives to preserve his existence, no one can deny. For if any distinction could be conceived on this point, it must arise from man's having a free will. But the freer we conceived man to be, the more we should be forced to maintain, that he must of necessity preserve his existence and be in possession of his senses; as anyone will easily grant me, that does not confound liberty with contingency. For liberty is a virtue, or excellence. Whatever, therefore, convicts a man of weakness cannot be ascribed to his liberty. And so man can by no means be called free, because he is able not to exist or not to use his reason, but only in so far as he preserves the power of existing and operating according to the laws of human nature. The more, therefore, we consider man to be free, the less we can say, that he can neglect to use reason, or choose evil in preference to good; and, therefore, God, Who exists in absolute liberty, also understands and operates of necessity, that is, exists, understands, and operates according to the necessity of His own nature. For there is no doubt, that God operates by the same liberty whereby He exists. As then He exists by the necessity of His own nature, by the necessity of His own nature also He acts, that is, He acts with absolute liberty.　　　—P T-II

See Falsity; God, Nature and Properties of; Mind

FRIENDSHIP

I value, above all other things out of my own control, the joining hands of friendship with men who are sincere lovers of truth. I believe that nothing in the world, of things outside our own control, brings more peace than the possibility of affectionate intercourse with such men; it is just as impossible that the love we bear them can be disturbed (inasmuch as it is founded on the desire each feels for the knowledge of truth), as that truth once perceived should not be assented to. It is, moreover, the highest and most pleasing source of happiness derivable from things not under our own control. Nothing save truth has power closely to unite different feelings and dispositions.

　　　　　　　　　　　　　　　　　—C-XXXII-B

Between friends all things, and especially things spiritual, ought to be in common.　　　　　　　　—C-II-O

See Emotions, Jealousy, Rational Life

G

GENERAL NOTIONS
See Ideas

GENTILES
See Miracles

GHASDAI
See Mode

GLORY
See Intellectual Love

GOD

All who have any education know that God has no right hand nor left; that He is not moved nor at rest, nor in a particular place, but that He is absolutely infinite and contains in Himself all perfections.

These things, I repeat, are known to whoever judges of things by the perception of pure reason, and not according as his imagination is affected by his outward senses, following the example of the masses who imagine a bodily Deity, holding a royal court with a throne on the convexity of heaven, above the stars, which are believed to be not very far off from the earth.

To these and similar opinions very many narrations in Scripture are adapted, and should not, therefore, be mistaken by philosophers for realities.   —T P-VI

The existence of God and His essence are one and the same.   —E-I

God is the indwelling and not the transient cause of all things.   —E-I

Whatsoever is, is in God, and without God nothing can be, or be conceived.   —E-I

God acts solely by the laws of His own nature.   —E-I

God, Whom I define as a Being consisting in infinite attributes, whereof each is infinite or supremely perfect after its kind.   —C-II-O

God is of all things the cause immanent, as the phrase is, not transient. I say that all things are in God and move in God, thus agreeing with Paul, and, perhaps, with all the ancient philosophers, though the phraseology may be different; I will even venture to affirm that I agree with all the ancient Hebrews.   —C-XXI-O

God we mean a Being supremely perfect and absolutely infinite.   —C-II-O

God is without passions, neither is he affected by any emotion of pleasure or pain.
Strictly speaking, God does not love or hate anyone. For God is not affected by any emotion of pleasure or pain, consequently He does not love or hate anyone.   —E-V

By *God*, I mean a being absolutely infinite—that is, a substance consisting in infinite attributes, of which each expresses eternal and infinite essentiality.
I say absolutely infinite, not infinite after its kind: for, of a thing infinite only after its kind, infinite attributes may be denied; but that which is absolutely infinite, contains in its essence whatever expresses reality, and involves no negation.   —E-I

See Bondage; Communion with God; Essence; Eternity; Extension; Falsity; Freedom, Human; God, Nature and Properties of; Ideas; Immortality of the Soul; Intellect; Intellectual Love; Knowledge; Law of Nature; Love; Miracles; Natural Right; Nature; Privation; Sin; Substance; Thought; Well-Being

GODLESSNESS
See Gratitude

GOD, NATURE AND PROPERTIES OF

He necessarily exists, He is one: He is, and acts solely by the necessity of His own nature; He is free cause of all things; all things are in God, and so depend on Him, that without Him they could neither exist nor be conceived; lastly, all things are predetermined by God, not through His free will or absolute fiat, but from the very nature of God or infinite power.

All misconceptions about God spring from the notion commonly entertained, that all things in nature act as men themselves act, namely, with an end in view. It is accepted as certain, that God Himself directs all things to a definite goal (for it is said that God made all things for man, and man that he might worship Him). I will, therefore, consider this opinion, asking first, why it obtains general credence, and why all men are naturally so prone to adopt it? secondly, I will point out its falsity; and, lastly, I will show how it has given rise to prejudices about good and bad, right and wrong, praise and blame, order and confusion, beauty and ugliness, and the like. However, this is not the place to deduce these misconceptions from the nature of the human mind: it will be sufficient here, if I assume as a starting point, what ought to be universally admitted, namely, that all men are born ignorant of the causes of things, that all have the desire to seek for what is useful to them, and that they are conscious of such desire.

Herefrom it follows, first, that men think themselves free-willed inasmuch as they are conscious of their volitions and desires, and never even dream, in their ignorance, of the causes which have disposed them so to wish and desire. Secondly, that men do all things for an end, namely, for that which is useful to them, and which they seek. Thus it comes to pass that they only look for a knowledge of the final causes of events, and when these are learned, they are content, as having no cause for further doubt. If they cannot learn such causes from external sources, they are compelled to turn to considering themselves, and reflecting what end would have induced them personally to bring about the given event, and thus they necessarily judge other natures by their own. Further, as they find in themselves and outside themselves many means which assist them not a little in their search for what is useful, for instance, eyes for seeing, teeth for chewing, herbs and animals for yielding food, the sun for giving light, the sea for breeding fish, &c., they come to look on the whole of nature as a means for obtaining such conveniences.

Now as they are aware, that they found these conveniences and did not make them, they think they have cause for believing, that some other being has made them for their use. As they look upon things as means, they cannot believe them to be self-created; but, judging from the means which they are accustomed to prepare for themselves, they are bound to believe in some ruler or rulers of the universe endowed with human freedom, who have arranged and adapted everything for human use. They are bound to estimate the nature of such rulers (having no information on the subject) in accordance with their own nature, and therefore they assert that the gods ordained everything for the use of man, in order to bind man to themselves and obtain from him the highest honor. Hence also it follows, that everyone thought out for himself, according to his abilities, a different way of worshipping God, so that God might love him more than his fellows, and direct the whole course of nature for the satisfaction of his blind cupidity and insatiable avarice. Thus the prejudice developed into superstition, and took deep root in the human mind; and for this reason everyone strove most zealously to understand and explain the final causes of things; but in their endeavor to show that nature does nothing in vain, *i.e.*, nothing

which is useless to man, they only seem to have demon-
strated that nature, the gods, and men are all mad together.
Consider, I pray you, the result: among the many helps of
nature they were bound to find some hindrances, such as
storms, earthquakes, diseases, &c.: so they declare that
such things happen, because the gods are angry at some
wrong done them by men, or at some fault committed in
their worship. Experience day by day protested and showed
by infinite examples, that good and evil fortunes fall to
the lot of pious and impious alike; still they would not
abandon their inveterate prejudice, for it was more easy
for them to class such contradictions among other unknown
things of whose use they were ignorant, and thus to retain
their actual and innate condition of ignorance, than to destroy the whole fabric of their reasoning and start afresh.

They therefore laid down as an axiom, that God's judgments far transcend human understanding. Such a doctrine
might well have sufficed to conceal the truth from the
human race for all eternity, if mathematics had not furnished another standard of verity in considering solely the
essence and properties of figures without regard to their
final causes. There are other reasons (which I need not
mention here), besides mathematics, which might have
caused men's minds to be directed to these general prejudices, and have led them to the knowledge of the truth.

I have now sufficiently explained my first point. There
is no need to show at length, that nature has no particular
goal in view, and that final causes are mere human figments. However, I will add a few remarks, in order to
overthrow this doctrine of a final cause utterly. That which
is really a cause it considers as an effect, and *vice versâ*: it
makes that which is by nature first to be last, and that which
is highest and most perfect to be most imperfect. Passing
over the questions of cause and priority as self-evident, it
is plain that the effect is most perfect which is produced
immediately by God; the effect which requires for its pro-

duction several intermediate causes is, in that respect, more imperfect. But if those things which were made immediately by God were made to enable Him to attain His end, then the things which come after, for the sake of which the first were made, are necessarily the most excellent of all.

Further, this doctrine does away with the perfection of God: for, if God acts for an object, He necessarily desires something which He lacks. Certainly, theologians and metaphysicians draw a distinction between the object of want and the object of assimilation; still they confess that God made all things for the sake of Himself, not for the sake of creation. They are unable to point to anything prior to creation, except God Himself, as an object for which God should act, and are therefore driven to admit (as they clearly must), that God lacked those things for whose attainment He created means, and further that He desired them.

We must not omit to notice that the followers of this doctrine, anxious to display their talent in assigning final causes, have imported a new method of argument in proof of their theory—namely, a reduction, not to the impossible, but to ignorance; thus showing that they have no other method of exhibiting their doctrine. For example, if a stone falls from a roof on to someone's head, and kills him, they will demonstrate by their new method, that the stone fell in order to kill the man; for, if it had not by God's will fallen with that object, how could so many circumstances (and there are often many concurrent circumstances) have all happened together by chance? Perhaps you will answer that the event is due to the facts that the wind was blowing, and the man was walking that way. "But why," they will insist, "was the wind blowing, and why was the man at that very time walking that way?" If you again answer, that the wind had then sprung up because the sea had begun to be agitated the day before, the weather being previously calm, and that the man had been invited by a friend, they will again insist: "But why was the sea agitated, and why was the man invited at that time?" So they will pursue their questions from cause to cause, till at last you take refuge in the will of God—in other words, the sanctuary of ignorance. So, again, when they survey the frame of the human body, they are amazed; and being ignorant of the causes of so great a work of art, conclude that it has been fashioned, not mechanically, but by divine and supernatural skill, and has been so put together that one part shall not hurt another.

Hence anyone who seeks for the true causes of miracles, and strives to understand natural phenomena as an intelligent being, and not to gaze at them like a fool, is set down and denounced as an impious heretic by those, whom the masses adore as the interpreters of nature and the gods. Such persons know that, with the removal of ignorance, the wonder which forms their only available means for proving and preserving their authority would vanish also. But I now quit this subject, and pass on to my third point.

After men persuaded themselves, that everything which is created is created for their sake, they were bound to consider as the chief quality in everything that which is most useful to themselves, and to account those things the best of all which have the most beneficial effect on mankind. Further, they were bound to form abstract notions for the explanation of the nature of things, such as *goodness, badness, order, confusion, warmth, cold, beauty, deformity,* and so on; and from the belief that they are free agents arose the further notions *praise* and *blame, sin* and *merit.*

I will speak of these latter hereafter, when I treat of human nature; the former I will briefly explain here.

Everything which conduces to health and the worship of God they have called *good,* everything which hinders these objects they have styled *bad*; and inasmuch as those who do not understand the nature of things do not verify phenomena in any way, but merely imagine them after a fashion, and mistake their imagination for understanding, such persons firmly believe that there is an *order* of things, being really ignorant both of things and their own nature. When phenomena are of such a kind, that the impression they make on our senses requires little effort of imagination, and can consequently be easily remembered, we say that they are *well-ordered*; if the contrary, that they are *ill-ordered* or *confused*. Further, as things which are easily imagined are more pleasing to us, men prefer order to confusion—as though there were any order in nature, except in relation to our imagination—and say that God has created all things in order; thus, without knowing it, attributing imagination to God, unless, indeed, they would have it that God foresaw human imagination, and arranged everything, so that it should be most easily imagined. If this be their theory, they would not, perhaps, be daunted by the fact that we find an infinite number of phenomena, far surpassing our imagination, and very many others which confound its weakness. But enough has been said on this subject. The other abstract notions are nothing but modes of imagining, in which the imagination is differently affected, though they are considered by the ignorant as the chief attributes of things, inasmuch as they believe that everything was created for the sake of themselves; and, according as they are affected by it, style it good or bad, healthy or rotten and corrupt. For instance, if the ˙motion which objects we see communicate to our nerves be conducive to health, the objects causing it are styled *beautiful*; if a contrary motion be excited, they are styled *ugly*.

Things which are perceived through our sense of smell are styled fragrant or fetid; if through our taste, sweet or bitter, full-flavored or insipid; if through our touch, hard or soft, rough or smooth, &c.

Whatsoever affects our ears is said to give rise to noise, sound, or harmony. In this latter case, there are men lunatic enough to believe, that even God himself takes pleasure in harmony; and philosophers are not lacking who have persuaded themselves, that the motion of the heavenly bodies gives rise to harmony—all of which instances sufficiently show that everyone judges of things according to the state of his brain, or rather mistakes for things the forms of his imagination. We need no longer wonder that there have arisen all the controversies we have witnessed, and finally scepticism: for, although human bodies in many respects agree, yet in very many others they differ; so that what seems good to one seems bad to another; what seems well ordered to one seems confused to another; what is pleasing to one displeases another, and so on. It is commonly said: "So many men, so many minds; everyone is wise in his own way; brains differ as completely as palates." All of which proverbs show, that men judge of things according to their mental disposition, and rather imagine than understand: for, if they understood phenomena, they would, as mathematics attest, be convinced if not attracted, by what I have urged.

We have now perceived, that all the explanations commonly given of nature are mere modes of imagining, and do not indicate the true nature of anything, but only the constitution of the imagination; and, although they have names, as though they were entities, existing externally to the imagination, I call them entities imaginary rather than real; and, therefore, all arguments against us drawn from such abstractions are easily rebutted.

Many argue in this way. If all things follow from a necessity of the absolute perfect nature of God, why are there so many imperfections in nature? such, for instance, as things corrupt to the point of putridity, loathsome deformity, confusion, evil, sin, &c. But these reasoners are, as I have said, easily confuted, for the perfection of things is to be reckoned only from their own nature and power; things are not more or less perfect, according as they delight or offend human senses, or according as they are serviceable or repugnant to mankind. To those who ask why God did not so create all men, that they should be governed only by reason, I give no answer but this: because matter was not lacking to Him for the creation of every degree of perfection from highest to lowest; or, more strictly, because the laws of His nature are so vast, as to suffice for the production of everything conceivable by an infinite intelligence.

We doubt of the existence of God, and consequently of all else, so long as we have no clear and distinct idea of God, but only a confused one. For as he who knows not rightly the nature of a triangle, knows not that its three angles are equal to two right angles, so he who conceives the Divine nature confusedly, does not see that it pertains to the nature of God to exist. Now, to conceive the nature of God clearly and distinctly, it is necessary to pay attention to a certain number of very simple notions, called general notions, and by their help to associate the conceptions which we form of the attributes of the Divine nature. It then, for the first time, becomes clear to us, that God exists necessarily, that He is omnipresent, and that all our conceptions involve in themselves the nature of God and are conceived through it. Lastly, we see that all our adequate ideas are true.   —T P-VI

The doctrines added by certain churches, such as that God took upon Himself human nature, I have expressly said that I do not understand; in fact, to speak the truth, they seem to me no less absurd than would a statement, that a circle had taken upon itself the nature of a square.
                                                   —C-XXI-O

GOOD AND BAD

By *good* I here mean every kind of pleasure, and all that conduces thereto, especially that which satisfies our longings, whatsoever they may be. By *evil*, I mean every kind of pain, especially that which frustrates our longings. We in no case desire a thing because we deem it good, but, contrariwise, we deem a thing good because we desire it: consequently we deem evil that which we shrink from; everyone, therefore, according to his particular emotions, judges or estimates what is good, what is bad, what is better, what is worse, what is best, and what is worst. Thus a miser thinks that abundance of money is the best, and want of money the worst; an ambitious man desires nothing so much as glory, and fears nothing so much as ignominy.

—E-III

Why does it happen that sometimes, although we see that a certain thing is good or bad, we nevertheless do not find in us the power either to do the good or to abstain from the bad, and sometimes, however, we do indeed [find this power in us]? This we can easily understand if we consider the causes that we assigned to opinions, which we stated to be the causes of all affects. These, we then said, [arise] either from hearsay, or from experience. And since all that we find in ourselves has greater power over us than that which comes to us from outside, it certainly follows that speculation can be the cause of the extinction of opinions which we have got from hearsay only (and this is so because reason has not like these come to us from outside), but by no means of those which we have got from experience. For the power which the thing itself gives us is always greater than that which we obtain by way of consequence through a second thing. For more power comes to us from the understanding of proportion itself, than from the understanding of the rule of proportion. And it is for this reason that we have said so often that one love may be extinguished by another which is greater, because in saying this we did not, by any means, intend to refer to desire which does not, like love, come from true knowledge, but comes from fancy.

—G-2-XXI

By *good* I mean that which we certainly know to be useful to us.

—E-IV

The knowledge of good and evil is nothing else but the emotions of pleasure or pain, in so far as we are conscious thereof.   —E-IV

A true knowledge of good and evil cannot check any emotion by virtue of being true, but only in so far as it is considered as an emotion.   —E-IV

In so far as a thing is in harmony with our nature, it is necessarily good.

Hence it follows, that, in proportion as a thing is in harmony with our nature, so is it more useful or better for us, and *vice versâ*, in proportion as a thing is more useful for us, so is it more in harmony with our nature. For, in so far as it is not in harmony with our nature, it will necessarily be different therefrom or contrary thereto. If different, it can neither be good nor bad; if contrary, it will be contrary to that which is in harmony with our nature, that is, contrary to what is good—in short, bad. Nothing, therefore, can be good, except in so far as it is in harmony with our nature; and hence a thing is useful, in proportion as it is in harmony with our nature, and *vice versâ*.   —E-IV

No individual thing, which is entirely different from our own nature, can help or check our power of activity, and absolutely nothing can do us good or harm, unless it has something in common with our nature.   —E-IV

A thing cannot be bad for us through the quality which it has in common with our nature, but it is bad for us in so far as it is contrary to our nature.   —E-IV

Every man, by the laws of his nature, necessarily desires or shrinks from that which he deems to be good or bad.
                                                        —E-IV

See Appetite; Bondage; Essence; God, Nature and Properties of; Happiness; Natural Right; Rational Life; Reason

GOVERNMENT

A commonwealth is always in greater danger from its citizens than from its enemies, for the good are few.

—P T-VI

A civil state, which has not done away with the causes of seditions, where war is a perpetual object of fear, and where, lastly, the laws are often broken, differs but little from the mere state of nature, in which everyone lives after his own mind at the great risk of his life. —P T-V

A commonwealth is most powerful and most independent, which is founded and guided by reason. —P T-V

A commonwealth does wrong, when it acts against the dictate of reason. For a commonwealth is most independent when it acts according to the dictate of reason; so far, then, as it acts against reason, it fails itself, or does wrong.

—P T-IV

Where men have general rights, and are all guided, as it were, by one mind, it is certain that every individual has the less right the more the rest collectively exceed him in power; that is, he has, in fact, no right over nature but that which the common law allows him. But whatever he is ordered by the general consent, he is bound to execute, or may rightfully be compelled thereto.

This right, which is determined by the power of a multitude, is generally called government. —P T-II

See Democracy, Liberty, Tyranny, Wrongdoing

GRATITUDE

Only free men are thoroughly grateful one to another.

The good will, which men who are led by blind desire have for one another, is generally a bargaining or enticement, rather than pure good will. Moreover, ingratitude is not an emotion. Yet it is base, inasmuch as it generally shows, that a man is affected by excessive hatred, anger, pride, avarice, &c. He who, by reason of his folly, knows not how to return benefits, is not ungrateful, much less he who is not gained over by the gifts of a courtesan to serve her lust, or by a thief to conceal his thefts, or by any similar persons. Contrariwise, such an one shows a constant mind, inasmuch as he cannot by any gifts be corrupted, to his own or the general hurt. —E-IV

Gratitude is the desire or zeal springing from love, whereby we endeavor to benefit him, who with similar feelings of love has conferred a benefit on us. —E-III

Gratitude is the inclinations which the soul has to wish and to do some good to one's neighbor. I say, to wish, [this happens] when good is returned to one who has done some good; I say, to do, [this is the case] when we ourselves have obtained or received some good.

I am well aware that almost all people consider these affects to be good; but, notwithstanding this, I venture to say that they can have no place in a perfect man. For a perfect man is moved to help his fellow-man by sheer necessity only, and by no other cause, and therefore he feels it all the more to be his duty to help the most godless, seeing that his misery and need are so much greater. —G 2-XIII

He who has conferred a benefit on anyone from motives of love or honor will feel pain, if he sees that the benefit is received without gratitude. —E-III

If anyone conceives that he is loved by another, and believes that he has given no cause for such love, he will love that other in return.

If he believes that he has given just cause for the love, he will take pride therein; this is what most often happens, and we said that its contrary took place whenever a man conceives himself to be hated by another. This reciprocal love, and consequently the desire of benefiting him who loves us, and who endeavors to benefit us, is called *grati-*

tude or *thankfulness*. It thus appears that men are much more prone to take vengeance than to return benefits.

He who imagines, that he is loved by one whom he hates, will be a prey to conflicting hatred and love.

If hatred be the prevailing emotion, he will endeavor to injure him who loves him; this emotion is called cruelty, especially if the victim be believed to have given no ordinary cause for hatred. —E-III

See Passions, Rational Life

GRIEF

Grief is a certain kind of sorrow arising from the contemplation of some good which we have lost, and [lost] in such a way that there is no hope of recovering the same. It makes its imperfection so manifest that as soon as we only examine it we think it bad. For we have already shown above that it is bad to bind and link ourselves to things which may easily, or at some time, fail us, and which we cannot have when we want them. And since it is a certain kind of sorrow, we have to shun it, as we have already remarked above, when we were treating of sorrow.

I think, now, that I have already shown and proved sufficiently that it is only thought that leads us to the knowledge of good and evil. And so when we come to prove that Knowledge is the first and principal cause of all these passions, it will be clearly manifest that if we use our Intelligence and Speculation aright, it should be impossible for us ever to fall a prey to one of these passions which we ought to reject. I say our Intelligence, because I do not think that Speculation alone is competent to free us from all these. —G 2-XIV

See Stimulation

GUIDANCE OF REASON
See Ideas

H

HAPPINESS

After experience had taught me that all the usual surroundings of social life are vain and futile; seeing that none
of the objects of my fears contained in themselves anything
either good or bad, except in so far as the mind is affected
by them, I finally resolved to inquire whether there might
be some real good having power to communicate itself,
which would affect the mind singly, to the exclusion of all
else: whether, in fact, there might be anything of which
the discovery and attainment would enable me to enjoy continuous, supreme, and unending happiness. I say "I *finally*
resolved," for at first sight it seemed unwise willingly to
lose hold on what was sure for the sake of something then
uncertain. I could see the benefits which are acquired
through fame and riches, and that I should be obliged to
abandon the quest of such objects, if I seriously devoted
myself to the search for something different and new. I
perceived that if true happiness chanced to be placed in the
former I should necessarily miss it; while if, on the other
hand, it were not so placed, and I gave them my whole
attention, I should equally fail.

I therefore debated whether it would not be possible to
arrive at the new principle, or at any rate at a certainty
concerning its existence, without changing the conduct and
usual plan of my life; with this end in view I made many
efforts, but in vain. For the ordinary surroundings of life
which are esteemed by men (as their actions testify) to be
the highest good, may be classed under the three heads—
Riches, Fame, and the Pleasures of Sense: with these three
the mind is so absorbed that it has little power to reflect

on any different good. By sensual pleasure the mind is enthralled to the extent of quiescence, as if the supreme good were actually attained, so that it is quite incapable of thinking of any other object; when such pleasure has been gratified it is followed by extreme melancholy, whereby the mind, though not enthralled, is disturbed and dulled.

The pursuit of honors and riches is likewise very absorbing, especially if such objects be sought simply for their own sake, inasmuch as they are then supposed to constitute the highest good. In the case of fame the mind is still more absorbed, for fame is conceived as always good for its own sake, and as the ultimate end to which all actions are directed. Further, the attainment of riches and fame is not followed as in the case of sensual pleasures by repentance, but, the more we acquire, the greater is our delight, and, consequently, the more we are incited to increase both the one and the other; on the other hand, if our hopes happen to be frustrated we are plunged into the deepest sadness. Fame has the further drawback that it compels its votaries to order their lives according to the opinions of their fellow men, shunning what they usually shun, and seeking what they usually seek.

When I saw that all these ordinary objects of desire would be obstacles in the way of a search for something different and new—nay, that they were opposed thereto, that either they or it would have to be abandoned, I was forced to inquire which would prove the most useful to me: for, as I say, I seemed to be willingly losing hold on a sure good for the sake of something uncertain. However, after I had reflected on the matter, I came in the first place to the conclusion that by abandoning the ordinary objects of pursuit, and betaking myself to a new quest, I should be leaving a good, uncertain by reason of its own nature, as may be gathered from what has been said, for the sake of a good not uncertain in its nature (for I sought for a fixed good), but only in the possibility of its attainment.

Further reflection convinced me, that if I could really get to the root of the matter I should be leaving certain evils for a certain good. I thus perceived that I was in a state of great peril, and I compelled myself to seek with all my strength for a remedy, however uncertain it might be; as a sick man struggling with a deadly disease, when he sees that death will surely be upon him unless a remedy be found, is compelled to seek such a remedy with all his strength, inasmuch as his whole hope lies therein. All the objects pursued by the multitude not only bring no remedy that tends to preserve our being, but even act as hindrances, causing the death not seldom of those who possess them, and always of those who are possessed by them. There are many examples of men who have suffered persecution even to death for the sake of their riches, and of men who in pursuit of wealth have exposed themselves to so many dangers, that they have paid away their life as a penalty for their folly. Examples are no less numerous of men, who have endured the utmost wretchedness for the sake of gaining or preserving their reputation. Lastly, there are innumerable cases of men, who have hastened their death through over-indulgence in sensual pleasure. All these evils seem to have risen from the fact, that happiness or unhappiness is made wholly to depend on the quality of the object which we love. When a thing is not loved, no quarrels will arise concerning it—no sadness will be felt if it perishes—no envy if it is possessed by another—no fear, no hatred, in short no disturbance of the mind. All these arise from the love of what is perishable, such as the objects already mentioned. But love towards a thing eternal and infinite feeds the mind wholly with joy, and is itself unmingled with any sadness, wherefore it is greatly to be desired and sought for with all our strength. Yet it was not at random that I used the words, "If I could go to the root of the matter," for, though what I have urged was perfectly clear to my mind, I could not forthwith lay aside all love of riches, sensual enjoyment, and fame. One thing was evident, namely, that while my mind was employed with these thoughts it turned away from its former objects of desire, and seriously considered the search for a new principle; this state of things was a great comfort to me, for I perceived that the evils were not such as to resist all remedies. Although these intervals were at first rare, and of very short duration, yet afterwards, as the true good became more and more discernible to me, they became more frequent and more lasting; especially after I had recognized that the acquisition of wealth, sensual pleasure, or fame, is only a hindrance, so long as they are sought as ends not as means; if they be sought as means, they will be under restraint, and, far from being hindrances, will further not a little the end for which they are sought, as I will show in due time.

I will here only briefly state what I mean by true good, and also what is the nature of the highest good. In order that this may be rightly understood, we must bear in mind that the terms good and evil are only applied relatively, so that the same thing may be called both good and bad, according to the relations in view, in the same way as it may be called perfect or imperfect. Nothing regarded in its own nature can be called perfect or imperfect; especially when we are aware that all things which come to pass, come to pass according to the eternal order and fixed laws of nature. However, human weakness cannot attain to this order in its own thoughts, but meanwhile man conceives a human character much more stable than his own, and sees that there is no reason why he should not himself acquire such a character. Thus he is led to seek for means which will bring him to this pitch of perfection, and calls everything which will serve as such means a true good. The chief good is that he should arrive, together with other individuals if possible, at the possession of the aforesaid character. What that character is we shall show in due time, namely, that it is the knowledge of the union existing between the mind and the whole of nature. This, then, is the end for which I strive, to attain to such a character myself, and to endeavor that many should attain to it with me. In other words, it is part of my happiness to lend a helping hand, that many others may understand even as I do, so that their understanding and desire may entirely agree with my own. In order to bring this about, it is necessary to understand as much of nature as will enable us to attain to the aforesaid character, and also to form a social order such as is most conducive to the attainment of this character by the greatest number with the least difficulty and danger. We must seek the assistance of Moral Philosophy and the Theory of Education; further, as health is no insignificant means for attaining our end, we must also include the whole science of Medicine, and, as many difficult things are by contrivance rendered easy, and we can in this way gain much time and convenience, the science of Mechanics must in no way be despised. But, before all things, a means must be devised for improving the understanding and purifying it, as far as may be at the outset, so that it may apprehend things without error, and in the best possible way.

Thus it is apparent to everyone that I wish to direct all sciences to one end and aim, so that we may attain to the supreme human perfection which we have named; and, therefore, whatsoever in the sciences does not serve to promote our object will have to be rejected as useless. To sum up the matter in a word, all our actions and thoughts must be directed to this one end. Yet, as it is necessary that while we are endeavoring to attain our purpose, and bring the understanding into the right path, we should carry on our life, we are compelled first of all to lay down certain rules of life as provisionally good, to wit the following:—

I. To speak in a manner intelligible to the masses, and to comply with every general custom that does not hinder the attainment of our purpose. For we can gain from the multitude no small advantages, provided that we strive to accommodate ourselves to its understanding as far as possible: moreover, we shall in this way gain a friendly audience for the reception of the truth.

II. To indulge ourselves with pleasures only in so far as they are necessary for preserving health.

III. Lastly, to endeavor to obtain only sufficient money or other commodities to enable us to preserve our life and health, and to follow such general customs as are consistent with our purpose.

See Blessedness, Desire, Ideas, Intellectual Love, Passions, Passive and Active, Rational Life

HARMONY

In so far as men are a prey to passion, they cannot, in that respect, be said to be naturally in harmony.

This is also self-evident; for, if we say that white and black only agree in the fact that neither is red, we absolutely affirm that they do not agree in any respect. So, if we say that a man and a stone only agree in the fact that both are finite—wanting in power, not existing by the necessity of their own nature, or, lastly, indefinitely surpassed by the power of external causes—we should certainly affirm that a man and a stone are in no respect alike; therefore, things which agree only in negation, or in qualities which neither possess, really agree in no respect.   —E-IV

See Good and Bad, Natural Right, Rational Life, Tyranny

HATE

He, who conceives himself to be hated by another, and believes that he has given him no cause for hatred, will hate that other in return.

He who thinks that he has given just cause for hatred will be affected with shame; but this case rarely happens. This reciprocation of hatred may also arise from the hatred, which follows an endeavor to injure the object of our hate, He therefore who conceives that he is hated by another will conceive his enemy as the cause of some evil or pain; thus he will be affected with pain or fear, accompanied by the idea of his enemy as cause; in other words, he will be affected with hatred towards his enemy, as I said above.

He who conceives, that one whom he loves hates him, will be a prey to conflicting hatred and love. For, in so far as he conceives that he is an object of hatred, he is determined to hate his enemy in return. But, by the hypothesis, he nevertheless loves him: wherefore he will be a prey to conflicting hatred and love.

If a man conceives that one, whom he has hitherto regarded without emotion, has done him any injury from motives of hatred, he will forthwith seek to repay the injury in kind. —E-III

If a man has begun to hate an object of his love, so that love is thoroughly destroyed, he will, causes being equal, regard it with more hatred than if he had never loved it, and his hatred will be in proportion to the strength of his former love. —E-III

He who hates anyone will endeavor to do him an injury, unless he fears that a greater injury will thereby accrue to himself; on the other hand, he who loves anyone will, by the same law, seek to benefit him. —E-III

If a man conceives, that anyone similar to himself hates anything also similar to himself, which he loves, he will hate that person. —E-III

Simply from the fact that we have regarded a thing with the emotion of pleasure or pain, though that thing be not the efficient cause of the emotion, we can either love or hate it. —E-III

Hate is nothing else but *pain accompanied by the idea of an external cause.*

He who hates endeavors to remove and destroy the object of his hatred. —E-III

Hatred is an inclination to ward off from us that which has caused us some harm. Now it is to be remarked that we perform our actions in two ways, namely, either with or without passion. With passion, as is commonly seen in the [conduct of] masters towards their servants who have done something amiss. Without passion, as is related of Socrates, who, when he was compelled to chastise his slave for [the latter's own] good, never did so when he felt that he was enraged against his slave.

Now that we see that our actions are performed by us either with, or without passion, we think that it is clear that those things which hinder or have hindered us can be removed, when necessary, without any perturbation on our part. And so, which is better: that we should flee from the things with aversion and hatred, or that, with the strength of reason, we should (for we think it possible) endure them without loss of temper? First of all, it is certain that when we do what we have to do without passion, then no evil can result therefrom. And, since there is no mean between good and evil, we see that, as it is bad to do anything in a passion, so it must be good to act without it.

But let us examine whether there is any harm in fleeing from things with hatred and aversion.

As regards the hatred which comes from superficial opinion, it is certain that it should have no place in us, because we know that one and the same thing is good for us at one time, bad for us at another time, as is always the case with medicinal herbs.

It therefore depends, in the end, on whether the hatred arises in us only through superficial opinion, and not also through true reasoning. But to ascertain this properly we deem it right to explain distinctly what hatred is, and to distinguish it from aversion.

Now I say that *Hatred* is a perturbation of the soul against some one who has done some ill to us willingly and knowingly. But *aversion* is the perturbation which arises in us against a thing on account of some infirmity or injury which we either know or think is in it by nature. I say, by nature; for when we do not suppose or think that it is so, then, even if we have suffered some hindrance or injury from it, we have no aversion for it, because we may, on the contrary, expect something useful from it. Thus, when some one is hurt by a stone or a knife, he does not on that account feel any aversion for the same.

After these observations let us now briefly consider the consequences of both of them. From hatred there ensues sorrow; and when the hatred is great, it produces anger, which not only, like hatred, seeks to flee from what is hated, but also to annihilate it, when that is practicable: from this great hatred comes also envy. But from aversion there comes a certain sorrow, because we consider ourselves to be deprived of something which, since it is real, must always have its essence and perfection.

From what has just been said it may be easily understood that, if we use our Reason aright, we can feel no hatred or aversion for anything, because, if we do, we deprive ourselves of that perfection which is to be found in everything. We see likewise with our Reason that we can never [reasonably] feel any hatred whatever against anybody, because whatsoever exists in Nature, if we entertain any wish about it, then we must always improve it, whether for our sake or for the sake of the thing itself. And since a perfect man is the best thing for us that we know of all that we have around us or before our eyes, it is by far the best both for us and for all people individually that we should at all times seek to educate them to this perfect state. For only then can we reap the greatest benefit from them, and they from us. The means thereto is, to give regard to them always in the manner in which we are constantly taught and exhorted to do by our good Conscience; for this never prompts us to our undoing, but always to our happiness and well-being.

In conclusion, we say that Hatred and Aversion have in them as many imperfections as Love, on the contrary, has perfections. For this always produces improvement, invigoration, and enlargement, which constitute perfection; while Hatred, on the contrary, always makes for desolation, enervation, and annihilation, which constitute imperfection itself.   —G 2-VI

Hatred is increased by being reciprocated, and can on the other hand be destroyed by love.   —E-III

Hatred can never be good.
When we hate a man, we endeavor to destroy him, we endeavor to do something that is bad.
Here, and in what follows, I mean by hatred only hatred towards men.
Envy, derision, contempt, anger, revenge, and other emotions attributable to hatred, or arising therefrom, are bad.
Whatsoever we desire from motives of hatred is base, and in a State unjust.
Between derision and laughter I recognize a great difference. For laughter, as also jocularity, is merely pleasure; therefore, so long as it be not excessive, it is in itself good. Assuredly nothing forbids man to enjoy himself, save grim and gloomy superstition. For why is it more lawful to satiate one's hunger and thirst than to drive away one's melancholy? I reason, and have convinced myself as follows: No deity, nor anyone else, save the envious, takes pleasure in my infirmity and discomfort, nor sets down to my virtue the tears, sobs, fear, and the like, which are signs of infirmity of spirit; on the contrary, the greater the pleasure wherewith we are affected, the greater the perfection whereto we pass; in other words, the more must we necessarily partake of the divine nature. Therefore, to make use of what comes in our way, and to enjoy it as much as possible (not to the point of satiety, for that would not be

enjoyment) is the part of a wise man. I say it is the part of a wise man to refresh and recreate himself with moderate and pleasant food and drink, and also with perfumes, with the soft beauty of growing plants, with dress, with music, with many sports, with theatres, and the like, such as every man may make use of without injury to his neighbor. For the human body is composed of very numerous parts, of diverse nature, which continually stand in need of fresh and varied nourishment, so that the whole body may be equally capable of performing all the actions, which follow from the necessity of its own nature; and, consequently, so that the mind may also be equally capable of understanding many things simultaneously. This way of life, then, agrees best with our principles, and also with general practice; therefore, if there be any question of another plan, the plan we have mentioned is the best, and in every way to be commended. There is no need for me to set forth the matter more clearly or in more detail. —E-IV

Hatred, the exact opposite of love, arises from error which is the outcome of superficial opinion. For when some one has come to the conclusion that a certain thing is good, and another happens to do something to the detriment of the same thing, then there arises in him a hatred against the one who did it, and this, as we shall explain afterwards, could never happen if the true good were known. For, in comparison with the true good, all indeed that is, or is conceived, is naught but wretchedness itself; and is not such a lover of what is wretched much more deserving of pity than of hatred?

Hatred, lastly, comes also from mere hearsay, as we see it in the Turks against Jews and Christians, in the Christians against the Jews and Turks, &c. For, how ignorant is the one multitude of the religion and morals of the others! —G 2-III

[123]

Love or hatred towards, for instance, Peter is destroyed, if the pleasure involved in the former, or the pain involved in the latter emotion, be associated with the idea of another cause: and will be diminished in proportion as we conceive Peter not to have been the sole cause of either emotion.

—E-III

Joy arising from the fact, that anything we hate is destroyed, or suffers other injury, is never unaccompanied by a certain pain in us.

Whenever we remember anything, even if it does not actually exist, we regard it only as present, and the body is affected in the same manner; wherefore, in so far as the remembrance of the thing is strong, a man is determined to regard it with pain; this determination, while the image of the thing in question lasts, is indeed checked by the remembrance of other things excluding the existence of the aforesaid thing, but is not destroyed: hence, a man only feels pleasure in so far as the said determination is checked: for this reason the joy arising from the injury done to what we hate is repeated, every time we remember that object of hatred. For, as we have said, when the image of the thing in question is aroused, inasmuch as it involves the thing's existence, it determines the man to regard the thing with the same pain as he was wont to do, when it actually did exist. However, since he has joined to the image of the thing other images, which exclude its existence, this determination to pain is forthwith checked, and the man rejoices afresh as often as the repetition takes place.

This is the cause of men's pleasure in recalling past evils, and delight in narrating dangers from which they have escaped. For when men conceive a danger, they conceive it as still future, and are determined to fear it; this determination is checked afresh by the idea of freedom, which became associated with the idea of the danger when they escaped therefrom: this renders them secure afresh: therefore they rejoice afresh.

—E-III

Hatred which is completely vanquished by love passes into love: and love is thereupon greater than if hatred had not preceded it.

Though this be so, no one will endeavor to hate anything, or to be affected with pain, for the sake of enjoying this greater pleasure; that is, no one will desire that he should be injured, in the hope of recovering from the injury, nor long to be ill for the sake of getting well. For everyone will always endeavour to persist in his being, and to ward off pain as far as he can. If the contrary is conceivable, namely, that a man should desire to hate someone, in order that he might love him the more thereafter, he will always desire to hate him. For the strength of the love is in proportion to the strength of the hatred, wherefore the man would desire, that the hatred be continually increased more and more, and, for a similar reason, he would desire to become more and more ill, in order that he might take a greater pleasure in being restored to health: in such a case he would always endeavor to be ill, which is absurd. —E-III

He who conceives that the object of his hate is destroyed will feel pleasure.   —E-III

We cannot hate a thing which we pity, because its misery affects us painfully.   —E-III

He who conceives, that an object of his hatred is painfully affected, will feel pleasure. Contrariwise, if he thinks that the said object is pleasurably affected, he will feel pain. Each of these emotions will be greater or less, according as its contrary is greater or less in the object of hatred.

This pleasure can scarcely be felt unalloyed, and without any mental conflict. For in so far as a man conceives that something similar to himself is affected by pain, he will himself be affected in like manner; and he will have the contrary emotion in contrary circumstances.   —E-III

Love or hatred towards a thing, which we conceive to be free, must, other conditions being similar, be greater than if it were felt towards a thing acting by necessity.

Hence it follows, that men, thinking themselves to be free, feel more love or hatred towards one another than towards anything else. —E-III

No one can hate God.

Love towards God cannot be turned into hate.

It may be objected that, as we understand God as the cause of all things, we by that very fact regard God as the cause of pain. But I make answer, that, in so far as we understand the causes of pain, it to that extent ceases to be a passion, that is, it ceases to be pain; therefore, in so far as we understand God to be the cause of pain, we to that extent feel pleasure. —E-V

If we conceive that a thing, which is wont to affect us painfully, has any point of resemblance with another thing which is wont to affect us with an equally strong emotion of pleasure, we shall hate the first-named thing, and at the same time we shall love it. —E-III

See Adequate Ideas, Class Hatred, Compassion, Derision, Enmity, Fame, Gratitude, Kindness, Rational Life, Wisdom

HEALTHY LIFE
See Race

HEBREW
The writers of the Old Testament and the New Testament were Hebrews: therefore, a knowledge of the Hebrew language is before all things necessary, not only for the comprehension of the Old Testament, which was written in that tongue, but also of the New: for although the latter was published in other languages, yet its characteristics are Hebrew. —T P-VII

See God

HERETIC
See Faith; God, Nature and Properties of

HIGH-MINDEDNESS
See Emotions, Lust, Wisdom

HISTORY
It is very rare for men to relate an event simply as it happened, without adding any element of their own judgment. When they see or hear anything new, they are, unless strictly on their guard, so occupied with their own preconceived opinions that they perceive something quite different from the plain facts seen or heard, especially if such facts surpass the comprehension of the beholder or hearer, and, most of all, if he is interested in their happening in a given way.

Thus men relate in chronicles and histories their own opinions rather than actual events, so that one and the same event is so differently related by two men of different opinions, that it seems like two separate occurrences; and, further, it is very easy from historical chronicles to gather the personal opinions of the historian. —T P-VI

HOLY GHOST
When people declare, as all are ready to do, that the Bible is the Word of God teaching man true blessedness and the way of salvation, they evidently do not mean what they say; for the masses take no pains at all to live according to Scriptures, and we see most people endeavoring to hawk about their own commentaries as the word of God, and giving their best efforts, under the guise of religion, to compelling others to think as they do: we generally see, I say, theologians anxious to learn how to wring their inventions and sayings out of the sacred text, and to fortify them with Divine authority. Such persons never display less scruple or more zeal than when they are interpreting Scripture or the mind of the Holy Ghost; if we ever see them

perturbed, it is not that they fear to attribute some error to the Holy Spirit, and to stray from the right path, but that they are afraid to be convicted of error by others, and thus to overthrow and bring into contempt their own authority. But if men really believed what they verbally testify of Scripture, they would adopt quite a different plan of life: their minds would not be agitated by so many contentions, nor so many hatreds, and they would cease to be excited by such a blind and rash passion for interpreting the sacred writings, and excogitating novelties in religion. On the contrary, they would not dare to adopt, as the teaching of Scripture, anything which they could not plainly deduce therefrom: lastly, those sacrilegious persons who have dared, in several passages, to interpolate the Bible, would have shrunk from so great a crime, and would have stayed their sacrilegious hands.

Ambition and unscrupulousness have waxed so powerful, that religion is thought to consist, not so much in respecting the writings of the Holy Ghost, as in defending human commentaries, so that religion is no longer identified with charity, but with spreading discord and propagating insensate hatred disguised under the name of zeal for the Lord, and eager ardor.

To these evils we must add superstition, which teaches men to despise reason and nature, and only to admire and venerate that which is repugnant to both: whence it is not wonderful that for the sake of increasing the admiration and veneration felt for Scripture, men strive to explain it so as to make it appear to contradict, as far as possible, both one and the other: thus they dream that most profound mysteries lie hid in the Bible, and weary themselves out in the investigation of these absurdities, to the neglect of what is useful. Every result of their diseased imagination they attribute to the Holy Ghost, and strive to defend with the utmost zeal and passion; for it is an observed fact that

men employ their reason to defend conclusions arrived at by
reason, but conclusions arrived at by the passions are de-
fended by the passions. —T P-VII

HONEST MAN
See Essence

HOLY SPIRIT
See Holy Ghost, Religion, Theology

HONOR
See Ambition, Fame, Happiness, Natural Right

HOPE
When we think that a certain thing which is yet to come
is good and that it can happen, the soul assumes, in consequence of this, that form which we call *hope*, which is
nothing else than a certain kind of joy, though mingled with
some sorrow. —G 2-IX

Hope is nothing else but *an inconstant pleasure, arising
from the image of something future or past, whereof we do
not yet know the issue.*

If the element of doubt be removed from these emotions,
hope becomes *Confidence* and fear becomes *Despair.* In
other words, *Pleasure or Pain arising from the image of
something concerning which we have hoped or feared.*
—E-III

See Confidence, Fear, Repentance

HORROR
If a man's anger, envy, &c., be what we wonder at, the
emotion is called *Horror*. —E-III

HOSEA
See Words

HUMAN AID
See Favors

HUMAN BODY
See Body, Hate

HUMAN CONDUCT

Most writers on the emotions and on human conduct seem to be treating rather of matters outside nature than of natural phenomena following nature's general laws. They appear to conceive man to be situated in nature as a kingdom within a kingdom: for they believe that he disturbs rather than follows nature's order, that he has absolute control over his actions, and that he is determined solely by himself. They attribute human infirmities and fickleness, not to the power of nature in general, but to some mysterious flaw in the nature of man, which accordingly they bemoan, deride, despise, or, as usually happens, abuse: he, who succeeds in hitting off the weakness of the human mind more eloquently or more acutely than his fellows, is looked upon as a seer. Still there has been no lack of very excellent men (to whose toil and industry I confess myself much indebted), who have written many noteworthy things concerning the right way of life, and have given much sage advice to mankind. But no one, so far as I know, has defined the nature and strength of the emotions, and the power of the mind against them for their restraint.

I do not forget, that the illustrious Descartes, though he believed, that the mind has absolute power over its actions, strove to explain human emotions by their primary causes, and, at the same time, to point out a way, by which the mind might attain to absolute dominion over them. However, in my opinion, he accomplishes nothing beyond a display of the acuteness of his own great intellect, as I will show in the proper place. For the present I wish to revert to those, who would rather abuse or deride human emotions than understand them. Such persons will, doubtless think it strange that I should attempt to treat of human vice and folly geometrically, and should wish to set forth with rigid reasoning those matters which they cry out against as repugnant to reason, frivolous, absurd, and dreadful. However, such is my plan.

Nothing comes to pass in nature, which can be set down to a flaw therein; for nature is always the same, and everywhere one and the same in her efficacy and power of action; that is, nature's laws and ordinances, whereby all things come to pass and change from one form to another, are everywhere and always the same; so that there should be one and the same method of understanding the nature of all things whatsoever, namely, through nature's universal laws and rules. Thus the passions of hatred, anger, envy, and so on, considered in themselves, follow from this same necessity and efficacy of nature; they answer to certain definite causes, through which they are understood, and possess certain properties as worthy of being known as the properties of anything else, whereof the contemplation in itself affords us delight. I treat of the nature and strength of the emotions according to the same method, as I employed in my investigations concerning God and the mind. I consider human actions and desires in exactly the same manner, as though I were concerned with lines, planes, and solids.

—E-III

HUMAN LAWS
See Law

HUMAN MIND
See Beauty, Body, Body and Mind, Knowledge

HUMILITY
Humility is pain arising from a man's contemplation of his own weakness of body or mind.

Self-complacency is opposed to humility, in so far as we thereby mean pleasure arising from a contemplation of our own power of action; but, in so far as we mean thereby pleasure accompanied by the idea of any action which we believe we have performed by the free decision of our mind, it is opposed to repentance.

—E-III

Humility is felt when any one knows his own imperfection, without regard to the contempt [of others] for himself; so that Humility does not refer to anything outside the humble man. —G 2-VIII

Pain, accompanied by the idea of our own weakness, is called humility. —E-III

See Inferiority, Feeling of; Pride; Repentance; Self-Abasement; Virtue

HYPOCRITES
See Inferiority, Feeling of

I

IDEAS

That which is common to all, and which is equally in a part and in the whole, does not constitute the essence of any particular thing.   —E-II

Falsity consists solely in the privation of knowledge involved in ideas which are fragmentary and confused. Wherefore, a false idea, inasmuch as it is false, does not involve certainty. When we say, then, that a man acquiesces in what is false, and that he has no doubts on the subject, we do not say that he is certain, but only that he does not doubt, or that he acquiesces in what is false, inasmuch as there are no reasons, which should cause his imagination to waver. Thus, although the man be assumed to acquiesce in what is false, we shall never say that he is certain. For by certainty we mean something positive, not merely the absence of doubt.

However, in order that the foregoing proposition may be fully explained, I will draw attention to a few additional points, and I will furthermore answer the objections which may be advanced against our doctrine. Lastly, in order to remove every scruple, I have thought it worth while to point out some of the advantages, which follow therefrom. I say "some," for they will be better appreciated from what we shall set forth in the fifth part.

I begin, then, with the first point, and warn my readers to make an accurate distinction between an idea, or conception of the mind, and the images of things which we imagine. It is further necessary that they should distinguish between idea and words, whereby we signify things. These three—namely, images, words, and ideas—are by many persons either entirely confused together, or not distinguished with sufficient accuracy or care, and hence people are generally in ignorance, how absolutely necessary is a knowledge of this doctrine of the will, both for philosophic purposes and for the wise ordering of life. Those who think that ideas consist in images which are formed in us by contact with external bodies, persuade themselves that the ideas of those things, whereof we can form no mental picture, are not ideas, but only figments, which we invent by the free decree of our will; they thus regard ideas as though they were inanimate pictures on a panel, and, filled with this misconception, do not see that an idea, inasmuch as it is an idea, involves an affirmation or negation.

Again, those who confuse words with ideas, or with the affirmation which an idea involves, think that they can wish something contrary to what they feel, affirm, or deny. This misconception will easily be laid aside by one, who reflects on the nature of knowledge, and seeing that it in no wise involves the conception of extension, will therefore clearly understand, that an idea (being a mode of thinking) does not consist in the image of anything, nor in words. The essence of words and images is put together by bodily motions, which in no wise involve the conception of thought.

These few words on this subject will suffice: I will therefore pass on to consider the objections, which may be raised against our doctrine. Of these, the first is advanced by those, who think that the will has a wider scope than the understanding, and that therefore it is different therefrom. The reason for their holding the belief, that the will has wider scope than the understanding, is that they assert, that they have no need of an increase in their faculty of assent, that is of affirmation or negation, in order to assent to an infinity of things which we do not perceive, but that they have need of an increase in their faculty of understanding. The will is thus distinguished from the intellect, the latter being finite and the former infinite. Secondly, it may be objected that experience seems to teach us especially clearly, that we are able to suspend our judgment before assenting to things which we perceive; this is confirmed by the fact that no one is said to be deceived, in so far as he perceives anything, but only in so far as he assents or dissents.

For instance, he who feigns a winged horse, does not therefore admit that a winged horse exists; that is, he is not deceived, unless he admits in addition that a winged horse does exist. Nothing therefore seems to be taught more clearly by experience, than that the will or faculty of assent is free and different from the faculty of understanding. Thirdly, it may be objected that one affirmation does not apparently contain more reality than another; in other words, that we do not seem to need for affirming, that what is true is true, any greater power than for affirming, that what is false is true. We have, however, seen that one idea has more reality or perfection than another, for as objects are some more excellent than others, so also are the ideas of them some more excellent than others; this also seems to point to a difference between the understanding and the will. Fourthly, it may be objected, if man does not act from free will, what will happen if the incentives to action are equally balanced, as in the case of Buridan's ass? Will he perish of hunger and thirst? If I say that he would, I shall seem to have in my thoughts an ass or the statue of a man rather than an actual man. If I say that he would not, he would then determine his own action, and would consequently possess the faculty of going and doing whatever he liked. Other objections might also be raised, but, as I am not bound to put in evidence everything that anyone may dream, I will only set myself to the task of refuting those I have mentioned, and that as briefly as possible.

To the *first* objection I answer, that I admit that the will has a wider scope than the understanding, if by the understanding be meant only clear and distinct ideas; but I deny that the will has a wider scope than the perceptions, and the faculty of forming conceptions; nor do I see why the faculty of volition should be called infinite, any more than the faculty of feeling: for, as we are able by the same faculty of volition to affirm an infinite number of things (one after the other, for we cannot affirm an infinite number simultaneously), so also can we, by the same faculty of feeling, feel or perceive (in succession) an infinite number of bodies. If it be said that there is an infinite number of things which we cannot perceive, I answer, that we cannot attain to such things by any thinking, nor, consequently, by any faculty of volition. But, it may still be urged, if God wished to bring it about that we should perceive them, he would be obliged to endow us with a greater faculty of perception, but not a greater faculty of volition than we have already. This is the same as to say that, if God wished to bring it about that we should understand an infinite number of other entities, it would be necessary for him to give us a greater understanding, but not a more universal idea of entity than that which we have already, in order to grasp such infinite entities. We have shown that will is a universal entity or idea, whereby we explain all particular volitions—in other words, that which is common to all such volitions.

As, then, our opponents maintain that this idea, common or universal to all volitions, is a faculty, it is little to be wondered at that they assert, that such a faculty extends itself into the infinite, beyond the limits of the understanding: for what is universal is predicated alike of one, of many, and of an infinite number of individuals.

To the *second* objection I reply by denying, that we have a free power of suspending our judgment: for, when we say that anyone suspends his judgment, we merely mean that he sees, that he does not perceive the matter in question adequately. Suspension of judgment is, therefore, strictly speaking, a perception, and not free will. In order to illustrate the point, let us suppose a boy imagining a horse, and perceiving nothing else. Inasmuch as this imagination in-

SPINOZA DICTIONARY

volves the existence of the horse, and the boy does not perceive anything which would exclude the existence of the
horse, he will necessarily regard the horse as present: he
will not be able to doubt of its existence, although he be
not certain thereof. We have daily experiences of such a
state of things in dreams; and I do not suppose that there
is anyone, who would maintain that, while he is dreaming,
he has the free power of suspending his judgment concerning the things in his dream, and bringing it about that he
should not dream those things, which he dreams that he
sees; yet it happens, notwithstanding, that even in dreams
we suspend our judgment, namely, when we dream that we
are dreaming.

Further, I grant that no one can be deceived, so far as
actual perception extends—that is, I grant that the mind's
imaginations, regarded in themselves, do not involve error;
but I deny, that a man does not, in the act of perception,
make any affirmation. For what is the perception of a
winged horse, save affirming that a horse has wings? If the
mind could perceive nothing else but the winged horse, it
would regard the same as present to itself: it would have no
reasons for doubting its existence, nor any faculty of dissent,
unless the imagination of a winged horse be joined to an
idea which precludes the existence of the said horse, or unless the mind perceives that the idea which it possesses of a
winged horse is inadequate, in which case it will either
necessarily deny the existence of such a horse, or will necessarily be in doubt on the subject.

I think that I have anticipated my answer to the *third*
objection, namely, that the will is something universal
which is predicated of all ideas, and that it only signifies
that which is common to all ideas, namely, an affirmation,
whose adequate essence must, therefore, in so far as it is
thus conceived in the abstract, be in every idea, and be, in
this respect alone the same in all, not in so far as it is considered as constituting the idea's essence: for, in this respect,

particular affirmations differ one from the other, as much as do ideas. For instance, the affirmation which involves the idea of a circle, differs from that which involves the idea of a triangle, as much as the idea of a circle differs from the idea of a triangle.

Further, I absolutely deny, that we are in need of an equal power of thinking, to affirm that that which is true is true, and to affirm that that which is false is true. These two affirmations, if we regard the mind, are in the same relation to one another as being and not-being; for there is nothing positive in ideas, which constitutes the actual reality of falsehood.

We must therefore conclude, that we are easily deceived, when we confuse universals with singulars, and the entities of reason and abstractions with realities. As for the *fourth* objection, I am quite ready to admit, that a man placed in the equilibrium described (namely, as perceiving nothing but hunger and thirst, a certain food and a certain drink, each equally distant from him) would die of hunger and thirst. If I am asked, whether such an one should not rather be considered an ass than a man; I answer, that I do not know, neither do I know how a man should be considered, who hangs himself, or how we should consider children, fools, madmen, &c.

It remains to point out the advantages of a knowledge of this doctrine as bearing on conduct, and this may be easily gathered from what has been said. The doctrine is good,

1. Inasmuch as it teaches us to act solely according to the decree of God, and to be partakers in the Divine nature, and so much the more, as we perform more perfect actions and more and more understand God. Such a doctrine not only completely tranquillizes our spirit, but also shows us where our highest happiness or blessedness is, namely, solely in the knowledge of God, whereby we are led to act only as love and piety shall bid us. We may thus clearly understand, how far astray from a true estimate of virtue are those who

expect to be decorated by God with high rewards for their virtue, and their best actions, as for having endured the direct slavery; as if virtue and the service of God were not in itself happiness and perfect freedom.

2. Inasmuch as it teaches us, how we ought to conduct ourselves with respect to the gifts of fortune, or matters which are not in our own power, and do not follow from our nature. For it shows us, that we should await and endure fortune's smiles or frowns with an equal mind, seeing that all things follow from the eternal decree of God by the same necessity, as it follows from the essence of a triangle, that the three angles are equal to two right angles.

3. This doctrine raises social life, inasmuch as it teaches us to hate no man, neither to despise, to deride, to envy, or to be angry with any. Further, as it tells us that each should be content with his own, and helpful to his neighbor, not from any womanish pity, favor, or superstition, but solely by the guidance of reason, according as the time and occasion demand.

4. Lastly, this doctrine confers no small advantage on the commonwealth; for it teaches how citizens should be governed and led, not so as to become slaves, but so that they may freely do whatsoever things are best. —E-II

Those things, which are common to all, and which are equally in a part and in the whole, cannot be conceived except adequately. —E-II

No one, who has a true idea, is ignorant that a true idea involves the highest certainty. For to have a true idea is only another expression for knowing a thing perfectly, or as well as possible. No one, indeed, can doubt of this, unless he thinks that an idea is something lifeless, like a picture on a panel, and not a mode of thinking—namely, the very act of understanding. And who, I ask, can know that he understands anything, unless he do first understand it? In other words, who can know that he is sure of a thing, unless he be first sure of that thing? Further, what can there be more clear, and more certain, than a true idea as a standard of truth? Even as light displays both itself and darkness, so is truth a standard both of itself and of falsity. —E-II

Every idea of every body, or of every particular thing actually existing, necessarily involves the eternal and infinite essence of God. —E-II

Every idea, which in us is absolute or adequate and perfect, is true. —E-II

Whatsoever ideas in the mind follow from ideas which are therein adequate, are also themselves adequate.

I have thus set forth the cause of those notions, which are common to all men, and which form the basis of our reasoning. But there are other causes of certain axioms or notions, which it would be to the purpose to set forth by this method of ours; for it would thus appear what notions are more useful than others, and what notions have scarcely any use at all. Furthermore, we should see what notions are common to all men, and what notions are only clear and distinct to those who are unshackled by prejudice, and we should detect those which are ill-founded. I will briefly set down the causes, whence are derived the terms styled *transcendental*, such as Being, Thing, Something. These terms arose from the fact, that the human body, being limited, is only capable of distinctly forming a certain number of images within itself at the same time; if this number be exceeded, the images will begin to be confused; if this number of images, which the body is capable of forming distinctly within itself, be largely exceeded, all will become entirely confused one with another. This being so, it is evident that the human mind can distinctly imagine as many things simultaneously, as its body can form images simultaneously. When the images become quite confused in the body, the mind also imagines all bodies confusedly without any distinction, and will comprehend them, as it were, under one attribute, namely, under the attribute of Being, Thing, &c. The same conclusion can be drawn from the fact that images are not always equally vivid, and from other analogous causes, which there is no need to explain here; for the purpose which we have in view it is sufficient for us to consider one only. All may be reduced to this, that these terms represent ideas in the highest degree confused.

From similar causes arise those notions, which we call *general*, such as man, horse, dog, &c. They arise, to wit, from the fact that so many images, for instance, of men, are formed simultaneously in the human mind, that the powers of imagination break down, not indeed utterly, but to the extent of the mind losing count of small differences between individuals (*e.g.* color, size, &c.) and their definite number, and only distinctly imagining that, in which all the individuals, in so far as the body is affected by them, agree; for that is the point, in which each of the said individuals chiefly affected the body; this the mind expresses by the name man, and this it predicates of an infinite number of particular individuals. For, as we have said, it is unable to imagine the definite number of individuals.

We must, however, bear in mind, that these general notions are not formed by all men in the same way, but vary in each individual according as the point varies, whereby the body has been most often affected and which the mind most easily imagines or remembers. For instance, those who have most often regarded with admiration the stature of man, will by the name of man understand an animal of erect stature; those who have been accustomed to regard some other attribute, will form a different general image of man, for instance, that man is a laughing animal, a two-footed animal without feathers, a rational animal, and thus, in other cases, everyone will form general images of things according to the habit of his body.

It is thus not to be wondered at, that among philosophers,

who seek to explain things in nature merely by the images formed of them, so many controversies have arisen.   —E-II

Inadequate and confused ideas follow by the same necessity, as adequate or clear and distinct ideas.   —E-II

There is nothing positive in ideas, which causes them to be called false.   —E-II

There is in the mind no volition or affirmation and negation, save that which an idea, inasmuch as it is an idea, involves.   —E-II

The knowledge of the eternal and infinite essence of God which every idea involves is adequate and perfect.   —E-II

He, who has a true idea, simultaneously knows that he has a true idea, and cannot doubt of the truth of the thing perceived.   —E-II

The idea of God, from which an infinite number of things follow in infinite ways, can only be one.   —E-II

All ideas, in so far as they are referred to God, are true.   —E-II

Even as thoughts and the ideas of things are arranged and associated in the mind, so are the modifications of body or the images of things precisely in the same way arranged and associated in the body.   —E-V

The idea of the mind is united to the mind in the same way as the mind is united to the body.   —E-II

By *idea* I mean the mental conception which is formed by the mind as a thinking thing.

I say *conception* rather than perception, because the word perception seems to imply that the mind is passive in respect to the object; whereas conception seems to express an activity of the mind.   .   —E-II

See Adequate Ideas, Emotions, Immortality of the Soul, Mind, Memory, Passive and Active, Things

IGNORANCE
See Favors, Miracles

IMAGES
See Ideas

IMAGINATION
Imagination is an idea, which indicates rather the present disposition of the human body than the nature of the external body; not indeed distinctly, but confusedly; whence it comes to pass, that the mind is said to err. For instance, when we look at the sun, we conceive that it is distant from us about two hundred feet; in this judgment we err, so long as we are in ignorance of its true distance; when its true distance is known, the error is removed, but not the imagination; or, in other words, the idea of the sun, which only explains the nature of that luminary, in so far as the body is affected thereby: wherefore, though we know the real distance, we shall still nevertheless imagine the sun to be near us. For, this is to be considered, we do not imagine the sun to be so near us, because we are ignorant of its true distance, but because the mind conceives the magnitude of the sun to the extent that the body is affected thereby. Thus, when the rays of the sun falling on the surface of water are reflected into our eyes, we imagine the sun as if it were in the water, though we are aware of its real position; and similarly other imaginations, wherein the mind is deceived, whether they indicate the natural disposition of the body, or that its power of activity is increased or diminished, are not contrary to the truth, and do not vanish at its presence. It happens indeed that, when we mistakenly fear an evil, the fear vanishes when we hear the true tidings; but the contrary also happens, namely, that we fear an evil which will certainly come, and our fear vanishes when we hear false tidings; thus imaginations do not vanish at the presence of the truth, in virtue of its being true, but because other imaginations, stronger than the first, supervene

and exclude the present existence of that which we imagined. —E-IV

It is only through our imagination that we consider things, whether in respect to the future or the past, as contingent.

How this way of looking at things arises, I will briefly explain. The mind always regards things as present to itself, even though they be not in existence, until some causes arise which exclude their existence and presence. Further, we showed that, if the human body has once been affected by two external bodies simultaneously, the mind, when it afterwards imagines one of the said external bodies, will straightway remember the other—that is, it will regard both as present to itself, unless there arise causes which exclude their existence and presence. Further, no one doubts that we imagine time, from the fact that we imagine bodies to be moved some more slowly than others, some more quickly, some at equal speed. Thus, let us suppose that a child yesterday saw Peter for the first time in the morning, Paul at noon, and Simon in the evening; then, that today he again sees Peter in the morning. It is evident that, as soon as he sees the morning light, he will imagine that the sun will traverse the same parts of the sky, as it did when he saw it on the preceding day; in other words, he will imagine a complete day, and, together with his imagination of the morning, he will imagine Peter; with noon, he will imagine Paul; and with evening, he will imagine Simon—that is, he will imagine the existence of Paul and Simon in relation to a future time; on the other hand, if he sees Simon in the evening, he will refer Peter and Paul to a past time, by imagining them simultaneously with the imagination of a past time. If it should at any time happen, that on some other evening the child should see James instead of Simon, he will, on the following morning, associate with his imagination of evening sometimes Simon, sometimes James, not both together: for the child is supposed to have seen, at evening, one or other of them, not both together. His imagination will therefore waver; and, with the imagination of future evenings, he will associate first one, then the other— that is, he will imagine them in the future, neither of them as certain, but both as contingent. This wavering of the imagination will be the same, if the imagination be concerned with things which we thus contemplate, standing in relation to time past or time present: consequently, we may imagine things as contingent, whether they be referred to time present, past, or future.   —E-II

We see how it comes about, as is often the case, that we regard as present things which are not. It is possible that the same result may be brought about by other causes; but I think it suffices for me to indicate one possible explanation, just as well as if I had pointed out the true cause. Indeed, I do not think I am very far from the truth, for all my assumptions are based on postulates, which rest, almost without exception, on experience, that cannot be controverted by those who have shown, as we have, that the human body, as we feel it, exists. Furthermore, we clearly understand what is the difference between the idea, say, of Peter, which constitutes the essence of Peter's mind, and the idea of the said Peter, which is in another man, say, Paul. The former directly answers to the essence of Peter's own body, and only implies existence so long as Peter exists; the latter indicates rather the disposition of Paul's body than the nature of Peter, and, therefore, while this disposition of Paul's body lasts, Paul's mind will regard Peter as present to itself, even though he no longer exists. Further, to retain the usual phraseology, the modifications of the human body, of which the ideas represent external bodies as present to us, we will call the images of things, though they do not recall the figures of things. When the mind regards bodies in this fashion, we say that it imagines. I will here draw attention to the fact, in order to indicate where error lies, that the imaginations of the mind, looked at in themselves, do not contain error. The mind does not err in the mere act of imagining, but only in so far as it is regarded as being without the idea, which excludes the existence of such things as it imagines to be present to it. If the mind, while imagining non-existent things as present to it, is at the same time conscious that they do not really exist, this power of imagination must be set down to the efficacy of its nature, and not to a fault, especially if this faculty of imagination depend solely on its own nature—that is, if this faculty of imagination be free. —E-II

The effects of the imagination arise either from bodily or mental causes. I will proceed to prove this, in order not to be too long, solely from experience. We know that fevers and other bodily ailments are the causes of delirium, and that persons of stubborn disposition imagine nothing but quarrels, brawls, slaughterings, and the like. We also see that the imagination is to a certain extent determined by the character of the disposition, for, as we know by experience, it follows in the tracks of the understanding in every respect, and arranges its images and words, just as the understanding arranges its demonstrations and connects one with another; so that we are hardly at all able to say, what will not serve the imagination as a basis for some image or other. This being so, I say that no effects of imagination springing from physical causes can ever be omens of future events; inasmuch as their causes do not involve any future events. But the effects of imagination, or images originating in the mental disposition, may be omens of some future event; inasmuch as the mind may have a confused presentiment of the future. It may, therefore, imagine a future event as forcibly and vividly, as though it were present; for instance a father (to take an example resembling your own) loves his child so much, that he and the beloved child are, as it were, one and the same. And since there must necessarily exist in thought the idea of the essence of the child's states and their results, and since the father, through his union with his child, is a part of the said child, the soul of the father must necessarily participate in the ideal essence of the child and his states, and in their results.

Again, as the soul of the father participates ideally in the consequences of his child's essence, he may sometimes imagine some of the said consequences as vividly as if they were present with him, provided that the following conditions are fulfilled:—I. If the occurrence in his son's career be remarkable. II. If it be capable of being readily imagined. III. If the time of its happening be not too remote. IV. If his body be sound, in respect not only of health but of freedom from every care or business which could outwardly trouble the senses. It may also assist the result, if we think of something which generally stimulates similar ideas. For instance, if while we are talking with this or that man we hear groans, it will generally happen that, when we think of the man again, the groans heard when we spoke with him will recur to our mind.   —C-XXX-P B

See God, Nature and Properties of; Mind; Passive and Active

IMITATION
See Emulation

IMMANENT CAUSE
See Freedom, Human

IMMORTALITY OF THE SOUL
The human mind cannot be absolutely destroyed with the body, but there remains of it something which is eternal.

This idea, which expresses the essence of the body under the form of eternity, is, as we have said, a certain mode of thinking, which belongs to the essence of the mind, and is necessarily eternal. Yet it is not possible that we should remember that we existed before our body, for our body can bear no trace of such existence, neither can eternity be defined in terms of time, or have any relation to time. But, notwithstanding, we feel and know that we are eternal. For the mind feels those things that it conceives by understanding, no less than those things that it remembers. For the eyes of the mind, whereby it sees and observes things, are none other than proofs. Thus, although we do not remember that we existed before the body, yet we feel that our mind, in so far as it involves the essence of the body, under the form of eternity, is eternal, and that thus its existence cannot be defined in terms of time, or explained through duration. Thus our mind can only be said to endure, and its existence can only be defined by a fixed time, in so far as it involves the actual existence of the body. Thus far only has it the power of determining the existence of things by time, and conceiving them under the category of duration. —E-V

The Soul is an Idea which is in the thinking thing, arising from the reality of a thing which exists in Nature. Whence it follows that according to the duration and change of the thing, so must also be the duration and change of the Soul. We remarked, at the same time, that the Soul can become united either *with* the body of which it is the Idea, or *with God*, without whom it can neither be, nor be known.

From this, then, it can easily be seen, (1) that, if it is united with the body alone, and that body happens to perish, then it must perish also; for when it is deprived of the body, which is the foundation of its love, it must perish with it. But (2) if it becomes united with some other thing which is and remains unchangeable, then, on the contrary, it must also remain unchangeable and lasting. For, in that case, through what shall it be possible for it to perish? Not through itself; for as little as it could begin to exist through itself when it did not yet exist, so little also can it change or perish through itself, now that it does exist.

Consequently, that thing which alone is the cause of its *existence*, must also (when it is about to perish) be the cause of its *non-existence*, because it happens to change itself or to perish. —G 2-XXIII

See Religion

IMPERFECTION
See Hate; Inferiority, Feeling of

IMPULSE
See Desire

INCLINATION
See Sympathy

INNER CAUSE
See Freedom, Human

INDIGNATION
Approval is not repugnant to reason, but can agree therewith and arise therefrom.

Indignation as we defined it is necessarily evil; we may, however, remark that, when the sovereign power for the sake of preserving peace punishes a citizen who has injured another, it should not be said to be indignant with the criminal, for it is not incited by hatred to ruin him, it is led by a sense of duty to punish him. —E-IV

Indignation is hatred towards one who has done evil to another.

I am aware that these terms are employed in senses somewhat different from those usually assigned. But my purpose is to explain, not the meaning of words, but the nature of things. I therefore make use of such terms, as may convey my meaning without any violent departure from their ordinary signification. —E-III

See Approval, Rational Life

INDIVIDUAL LIBERTY
See Democracy

INFERIORITY, FEELING OF

Culpable humility (inferiority) is this, when some one attributes to himself an imperfection which he has not. I am not speaking of those hypocrites who, without meaning it, humble themselves in order to deceive others; but only of those who really think they have the imperfections which they attribute to themselves.

From what has just been said it is evident, then, that just as Self-respect and True Humility are good and salutary, so, on the contrary, Conceit and Culpable Humility are bad and pernicious. —G 2·VIII

INFINITE INTELLECT
See Intellect, Passive and Active

INFINITE UNDERSTANDING
See Beauty

INFINITY

That an infinity of parts cannot be inferred from a multitude of parts, is plain when we consider that, if such a conclusion could be drawn from a multitude of parts, we should not be able to imagine a greater multitude of parts; the first-named multitude, whatever it was, would have to be the greater, which is contrary to fact. For in the whole space between two non-concentric circles we conceive a greater multitude of parts than in half that space, yet the number of parts in the half, as in the whole of the space, exceeds any assignable number. Again, from extension, as Descartes conceives it, to wit, a quiescent mass, it is absolutely impossible to prove the existence of bodies. For matter at rest, as it is in itself, will continue at rest, and will only be determined to motion by some more powerful external cause; for this reason I have not hesitated on occasion to affirm, that the Cartesian principles of natural things are useless, not to say absurd. —C-LXX-T

See Law of Nature, Mode, Substance

INFIRMITY
See Natural Right, Rational Life

INGRATITUDE
Ingratitude is a disregard or shaking off of Gratitude, as
Shamelessness is of Shame, and that without any rational
ground, but solely as the result either of greed or of immoderate self-love; and that is why it can have no place in
a perfect man.   —G 2-XIII
See Gratitude

INIQUITY
See Democracy

INJUSTICE
See Democracy, Natural Right

INTELLECT
Inasmuch as the intellect is the best part of our being, it
is evident that we should make every effort to perfect it as
far as possible if we desire to search for what is really profitable to us. For in intellectual perfection the highest good
should consist. Now, since all our knowledge, and the
certainty which removes every doubt, depend solely on the
knowledge of God;—firstly, because without God nothing
can exist or be conceived; secondly, because so long as we
have no clear and distinct idea of God we may remain in
universal doubt—it follows that our highest good and perfection also depend solely on the knowledge of God. Further, since without God nothing can exist or be conceived,
it is evident that all natural phenomena involve and express
the conception of God as far as their essence and perfection
extend, so that we have greater and more perfect knowledge
of God in proportion to our knowledge of natural phenomena: conversely (since the knowledge of an effect through
its cause is the same thing as the knowledge of a particular
property of a cause) the greater our knowledge of natural

phenomena, the more perfect is our knowledge of the essence of God (which is the cause of all things). So, then, our highest good not only depends on the knowledge of God, but wholly consists therein; and it further follows that man is perfect or the reverse in proportion to the nature and perfection of the object of his special desire; hence the most perfect and the chief sharer in the highest blessedness is he who prizes above all else, and takes especial delight in, the intellectual knowledge of God, the most perfect Being.

Hither, then, our highest good and our highest blessedness aim—namely, to the knowledge and love of God; therefore the means demanded by this aim of all human actions, that is, by God in so far as the idea of Him is in us, may be called the commands of God, because they proceed, as it were, from God Himself, inasmuch as He exists in our minds, and the plan of life which has regard to this aim may be fitly called the law of God.   —T P-IV

Intellect, in function finite, or in function infinite, must comprehend the attributes of God and the modifications of God, and nothing else.   —E-I

The intellect in function, whether finite or infinite, as will, desire, love, &c., should be referred to passive nature and not to active nature.   —E-I

From the necessity of the Divine nature must follow an infinite number of things in infinite ways—that is, all things which can fall within the sphere of infinite intellect. —E-I
See Free Will, Ideas, Passions

INTELLECTUAL LOVE

The intellectual love of the mind towards God is that very love of God whereby God loves Himself, not in so far as He is infinite, but in so far as He can be explained through the essence of the human mind regarded under the form of eternity; in other words, the intellectual love of the mind towards God is part of the infinite love wherewith God loves Himself.

Hence it follows that God, in so far as He loves Himself, loves man, and, consequently, that the love of God towards men, and the intellectual love of the mind towards God are identical.

From what has been said we clearly understand, wherein our salvation, or blessedness, or freedom, consists: namely, in the constant and eternal love towards God, or in God's love towards men. This love or blessedness is, in the Bible, called Glory, and not undeservedly. For whether this love be referred to God or to the mind, it may rightly be called acquiescence of spirit, which is not really distinguished from glory. In so far as it is referred to God, it is pleasure, if we may still use that term, accompanied by the idea of itself, and, in so far as it is referred to the mind, it is the same.

Again, since the essence of our mind consists solely in knowledge, whereof the beginning and the foundation is God, it becomes clear to us, in what manner and way our mind, as to its essence and existence, follows from the Divine nature and constantly depends on God. I have thought it worth while here to call attention to this, in order to show by this example how the knowledge of particular things, which I have called intuitive or of the third kind, is potent, and more powerful than the general knowledge, which I have styled knowledge of the second kind. For, although it has been shown in general terms, that all things (and consequently, also, the human mind) depend as to their essence and existence on God, yet that demonstration, though legitimate and placed beyond the chances of doubt, does not affect our mind so much, as when the same conclusion is derived from the actual essence of some particular thing, which we say depends on God.   —E-V

Love towards God cannot be stained by the emotion of envy or jealousy: contrariwise, it is the more fostered, in proportion as we conceive a greater number of men to be joined to God by the same bond of love.

We can in the same way show, that there is no emotion directly contrary to this love, whereby this love can be destroyed; therefore we may conclude, that this love towards God is the most constant of all the emotions, and that, in so far as it is referred to the body, it cannot be destroyed, unless the body be destroyed also. As to its nature, in so far as it is referred to the mind only, we shall presently inquire.

It appears that the mind's power over the emotions consists:—

I. In the actual knowledge of the emotion.

II. In the fact that it separates the emotions from the thought of an external cause, which we conceive confusedly.

III. In the fact, that, in respect to time, the emotions referred to things, which we distinctly understand, surpass those referred to what we conceive in a confused and fragmentary manner.

IV. In the number of causes whereby those modifications are fostered, which have regard to the common properties of things or to God.

V. Lastly, in the order wherein the mind can arrange and associate, one with another, its own emotions.

But, in order that this power of the mind over the emotions may be better understood, it should be specially observed that the emotions are called by us strong, when we compare the emotion of one man with the emotion of another, and see that one man is more troubled than another by the same emotion; or when we are comparing the various emotions of the same man one with another, and find that he is more affected or stirred by one emotion than by another. For the strength of every emotion is defined by a comparison of our own power with the power of an external cause. Now the power of the mind is defined by knowledge only, and its infirmity or passion is defined by the privation of knowledge only: it therefore follows, that that mind is most passive, whose greatest part is made up of inadequate ideas, so that it may be characterized more readily by its passive states than by its activities: on the other hand, that mind is most active, whose greatest part is made up of adequate ideas, so that, although it may contain as many inadequate ideas as the former mind, it may yet be more easily characterized by ideas attributable to human virtue, than by ideas which tell of human infirmity. Again, it must be observed, that spiritual unhealthiness and misfortunes can generally be traced to excessive love for something which is subject to many variations, and which we can never become masters of. For no one is solicitous or anxious about anything, unless he loves it; neither do wrongs, suspicions, enmities, &c. arise, except in regard to things whereof no one can be really master.

We may thus readily conceive the power which clear and distinct knowledge, and especially that third kind of knowledge, founded on the actual knowledge of God, possesses over the emotions: if it does not absolutely destroy them, in so far as they are passions; at any rate, it causes them to occupy a very small part of the mind. Further, it begets a love towards a thing immutable and eternal, whereof we may really enter into possession; neither can it be defiled with those faults which are inherent in ordinary love; but it may grow from strength to strength, and may engross the greater part of the mind, and deeply penetrate it.   —E-V

There is nothing in nature, which is contrary to this intellectual love, or which can take it away.   —E-V

God loves Himself with an infinite intellectual love   —E-V

The love towards God must hold the chief place in the mind.   —E-V

He, who loves God, cannot endeavor that God should love him in return.   —E-V

[155]

Whatsoever we understand by the highest (third) kind of knowledge, we take delight in, and our delight is accompanied by the idea of God as cause.

From the third kind of knowledge necessarily arises the intellectual love of God. From this kind of knowledge arises pleasure accompanied by the idea of God as cause, that is, the love of God; not in so far as we imagine him as present, but in so far as we understand him to be eternal; this is what I call the intellectual love of God.   —E-V

The intellectual love of God, which arises from the third kind of knowledge, is eternal.

Although this love towards God has no beginning, it yet possesses all the perfections of love. Nor is there here any difference, except that the mind possesses as eternal those same perfections which we feigned to accrue to it, and they are accompanied by the idea of God as eternal cause. If pleasure consists in the transition to a greater perfection, assuredly blessedness must consist in the mind being endowed with perfection itself.   —E-V

As the love of God is man's highest happiness and blessedness, and the ultimate end and aim of all human actions, it follows that he alone lives by the Divine law who loves God not from fear of punishment, or from love of any other object, such as sensual pleasure, fame, or the like; but solely because he has knowledge of God, or is convinced that the knowledge and love of God is the highest good. The sum and chief precept, then, of the Divine law is to love God as the highest good, namely, as we have said, not from fear of any pains and penalties, or from the love of any other object in which we desire to take pleasure. The idea of God lays down the rule that God is our highest good—in other words, that the knowledge and love of God is the ultimate aim to which all our actions should be directed. The worldling cannot understand these things, they appear foolishness to him, because he has too meagre a knowledge of God, and also because in this highest good he can discover nothing which he can handle or eat, or which affects the fleshly appetites wherein he chiefly delights, for it consists solely in thought and the pure reason. They, on the other hand, who know that they possess no greater gift than intellect and sound reason, will doubtless accept what I have said without question.   —T P-IV

See Passions

INTELLECTUAL PERFECTION
See Intellect

INTELLIGENCE
See Grief, Rational Life, Well-being

INTEMPERANCE
Intemperance is the excessive desire and love of drinking.   —E-III

INTEREST
See Society

INTREPID
I shall call a man *intrepid*, if he despises an evil which I am accustomed to fear; if I further take into consideration, that, in his desire to injure his enemies and to benefit those whom he loves, he is not restrained by the fear of an evil which is sufficient to restrain me, I shall call him *daring*.   —E-III

See Courage

INTUITION
See Intellectual Love, Knowledge

INWARD WORSHIP
See Worship

ISRAEL
If the foundations of their religion have not deserted

their minds they may even, if occasion offers, so changeable are human affairs, raise up their empire afresh, and that God may a second time elect them.   —T P-III

ISRAELITES
   See Words

J

JACOB
See Words

JEALOUSY
If anyone conceives, that an object of his love joins itself to another with closer bonds of friendship than he himself has attained to, he will be affected with hatred towards the loved object and with envy towards his rival.

This hatred towards an object of love joined with envy is called *Jealousy*, which accordingly is nothing else but a wavering of the disposition arising from combined love and hatred, accompanied by the idea of some rival who is envied. Further, this hatred towards the object of love will be greater, in proportion to the pleasure which the jealous man had been wont to derive from the reciprocated love of the said object; and also in proportion to the feelings he had previously entertained towards his rival. If he had hated him, he will forthwith hate the object of his love, because he conceives it is pleasurably affected by one whom he himself hates: and also because he is compelled to associate the image of his loved one with the image of him whom he hates. This condition generally comes into play in the case of love for a woman: for he who thinks, that a woman whom he loves gives herself to another, will feel pain, not only because his own desire is restrained, but also because, being compelled to associate the image of her he loves with the parts of shame and the excreta of another, he therefore shrinks from her.

We must add, that a jealous man is not greeted by his beloved with the same joyful countenance as before, and this also gives him pain as a lover.　　　—E-III

[159]

Jealousy is the anxiety which we feel that we may have the sole enjoyment and possession of something already acquired.　　　　　　　　—G 2-IX
See Lust

JEROBOAM
See Words

JEWS
See Hate, Miracles, Prophecy

JOB
See Books

JOY

Joy is pleasure accompanied by the idea of something past, which has had an issue beyond our hope.　　—E-III

Joy is pleasure arising from the image of something past whereof we doubted the issue.　　　　　　　—E-III

JUDGMENT
See Affections, History, Ideas

JUSTICE
See Democracy, Faith, Law, Natural Right, Private Property, Rational Life, Worship

K

KINDLINESS
See Ambition

KINDNESS
He, who lives under the guidance of reason, endeavors, as far as possible, to render back love, or kindness, for other men's hatred, anger, contempt, towards him.

He who chooses to avenge wrongs with hatred is assuredly wretched. But he, who strives to conquer hatred with love, fights his battle in joy and confidence; he withstands many as easily as one, and has very little need of fortune's aid. Those whom he vanquishes yield joyfully, not through failure, but through increase in their powers; all these consequences follow so plainly from the mere definitions of love and understanding, that I have no need to prove them in detail.   —E-IV

KNOWLEDGE
The human mind has an adequate knowledge of the eternal and infinite essence of God.

Hence we see, that the infinite essence and the eternity of God are known to all. Now as all things are in God, and are conceived through God, we can from this knowledge infer many things, which we may adequately know, and we may form that third kind of knowledge or intuitive intelligence. Men have not so clear a knowledge of God as they have of general notions, because they are unable to imagine God as they do bodies, and also because they have associated the name God with images of things that they are in the habit of seeing, as indeed they can hardly avoid doing, being, as they are, men, and continually affected by external bodies.   —E-II

In proportion as the mind is more capable of understanding things by the third kind of knowledge, it desires more to understand things by that kind.   —E-V

The endeavor or desire to know things by the third kind of knowledge cannot arise from the first, but from the second kind of knowledge.   —E-V

In proportion as the mind understands more things by the second and third kind of knowledge it is less subject to those emotions which are evil, and stands in less fear of death.

Hence we understand that death becomes less hurtful, in proportion as the mind's clear and distinct knowledge is greater, and, consequently, in proportion as the mind loves God more. Again, since from the third kind of knowledge arises the highest possible acquiescence, it follows that the human mind can attain to being of such a nature, that the part thereof which we have shown to perish with the body should be of little importance when compared with the part which endures.   —E-V

The third kind of knowledge depends on the mind, as its formal cause, in so far as the mind itself is eternal.

In proportion, therefore, as a man is more potent in this kind of knowledge, he will be more completely conscious of himself and of God; in other words, he will be more perfect and blessed, as will appear more clearly in the sequel. But we must here observe that, although we are already certain that the mind is eternal, in so far as it conceives things under the form of eternity, yet, in order that what we wish to show may be more readily explained and better understood, we will consider the mind itself, as though it had just begun to exist and to understand things under the form of eternity, as indeed we have done hitherto; this we may do without any danger of error, so long as we are careful not to draw any conclusion, unless our premises are plain.   —E-V

Knowledge of the first kind (based on superficial opinion) is the only source of falsity, knowledge of the second (based on reasonable speculation) and third (based on true intelligence) kinds is necessarily true.　　—E-II

The first kind of knowledge, we call *Opinionated Knowledge*, the second *Speculation*, but the third is what we call *Intuition*.

We call it *Opinion* because it is subject to error, and has no place when we are sure of anything, but only in those cases when we are said to guess and to surmise. The second we call *Speculation*, because the things we apprehend only with our speculation are not seen by us, but are only known to us through the conviction of our understanding that it must be so and not otherwise. But we call that *True Intuition* which comes, not from our being convinced by reasons, but from our feeling and enjoying the thing itself, and it surpasses the others by far.

After these preliminary remarks let us now turn to their effects. Of these we say this, namely, that from the first proceed all the "passions" which are opposed to good reason; from the second, the good desires; and from the third, true and sincere Love, with all its offshoots.

We thus maintain that Knowledge is the proximate cause of all the "passions" in the soul. For we consider it once for all impossible that any one, who neither thinks nor knows in any of the preceding ways and modes, should be capable of being incited to Love or Desire or any other mode of Will.　　—G 2-II

Knowledge of the second and third kinds, not knowledge of the first kind, teaches us to distinguish the true from the false.　　—E-II

KNOWLEDGE OF GOD
　　See Communion with God, Ideas, Intellect, Intellectual Love, Virtue, Well-Being

L

LAW

The word law, taken in the abstract, means that by which an individual, or all things, or as many things as belong to a particular species, act in one and the same fixed and definite manner, which manner depends either on natural necessity or on human decree. A law which depends on natural necessity is one which necessarily follows from the nature, or from the definition of the thing in question; a law which depends on human decree, and which is more correctly called an ordinance, is one which men have laid down for themselves and others in order to live more safely or conveniently, or from some similar reason.

For example, the law that all bodies impinging on lesser bodies, lose as much of their own motion as they communicate to the latter is a universal law of all bodies, and depends on natural necessity. So, too, the law that a man in remembering one thing, straightway remembers another either like it, or which he had perceived simultaneously with it, is a law which necessarily follows from the nature of man. But the law that men must yield, or be compelled to yield, somewhat of their natural right, and that they bind themselves to live in a certain way, depends on human decree. Now, though I freely admit that all things are predetermined by universal natural laws to exist and operate in a given, fixed, and definite manner, I still assert that the laws I have just mentioned depend on human decree.

(1) Because man, in so far as he is a part of nature, constitutes a part of the power of nature. Whatever, therefore, follows necessarily from the necessity of human nature

(that is, from nature herself, in so far as we conceive of her as acting through man) follows, even though it be necessarily, from human power. Hence the sanction of such laws may very well be said to depend on man's decree, for it principally depends on the power of the human mind; so that the human mind in respect to its perception of things as true and false, can readily be conceived as without such laws, but not without necessary law as we have just defined it.

(2) I have stated that these laws depend on human decree because it is well to define and explain things by their proximate causes. The general consideration of fate and the concatenation of causes would aid us very little in forming and arranging our ideas concerning particular questions. Let us add that as to the actual co-ordination and concatenation of things, that is how things are ordained and linked together, we are obviously ignorant; therefore, it is more profitable for right living, nay, it is necessary for us to consider things as contingent. So much about law in the abstract.

Now the word law seems to be only applied to natural phenomena by analogy, and is commonly taken to signify a command which men can either obey or neglect, inasmuch as it restrains human nature within certain originally exceeded limits, and therefore lays down no rule beyond human strength. Thus it is expedient to define law more particularly as a plan of life laid down by man for himself or others with a certain object.

However, as the true object of legislation is only perceived by a few, and most men are almost incapable of grasping it, though they live under its conditions, legislators, with a view to exacting general obedience, have wisely put forward another object, very different from that which necessarily follows from the nature of law: they promise to the observers of the law that which the masses chiefly desire, and threaten its violators with that which they chiefly

fear: thus endeavoring to restrain the masses, as far as may
be, like a horse with a curb; whence it follows that the
word law is chiefly applied to the modes of life enjoined
on men by the sway of others; hence those who obey the
law are said to live under it and to be under compulsion.
In truth, a man who renders everyone their due because he
fears the gallows, acts under the sway and compulsion of
others, and cannot be called just. But a man who does the
same from a knowledge of the true reason for laws and
their necessity, acts from a firm purpose and of his own
accord, and is therefore properly called just. This, I take
it, is Paul's meaning when he says, that those who live under the law cannot be justified through the law, for justice,
as commonly defined, is the constant and perpetual will to
render every man his due. Thus Solomon says (Prov. xxi.
15), "It is a joy to the just to do judgment," but the wicked
fear.

Law, then, being a plan of living which men have for a
certain object laid down for themselves or others, may, as it
seems, be divided into human law and Divine law.

By human law I mean a plan of living which serves only
to render life and the state secure.

By Divine law I mean that which only regards the highest
good, in other words, the true knowledge of God and love.

—T P-IV

See Evil

LAW OF NATURE

The law and ordinance of nature, under which all men
are born, and for the most part live, forbids nothing but
what no one wishes or is able to do, and is not opposed to
strifes, hatred, anger, treachery, or, in general, anything
that appetite suggests. For the bounds of nature are not the
laws of human reason, which do but pursue the true interest
and preservation of mankind, but other infinite laws, which
regard the eternal order of universal nature, whereof man

is an atom; and according to the necessity of this order only
are all individual beings determined in a fixed manner to
exist and operate. Whenever, then, anything in nature seems
to us ridiculous, absurd, or evil, it is because we have but a
partial knowledge of things, and are in the main ignorant
of the order and coherence of nature as a whole, and because we want everything to be arranged according to the
dictate of our own reason; although, in fact, what our reason pronounces bad, is not bad as regards the order and
laws of universal nature, but only as regards the laws of
our own nature taken separately.   —P T-II

God gives no laws to mankind so as to reward them
when they fulfill them [and to punish them when they
transgress them,] or, to state it more clearly, that God's
laws are not of such a nature that they could be transgressed.
For the regulations imposed by God on Nature, according
to which all things come into existence and continue to
exist, these, if we will call them laws, are such that they
can never be transgressed; such, for instance, is [the law]
that the weakest must yield to the strongest, that no cause
can produce more than it contains in itself, and the like,
which are of such a kind that they never change, and never
had a beginning, but all things are subjected and subordi-
nated to them. And, to say briefly something about them:
all laws that cannot be transgressed, are Divine laws; the
reason [is this], because whatsoever happens, is not contrary to, but in accordance with, His own decision. All laws
that can be transgressed are human laws; the reason [is
this], because all that people decide upon for their own
well-being does not necessarily, on that account, tend also
to the well-being of the whole of Nature, but may, on the
contrary, tend to the annihilation of many others things.

When the laws of Nature are stronger, the laws of men
are made null; the Divine laws are the final end for the sake
of which they exist, and not subordinate; human [laws] are

not. Still, notwithstanding the fact that men make laws for their own well-being, and have no other end in view except to promote their own well-being by them, this end of theirs may yet (in so far as it is subordinate to other ends which another has in view, who is above them, and lets them act thus as parts of Nature) serve that end [which] coincides with the eternal laws established by God from eternity, and so, together with all others, help to accomplish everything. For example, although the Bees, in all their work and the orderly discipline which they maintain among themselves, have no other end in view than to make certain provisions for themselves for the winter, still, man who is above them, has an entirely different end in view when he maintains and tends them, namely, to obtain honey for himself. So also [is it with] man, in so far as he is an individual thing and looks no further than his finite character can reach; but, in so far as he is also a part and tool of the whole of Nature, this end of man cannot be the final end of Nature, because she is infinite, and must make use of him, together also with all other things, as an instrument.

Thus far [we have been speaking] of the law imposed by God; it is now to be remarked also that man is aware of two kinds of law even in himself; I mean such a man who uses his understanding aright, and attains to the knowledge of God; and these [two kinds of law] result from his fellowship with God, and from his fellowship with the modes of Nature. Of these the one is necessary, and the other is not. For, as regards the law which results from his fellowship with God, since he can never be otherwise but must always necessarily be united with him, therefore he has, and always must have before his eyes the laws by which he must live for and with God. But as regards the law which results from his fellowship with the modes, since he can separate himself from men, this is not so necessary.

—G 2-XXIV

See Miracles

[169]

LEGISLATION
See Law

LIBERTY

If we hold to the principle that a man's loyalty to the state should be judged, like his loyalty to God, from his actions only—namely, from his charity towards his neighbors; we cannot doubt that the best government will allow freedom of philosophical speculation no less than of religious belief. I confess that from such freedom inconveniences may sometimes arise, but what question was ever settled so wisely that no abuses could possibly spring therefrom? He who seeks to regulate everything by law, is more likely to arouse vices than to reform them. It is best to grant what cannot be abolished, even though it be in itself harmful. How many evils spring from luxury, envy, avarice, drunkenness, and the like, yet these are tolerated—vices as they are—because they cannot be prevented by legal enactments. How much more then should free thought be granted, seeing that it is in itself a virtue that it cannot be crushed! Besides, the evil results can easily be checked, as I will show, by the secular authorities, not to mention that such freedom is absolutely necessary for progress in science and the liberal arts: no man follows such pursuits to advantage unless his judgment be entirely free and unhampered.

But let it be granted that freedom may be crushed, and men be so bound down, that they do not dare to utter a whisper, save at the bidding of their rulers; nevertheless this can never be carried to the pitch of making them think according to authority, so that the necessary consequences would be that men would daily be thinking one thing and saying another, to the corruption of good faith, that mainstay of government, and to the fostering of hateful flattery and perfidy, whence spring stratagems, and the corruption of every good art.

It is far from possible to impose uniformity of speech, for the more rulers strive to curtail freedom of speech, the more obstinately are they resisted; not indeed by the avaricious, the flatterers, and other numskulls, who think supreme salvation consists in filling their stomachs and gloating over their money-bags, but by those whom good education, sound morality, and virtue have rendered more free. Men, as generally constituted, are most prone to resent the branding as criminal of opinions which they believe to be true, and the proscription as wicked of that which inspires them with piety towards God and man; hence they are ready to forswear the laws and conspire against the authorities, thinking it not shameful but honorable to stir up seditions and perpetuate any sort of crime with this end in view. Such being the constitution of human nature, we see that laws directed against opinions affect the generous-minded rather than the wicked, and are adapted less for coercing criminals than for irritating the upright; so that they cannot be maintained without great peril to the state.

—T P-XX

Since, therefore, no one can abdicate his freedom of judgment and feeling; since every man is by indefeasible natural right the master of his own thoughts, it follows that men thinking in diverse and contradictory fashions, cannot, without disastrous results, be compelled to speak only according to the dictates of the supreme power. Not even the most experienced, to say nothing of the multitude, know how to keep silence. Men's common failing is to confide their plans to others, though there be need for secrecy, so that a government would be most harsh which deprived the individual of his freedom of saying and teaching what he thought; and would be moderate if such freedom were granted.

—T P-XX

This is taught not only by reason but by daily examples, that laws prescribing what every man shall believe and for-

[171]

bidding anyone to speak or write to the contrary, have often been passed, as sops or concessions to the anger of those who cannot tolerate men of enlightenment, and who, by such harsh and crooked enactments, can easily turn the devotion of the masses into fury and direct it against whom they will.   —T P-XX

The ultimate aim of government is not to rule, or restrain, by fear, nor to exact obedience, but contrariwise, to free every man from fear, that he may live in all possible security; in other words, to strengthen his natural right to exist and work without injury to himself or others.

No, the object of government is not to change men from rational beings into beasts or puppets, but to enable them to develop their minds and bodies in security, and to employ their reason unshackled; neither showing hatred, anger, or deceit, nor watched with the eyes of jealousy and injustice. In fact, the true aim of government is liberty. —T P-XX

As men's habits of mind differ, so that some more readily embrace one form of faith, some another, for what moves one to pray may move another only to scoff, I conclude, in accordance with what has gone before, that everyone should be free to choose for himself the foundations of his creed, and that faith should be judged only by its fruits; each would then obey God freely with his whole heart, while nothing would be publicly honored save justice and charity.

Having thus drawn attention to the liberty conceded to everyone by the revealed law of God, I pass on to another part of my subject, and prove that this same liberty can and should be accorded with safety to the state and the magisterial authority—in fact, that it cannot be withheld without great danger to peace and detriment to the community.

No one is bound to live as another pleases, but is the guardian of his own liberty. I show that these rights can only be transferred to those whom we depute to defend us, who acquire with the duties of defense the power of ordering our lives, and I thence infer that rulers possess rights only limited by their power, that they are sole guardians of justice and liberty, and that their subjects should act in all things as they dictate: nevertheless, since no one can so utterly abdicate his own power of self-defense as to cease to be a man, I conclude that no one can be deprived of his natural rights absolutely, but that subjects, either by tacit agreement, or by social contract, retain a certain number, which cannot be taken from them without great danger to the state.   —T P-PREFACE

See Democracy, Free Will, Society, Virtue

LIFE HEREAFTER
See Religion

LOVE

He who conceives that the object of his love is destroyed will feel pain; if he conceives that it is preserved he will feel pleasure.   —E-III

Love and desire may be excessive.

Mirth, which I have stated to be good, can be conceived more easily than it can be observed. For the emotions, whereby we are daily assailed, are generally referred to some part of the body which is affected more than the rest; hence the emotions are generally excessive, and so fix the mind in the contemplation of one object, that it is unable to think of others; and although men, as a rule, are prey to many emotions—and very few are found who are always assailed by one and the same—yet there are cases, where one and the same emotion remains obstinately fixed. We sometimes see men so absorbed in one object, that, although it be not present, they think they have it before them; when this is the case with a man who is not asleep, we say he is delirious or mad; nor are those persons who are inflamed with love, and who dream all night and all day about nothing but their mistress, or some woman, considered as less

[173]

mad, for they are made objects of ridicule. But when a miser thinks of nothing but gain or money, or when an ambitious man thinks of nothing but glory, they are not reckoned to be mad, because they are generally harmful, and are thought worthy of being hated. But, in reality, Avarice, Ambition, Lust, &c., are species of madness, though they may not be reckoned among diseases. —E-IV

Love, which is nothing else than the enjoyment of a thing and union therewith, we shall divide according to the qualities of its object; the object, that is, which man seeks to enjoy, and to unite himself with.

Now some objects are in themselves transient; others, indeed, are not transient by virtue of their cause. There is yet a third that is eternal and imperishable through its own power and might.

The transient are all the particular things which did not exist from all time, or have had a beginning.

The others are all those modes which we have stated to be the cause of the particular modes.

But the third is God, or, what we regard as one and the same, *Truth*.

Love, then, arises from the idea and knowledge that we have of a thing; and according as the thing shows itself greater and more glorious, so also is our love greater.

In two ways it is possible to free ourselves from love: either by getting to know something better or by discovering that the loved object, which is held by us to be something greater and glorious, brings in its train much woe and disaster.

It is also characteristic of love that we never think of emancipating ourselves from it (as from surprise and other passions); and this for the following two reasons: (1) because it is impossible, (2) because it is necessary that we should not be released from the same.

It is *impossible* because it does not depend on us, but

only on the good and useful which we discern in the object; it is necessary that these should never have become known to us, if we would not or should not love it; and this is not a matter of our free choice, or dependent on us, for if we knew nothing, it is certain that we should also be nothing.

It is *necessary* that we should not be released from it, because, owing to the weakness of our nature, we could not exist without enjoying something with which we become united, and from which we draw strength.

Now which of these three kinds of objects are we to choose or to reject?

As regards the *transient* (since, as remarked, we must, owing to the weakness of our nature, necessarily love something and become united with it in order to exist), it is certain that our nature becomes nowise strengthened through our loving, and becoming united with, these, for they are weak themselves, and the one cripple cannot carry the other. And not only do they not advance us, but they are even harmful to us. For we have said *that love is a union with the object which our understanding judges to be good and glorious*; and by this mean such a union whereby both the lover and what is loved become one and the same thing, or together constitute one whole. He, therefore, is indeed always wretched who is united to transient things. For, since these are beyond his power, and subject to many accidents, it is impossible that, when they are affected, he should be free from these effects. And, consequently, we conclude: If those who love transient things that have some measure of reality are so wretched, how wretched must they be who love honor, riches, and pleasures, which have no reality whatever!

Let this suffice to show us how reason teaches us to keep away from things so fleeting. For what we have just said shows us clearly the poison and the evil which lurk concealed in the love of these things. But we see this yet incomparably clearer when we observe from what glorious and excellent a good we are kept away through the enjoyment of this.

We said before that the things which are transient are beyond our power. But let us be well understood; we do not mean to say that we are a free cause depending upon nothing else; only when we say that some things are in, others beyond our power, we mean by those that are in our power such as we can produce through the order of or together with Nature, of which we are a part; by those which are not in our power, such as, being outside us, are not liable to suffer any change through us, because they are very far removed from our real essence as thus fashioned by Nature.

To proceed, we come now to the second kind of objects, which though eternal and imperishable, are not such through their own power. However, if we institute a brief inquiry here, we become immediately aware that these are only mere modes which depend immediately on God. And since the nature of these is such, they cannot be conceived by us unless we, at the same time, have a conception of God. In this, since He is perfect, our love must necessarily rest. And, to express it in a word, if we use our understanding aright it will be impossible for us not to love God.

The reasons why, are clear. *First of all,* because we find that God alone has essence only, and all other things are not essence but modes. And since the modes cannot be rightly understood without the entity on which they immediately depend; and [as] we have already shown before that if, when loving something, we get to know a better thing than that which we then love, we always prefer it immediately, and forsake the first; it follows, therefore, incontrovertibly that when we get to know God, who has all perfection in Himself, we must necessarily love Him.

Secondly, if we use our understanding well in acquiring a knowledge of things, then we must know them in [relation to] their causes. Now then, since God is a first cause of all other things, therefore, from the nature of the case the knowledge of God is, and remains, before the knowledge of all other things: because the knowledge of all other things must follow from the knowledge of the first cause. And true love results always from the knowledge that the thing is glorious and good. What else, then, can follow but that it can be lavished upon no one more ardently than upon the Lord our God? For He alone is glorious, and a perfect good.

So we see now, how we can make love strong, and also how it must rest only in God. —G 2-V

He who conceives, that the object of his love is affected pleasurably or painfully, will himself be affected pleasurably or painfully; and the one or the other emotion will be greater or less in the lover according as it is greater or less in the thing loved. —E-III

When we love a thing similar to ourselves we endeavor, as far as we can, to bring about that it should love us in return. —E-III

He who loves necessarily endeavors to have, and to keep present to him, the object of his love. —E-III

Love is pleasure, accompanied by the idea of an external cause.

This definition explains sufficiently clearly the essence of love; the definition given by those authors who say that love is *the lover's wish to unite himself to the loved object* expresses a property, but not the essence of love; and, as such authors have not sufficiently discerned love's essence, they have been unable to acquire a true conception of its properties, accordingly their definition is on all hands admitted to be very obscure. It must, however, be noted, that when I say that it is a property of love, that the lover should wish to unite himself to the beloved object, I do not here mean by *wish* consent, or conclusion, or a free decision of

loved object when it is absent, or of continuing in its
presence when it is at hand; for love can be conceived without either of these desires; but by *wish* I mean the contentment, which is in the lover, on account of the presence of
the beloved object, whereby the pleasure of the lover is
strengthened, or at least maintained.   —E-III

See Adequate Ideas, Class Hatred, Compassion, Emotions, Envy, Fame, Good and Bad, Gratitude, Hate, Intellectual Love, Kindness, Knowledge, Rational Life, Wisdom

LOVE OF FREEDOM
See Wisdom

LOVE OF GOD
See Intellect, Intellectual Love, Sin

LUST
Lust is desire and love in the matter of sexual intercourse.
Whether this desire be excessive or not, it is still called
lust.
Again, I have already pointed out, that temperance, sobriety, and chastity indicate rather a power than a passivity
of the mind. It may, nevertheless, happen, that an avaricious,
an ambitious, or a timid man may abstain from excess in
eating, drinking, or sexual indulgence, yet avarice, ambition,
and fear are not contraries to luxury, drunkenness, and
debauchery. For an avaricious man often is glad to gorge
himself with food and drink at another man's expense. An
ambitious man will restrain himself in nothing, so long as
he thinks his indulgences are secret; and if he lives among
drunkards and debauchees, he will, from the mere fact of
being ambitious, be more prone to those vices. Lastly, a
timid man does that which he would not. For though an
avaricious man should, for the sake of avoiding death, cast
his riches into the sea, he will none the less remain avaricious; so, also, if a lustful man is downcast, because he can-

not follow his bent, he does not, on the ground of absten-
tion, cease to be lustful. In fact, these emotions are not so
much concerned with the actual feasting, drinking, &c., as
with the appetites and love of such. Nothing, therefore, can
be opposed to these emotions, but high-mindedness and
valor, whereof I will speak presently.

The definitions of jealousy and other waverings of the
mind I pass over in silence, first, because they arise from
the compounding of the emotions already described; secondly, because many of them have no distinctive names,
which shows that it is sufficient for practical purposes to
have merely a general knowledge of them. However, it is
established from the definitions of the emotions, which we
have set forth, that they all spring from desire, pleasure, or
pain, or, rather, that there is nothing besides these three;
wherefore each is wont to be called by a variety of names in
accordance with its various relations and extrinsic tokens.
If we now direct our attention to these primitive emotions,
and to what has been said concerning the nature of the
mind, we shall be able thus to define the emotions, in so far
as they are referred to the mind only.   —E-III
See Blessedness, Emotions, Love, Rational Life

LUXURY

Luxury is excessive desire, or even love of living sumptu-
ously.   —E-III
See Emotions; Lust

M

MADNESS
See Love

MAN

We can only judge of a man by his works. If a man
abounds in the fruits of the Spirit, charity, joy, peace, long-
suffering, kindness, goodness, faith, gentleness, chastity,
against which, as Paul says (Gal. v. 22), there is no law,
such an one, whether he be taught by reason only or by the
Scripture only, has been in very truth taught by God, and is
altogether blessed.   —T P-V

It is impossible, that man should not be a part of Nature,
or that he should be capable of undergoing no changes,
save such as can be understood through his nature only as
their adequate cause.

Hence it follows, that man is necessarily always a prey to
his passions, that he follows and obeys the general order of
nature, and that he accommodates himself thereto, as much
as the nature of things demands.   —E-IV

See Desire; Envy; God, Nature and Properties of; Social Life

MANKIND
See Desire

MAN'S TRUE FREEDOM
See State

MARRIAGE
See Rational Life

MASSES

The multitude always strains after rarities and exceptions, and think little of the gifts of nature.　　　—T P·I
See Law, Utopia

MATTHEW
See Books

MEANING

Many errors, in truth, can be traced to this head, namely, that we do not apply names to things rightly. For instance, when a man says that the lines drawn from the center of a circle to its circumference are not equal, he then, at all events, assuredly attaches a meaning to the word circle different from that assigned by mathematicians. So again, when men make mistakes in calculation, they have one set of figures in their mind, and another on the paper. If we could see into their minds, they do not make a mistake; they seem to do so, because we think, that they have the same numbers in their mind as they have on the paper. If this were not so, we should not believe them to be in error, any more than I thought that a man was in error, whom I lately heard exclaiming that his entrance hall had flown into a neighbor's hen, for his meaning seemed to me sufficiently clear. Very many controversies have arisen from the fact, that men do not rightly explain their meaning, or do not rightly interpret the meaning of others. For, as a matter of fact, as they flatly contradict themselves, they assume now one side, now another, of the argument, so as to oppose the opinions, which they consider mistaken and absurd in their opponents.　　　—E-II

MEASURE
See Mode

MECHANISM OF THE HUMAN BODY
See Mind

MELANCHOLY

Mirth cannot be excessive, but is always good; contrariwise, melancholy is always bad.   —E-IV

See Emotions, Primary

MEMORY

Memory is a certain association of ideas involving the nature of things outside the human body, which association arises in the mind according to the order and association of the various modifications of the human body. I say, first, it is an association of those ideas only, which involve the nature of things outside the human body: not of ideas which answer to the nature of the said things: ideas of the modifications of the human body are, strictly speaking, those which involve the nature both of the human body and of external bodies. I say, secondly, that this association arises according to the order and association of the modifications of the human body, in order to distinguish it from that association of ideas, which arises from the order of the intellect, whereby the mind perceives things through their primary causes, and which is in all men the same.

And hence we can further clearly understand, why the mind from the thought of one thing, should straightway arrive at the thought of another thing, which has no similarity with the first; for instance, from the thought of the word *pomum* (an apple), a Roman would straightway arrive at the thought of the fruit apple, which has no similitude with the articulate sound in question, nor anything in common with it, except that the body of the man has often been affected by these two things; that is, that the man has often heard the word *pomum*, while he was looking at the fruit; similarly every man will go on from one thought to another, according as his habit has ordered the images of things in his body. For a soldier, for instance, when he sees the tracks of a horse in the sand, will at once pass from the thought of a horse to the thought of a horseman, and thence

[183]

to the thought of war, &c.; while a countryman will proceed from the thought of a horse to the thought of a plough, a field, &c.

Thus every man will follow this or that train of thought, according as he has been in the habit of conjoining and associating the mental images of things in this or that manner. —E-II

In proportion as a mental image is referred to more objects, so is it more frequent, or more often vivid, and occupies the mind more. —E-V

A mental image is more often vivid, in proportion as it is associated with a greater number of other images. —E-V

The mental images of things are more easily associated with the images referred to things which we clearly and distinctly understand, than with others. —E-V

MERCY
See Emotions

MERIT
See God, Nature and Properties of; Natural Right; Rational Life

MERRIMENT
See Emotions, Primary

MIND
The mind does not know itself, except in so far as it perceives the ideas of the modifications of the body. —E-II

The idea, which constitutes the actual being of the human mind, is not simple, but compounded of a great number of ideas. —E-II

We can only have a very inadequate knowledge of the duration of particular things external to ourselves.
All particular things are contingent and perishable. We have no adequate idea of their duration, and this is what

we must understand by the contingency and perishableness of things. For, except in this sense, nothing is contingent.

—E-II

The human mind does not involve an adequate knowledge of the parts composing the human body.   —E-II

Mind and body are one and the same thing, conceived first under the attribute of thought, secondly, under the attribute of extension. Thus it follows that the order or concatenation of things is identical, whether nature be conceived under the one attribute or the other; consequently the order of states of activity and passivity in our body is simultaneous in nature with the order of states of activity and passivity in the mind.

Nevertheless, though such is the case, and though there be no further room for doubt, I can scarcely believe, until the fact is proved by experience, that men can be induced to consider the question calmly and fairly, so firmly are they convinced that it is merely at the bidding of the mind, that the body is set in motion or at rest, or performs a variety of actions depending solely on the mind's will or the exercise of thought. However, no one has hitherto laid down the limits to the powers of the body, that is, no one has as yet been taught by experience what the body can accomplish solely by the laws of nature, in so far as she is regarded as extension. No one hitherto has gained such an accurate knowledge of the bodily mechanism, that he can explain all its functions; nor need I call attention to the fact that many actions are observed in the lower animals, which far transcend human sagacity, and that somnambulists do many things in their sleep, which they would not venture to do when awake: these instances are enough to show, that the body can by the sole laws of its nature do many things which the mind wonders at.

Again, no one knows how or by what means the mind moves the body, nor how many various degrees of motion it can impart to the body, nor how quickly it can move it. Thus, when men say that this or that physical action has its origin in the mind, which latter has dominion over the body, they are using words without meaning, or are confessing in specious phraseology that they are ignorant of the cause of the said action, and do not wonder at it.

But, they will say, whether we know or do not know the means whereby the mind acts on the body, we have, at any rate, experience of the fact that unless the human mind is in a fit state to think, the body remains inert. Moreover, we have experience, that the mind alone can determine whether we speak or are silent, and a variety of similar states which, accordingly, we say depend on the mind's decree. But, as to the first point, I ask such objectors, whether experience does not also teach, that if the body be inactive the mind is simultaneously unfitted for thinking? For when the body is at rest in sleep, the mind simultaneously is in a state of torpor also, and has no power of thinking, such as it possesses when the body is awake. Again, I think everyone's experience will confirm the statement, that the mind is not at all times equally fit for thinking on a given subject, but according as the body is more or less fitted for being stimulated by the image of this or that object, so also is the mind more or less fitted for contemplating the said object.

But, it will be urged, it is impossible that solely from the laws of nature considered as extended substance, we should be able to deduce the causes of buildings, pictures, and things of that kind, which are produced only by human art; nor would the human body, unless it were determined and led by the mind, be capable of building a single temple. However, I have just pointed out that the objectors cannot fix the limits of the body's power, or say what can be concluded from a consideration of its sole nature, whereas they have experience of many things being accomplished solely by the laws of nature, which they would never have believed possible except under the direction of mind: such are the

actions performed by somnambulists while asleep, and wondered at by their performers when awake. I would further
call attention to the mechanism of the human body, which
far surpasses in complexity all that has been put together by
human art, not to repeat what I have already shown, namely,
that from nature, under whatever attribute she be considered, infinite results follow. As for the second objection, I
submit that the world would be much happier, if men were
as fully able to keep silence as they are to speak. Experience
abundantly shows that men can govern anything more easily
than their tongues, and restrain anything more easily than
their appetites; whence it comes about that many believe,
that we are only free in respect to objects which we mod-
erately desire, because our desire for such can easily be
controlled by the thought of something else frequently remembered, but that we are by no means free in respect to
what we seek with violent emotion, for our desire cannot
then be allayed with the remembrance of anything else.

However, unless such persons had proved by experience
that we do many things which we afterwards repent of, and
again that we often, when assailed by contrary emotions, see
the better and follow the worse, there would be nothing to
prevent their believing that we are free in all things. Thus
an infant believes that of its own free will it desires milk,
an angry child believes that it freely desires vengeance, a
timid child believes that it freely desires to run away;
further, a drunken man believes that he utters from the free
decision of his mind words which, when he is sober, he
could willingly have withheld: thus, too, a delirious man, a
garrulous woman, a child, and others of like complexion,
believe that they speak from the free decision of their mind,
when they are in reality unable to restrain their impulse to
talk. Experience teaches us no less clearly than reason, that
men believe themselves to be free, simply because they are
conscious of their actions, and unconscious of the causes
whereby those actions are determined; and, further, it is

plain that the dictates of the mind are but another name for the appetites, and therefore vary according to the varying state of the body. Everyone shapes his actions according to his emotion, those who are assailed by conflicting emotions know not what they wish; those who are not attacked by any emotion are readily swayed this way or that. All these considerations clearly show that a mental decision and a bodily appetite, or determined state, are simultaneous, or rather are one and the same thing, which we call decision, when it is regarded under and explained through the attribute of thought, and a conditioned state, when it is regarded under the attribute of extension, and deduced from the laws of motion and rest. This will appear yet more plainly in the sequel.

For the present I wish to call attention to another point, namely, that we cannot act by the decision of the mind, unless we have a remembrance of having done so. For instance, we cannot say a word without remembering that we have done so. Again, it is not within the free power of the mind to remember or forget a thing at will. Therefore the freedom of the mind must in any case be limited to the power of uttering or not uttering something which it remembers. But when we dream that we speak, we believe that we speak from a free decision of the mind, yet we do not speak, or, if we do, it is by a spontaneous motion of the body. Again, we dream that we are concealing something, and we seem to act from the same decision of the mind as that, whereby we keep silence when awake concerning something we know. Lastly, we dream that from the free decision of our mind we do something, which we should not dare to do when awake.

Now I should like to know whether there be in the mind two sorts of decisions, one sort illusive, and the other sort free? If our folly does not carry us so far as this, we must necessarily admit, that the decision of the mind, which is believed to be free, is not distinguishable from the imagination or memory, and is nothing more than the affirmation, which an idea, by virtue of being an idea, necessarily involves. Wherefore these decisions of the mind arise in the mind by the same necessity, as the ideas of things actually existing. Therefore those who believe, that they speak or keep silence or act in any way from the free decision of their mind, do but dream with their eyes open. —E-III

The mind shrinks from conceiving those things, which diminish or constrain the power of itself and of the body. —E-III

Seeing that our mind subjectively contains in itself and partakes of the nature of God, and solely from this cause is enabled to form notions explaining natural phenomena and inculcating morality, it follows that we may rightly assert the nature of the human mind (in so far as it is thus conceived) to be a primary cause of Divine revelation. All that we clearly and distinctly understand is dictated to us out, by the idea and nature of God; not indeed through words, but in a way far more excellent and agreeing perfectly with the nature of the mind. —T P-I

Our mind is in certain cases active, and in certain cases passive. In so far as it has adequate ideas it is necessarily active, and in so far as it has inadequate ideas, it is necessarily passive. —E-III

The mind, both in so far as it has clear and distinct ideas, and also in so far as it has confused ideas, endeavors to persist in its being an indefinite period, and of this endeavor it is conscious. —E-III

See Adequate Ideas, Body, Body and Mind, Emotions, Ideas, Immortality of the Soul, Intellectual Love, Passive and Active

MIND, WEAKNESS OF

When the mind contemplates its own weakness, it feels pain thereat.

This pain is more and more fostered, if a man conceives that he is blamed by others. —E-III

MIRACLES

If events are found in the Bible which we cannot refer to their causes, nay, which seem entirely to contradict the order of nature, we must not come to a stand, but assuredly believe that whatever did really happen happened naturally. This view is confirmed by the fact that in the case of every miracle there were many attendant circumstances, though these were not always related, especially where the narrative was of a poetic character. —T P-VI

As men are accustomed to call Divine the knowledge which transcends human understanding, so also do they style Divine, or the work of God, anything of which the cause is not generally known: for the masses think that the power and providence of God are most clearly displayed by events that are extraordinary and contrary to the conception they have formed of nature, especially if such events bring them any profit or convenience: they think that the clearest possible proof of God's existence is afforded when nature, as they suppose, breaks her accustomed order, and consequently they believe that those who explain or endeavor to understand phenomena or miracles through their natural causes are doing away with God and His providence. They suppose, forsooth, that God is inactive so long as nature works in her accustomed order, and *vice versâ*, that the power of nature and natural causes are idle so long as God is acting: thus they imagine two powers distinct one from the other, the power of God and the power of nature, though the latter is in a sense determined by God, or (as most people believe now) created by Him. What they mean by either, and what they understand by God and nature they do not know, except that they imagine the power of God to be like that of some royal potentate, and nature's power to consist in force and energy.

The masses then style unusual phenomena "miracles," and partly from piety, partly for the sake of opposing the students of science, prefer to remain in ignorance of natural causes, and only to hear of those things which they know least, and consequently admire most. In fact, the common people can only adore God, and refer all things to His power by removing natural causes, and conceiving things happening out of their due course, and only admire the power of God when the power of nature is conceived of as in subjection to it.

This idea seems to have taken its rise among the early Jews who saw the Gentiles round them worshipping visible gods such as the sun, the moon, the earth, water, air, &c., and in order to inspire the conviction that such divinities were weak and inconstant, or changeable, told how they themselves were under the sway of an invisible God, and narrated their miracles, trying further to show that the God whom they worshipped arranged the whole of nature for their sole benefit: this idea was so pleasing to humanity that men go on to this day imagining miracles, so that they may believe themselves God's favorites, and the final cause for which God created and directs all things.

What pretension will not people in their folly advance! They have no single sound idea concerning either God or nature, they confound God's decrees with human decrees, they conceive nature as so limited that they believe man to be its chief part! —T P-VI

In order to make himself known to men, God can and need use neither words, nor miracles, nor any other created thing, but only himself. —G 2-XXIV

From miracles God's divinity cannot be proved, as I have already shown, and need not now repeat, for miracles could be wrought by false prophets. Wherefore the Divine origin of Scripture must consist solely in its teaching true virtue. —T P-VII

I have taken miracles and ignorance as equivalent terms, because those, who endeavor to establish God's existence and the truth of religion by means of miracles, seek to prove the obscure by what is more obscure and completely unknown, thus introducing a new sort of argument, the reduction, not to the impossible, as the phrase is, but to ignorance.

—C-XXIII-O

As regards miracles, I am of opinion that the revelation of God can only be established by the wisdom of the doctrine, not by miracles, or in other words by ignorance.

—C-XXI-O

For whatsoever we understand clearly and distinctly should be plain to us either in itself or by means of something else clearly and distinctly understood; wherefore from a miracle of a phenomenon which we cannot understand, we can gain no knowledge of God's essence, or existence, or indeed anything about God or nature; whereas when we know that all things are ordained and ratified by God, that the operations of nature follow from the essence of God, and that the laws of nature are eternal decrees and volitions of God, we must perforce conclude that our knowledge of God and of God's will increases in proportion to our knowledge and clear understanding of nature, as we see how she depends on her primal cause, and how she works according to eternal law. Wherefore so far as our understanding goes, those phenomena which we clearly and distinctly understand have much better right to be called works of God, and to be referred to the will of God than those about which we are entirely ignorant, although they appeal powerfully to the imagination, and compel men's admiration.

It is only phenomena that we clearly and distinctly understand, which heighten our knowledge of God, and most clearly indicate His will and decrees. Plainly, they are but triflers who, when they cannot explain a thing, run back to the will of God; this is, truly, a ridiculous way of expressing ignorance.

On the other hand, the laws of nature, as we have shown, extend over infinity, and are conceived by us as, after a fashion, eternal, and nature works in accordance with them in a fixed and immutable order; therefore, such laws indicate to us in a certain degree the infinity, the eternity, and the immutability of God.

We may conclude, then, that we cannot gain knowledge of the existence and providence of God by means of miracles, but that we can far better infer them from the fixed and immutable order of nature. By miracles, I here mean an event which surpasses, or is thought to surpass, human comprehension: for in so far as it is supposed to destroy or interrupt the order of nature or her laws, it not only can give us no knowledge of God, but, contrariwise, takes away that which we naturally have, and makes us doubt of God and everything else.

Neither do I recognize any difference between an event against the laws of nature and an event beyond the laws of nature (that is, according to some, an event which does not contravene nature, though she is inadequate to produce or effect it)—for a miracle is wrought in, and not beyond nature, though it may be said in itself to be above nature, and, therefore, must necessarily interrupt the order of nature, which otherwise we conceive of as fixed and unchangeable, according to God's decrees. If, therefore, anything should come to pass in nature which does not follow from her laws, it would also be in contravention to the order which God has established in nature forever through universal natural laws: it would, therefore, be in contravention to God's nature and laws, and, consequently, belief in it would throw doubt upon everything, and lead to Atheism.

—T P-VI

See God, Nature and Properties of; Religion

MIRTH

See Love, Melancholy

MODE

Now, as regards the *general Natura naturata,* or the modes, or creations which depend on, or have been created by, God immediately, of these we know no more than two, namely, *motion* in matter, and the *understanding* in the thinking thing. These, then, we say, have been from all eternity, and to all eternity will remain immutable. A work truly as great as becomes the greatness of the work-master.

—G I-IX

By *mode,* I mean the modifications of substance, or that which exists in, and is conceived through, something other than itself.　　　　　—E-I

The modifications of substance I call *modes.* Their definition, in so far as it is not identical with that of substance, cannot involve any existence. Hence, though they exist, we can conceive them as non-existent. From this it follows, that, when we are regarding only the essence of modes, and not the order of the whole of nature, we cannot conclude from their present existence, that they will exist or not exist in the future, or that they have existed or not existed in the past; whence it is abundantly clear, that we conceive the existence of substance as entirely different from the existence of modes. From this difference arises the distinction between *eternity* and *duration. Duration* is only applicable to the existence of modes; *eternity* is applicable to the existence of substance, that is, the infinite faculty of existence or being.

From what has been said it is quite clear that, when as is most often the case, we are regarding only the essence of modes and not the order of nature, we may freely limit the existence and duration of modes without destroying the conception we have formed of them; we may conceive them as greater or less, or may divide them into parts. Eternity and substance, being only conceivable as infinite, cannot be thus treated without our conception of them being destroyed. Wherefore it is mere foolishness, or even insanity, to say that extended substance is made up of parts or bodies really distinct from one another. It is as though one should attempt by the aggregation and addition of many circles to make up a square, or a triangle, or something of totally different essence. Wherefore the whole heap of arguments, by which philosophers commonly endeavor to show that extended substance is finite, falls to the ground by its own weight. For all such persons suppose, that corporeal substance is made up of parts. In the same way, others, who have persuaded themselves that a line is made up of points, have been able to discover many arguments to show that a line is not infinitely divisible. If you ask, why we are by nature so prone to attempt to divide extended substance, I answer, that quantity is conceived by us in two ways, namely, by abstraction or superficially, as we imagine it by the aid of the senses, or as substance, which can only be accomplished through the understanding. So that, if we regard quantity as it exists in the imagination (and this is the more frequent and easy method), it will be found to be divisible, finite, composed of parts, and manifold. But, if we regard it as it is in the understanding, and the thing be conceived as it is in itself (which is very difficult), it will then be found to be infinite, indivisible, and single.

Again, from the fact that we can limit duration and quantity at our pleasure, when we conceive the latter abstractedly as apart from substance, and separate the former from the manner whereby it flows from things eternal, there arise *time* and *measure*; *time* for the purpose of limiting duration, *measure* for the purpose of limiting quantity, so that we may, as far as is possible, the more readily imagine them. Further, inasmuch as we separate the modifications of substance from substance itself, and reduce them to classes, so that we may, as far as is possible, the more readily imagine them, there arises *number*, whereby we limit them. Whence it is clearly to be seen, that measure, time, and number, are merely modes of thinking, or, rather, of imagining. It is not to be wondered at, therefore, that all, who have endeavored to understand the course of nature by means of such notions, and without fully understanding even them, have entangled themselves so wondrously, that they have at last only been able to extricate themselves by breaking through every rule and admitting absurdities even of the grossest kind. For there are many things which cannot be conceived through the imagination but only through the understanding, for instance, substance, eternity, and the like; thus, if anyone tries to explain such things by means of conceptions which are mere aids to the imagination, he is simply assisting his imagination to run away with him. Nor can even the modes of substance ever be rightly understood, if we confuse them with entities of the kind mentioned, mere aids of the reason or imagination. In so doing we separate them from substance, and the mode of their derivation from eternity, without which they can never be rightly understood.

To make the matter yet more clear, take the following example: when a man conceives of duration abstractedly, and, confusing it with time, begins to divide it into parts, he will never be able to understand how an hour, for instance, can elapse. For in order that an hour should elapse, it is necessary that its half should elapse first, and afterwards half of the remainder, and again half of the half of the remainder, and if you go on thus to infinity, subtracting the half of the residue, you will never be able to arrive at the end of the hour. Wherefore many, who are not accustomed to distinguish abstractions from realities, have ventured to assert that duration is made up of instants, and so in wishing to avoid Charybdis have fallen into Scylla. It is the same thing to make up duration out of instants, as it is to make number simply by adding up noughts.

Further, as it is evident from what has been said, that neither number, nor measure, nor time, being mere aids to the imagination, can be infinite (for, otherwise, number would not be number, nor measure measure, nor time time); it is hence abundantly evident, why many who confuse these three abstractions with realities, through being ignorant of the true nature of things, have actually denied the infinite.

The wretchedness of their reasoning may be judged by mathematicians, who have never allowed themselves to be delayed a moment by arguments of this sort, in the case of things which they clearly and distinctly perceive. For not only have they come across many things, which cannot be expressed by number (thus showing the inadequacy of number for determining all things); but also they have found many things, which cannot be equalled by any number, but surpass every possible number. But they infer hence, that such things surpass enumeration, not because of the multitude of their component parts, but because their nature cannot, without manifest contradiction, be expressed in terms of number. As, for instance, in the case of two circles, non-concentric, whereof one encloses the other, no number can express the inequalities of distance which exist between the two circles, nor all the variations which matter in motion in the intervening space may undergo. This conclusion is not based on the excessive size of the intervening space. However small a portion of it we take, the inequalities of this small portion will surpass all numerical expression. Nor, again, is the conclusion based on the fact, as in other cases, that we do not know the maximum and the minimum of the said space. It springs simply from the fact, that the nature of the space between two non-concentric circles cannot be expressed in number. Therefore, he who would assign a numerical equivalent for the inequalities in question, would be bound, at the same time, to bring about that a circle should not be a circle.

The same result would take place—to return to my subject—if one were to wish to determine all the motions undergone by matter up to the present, by reducing them and their duration to a certain number and time. This would be the same as an attempt to deprive corporeal substance, which we cannot conceive except as existent, of its modifications, and to bring about that it should not possess the nature which it does possess.

From all that has been said, it is abundantly evident that certain things are in their nature infinite, and can by no means be conceived as finite; whereas there are other things, infinite in virtue of the cause from which they are derived, which can, when conceived abstractedly, be divided into parts, and regarded as finite. Lastly, there are some which are called infinite or, if you prefer, indefinite, because they cannot be expressed in number, which may yet be conceived as greater or less. It does not follow that such are equal, because they are alike incapable of numerical expression. This is plain enough, from the example given, and many others.

But I should like it first to be observed here, that the later Peripatetics have, I think, misunderstood the proof given by the ancients who sought to demonstrate the existence of God. This, as I find it in a certain Jew named Rabbi Ghasdai, runs as follows:—"If there be an infinite series of causes, all things which are, are caused. But nothing which is caused can exist necessarily in virtue of its own nature. Therefore there is nothing in nature, to whose essence existence necessarily belongs. But this is absurd. Therefore the premise is absurd also." Hence the force of the argument lies not in the impossibility of an actual infinite or an infinite series of causes; but only in the absurdity of the assumption that things, which do not necessarily exist by nature, are not conditioned for existence by a thing, which does by its own nature necessarily exist.   —C-XXIX-L M

See Existence, Love

MODE OF THINKING
  See Falsity, Ideas, Immortality of the Soul

MODESTY
  See Shame

MONEY
  See Happiness, Rational Life

MOSES
  See Freedom, Prophecy

MOTION
  If certain bodies composing an individual be compelled
to change the motion, which they have in one direction,
for motion in another direction, but in such a manner, that
they be able to continue their motions and their mutual
communication in the same relations as before, the individual will retain its own nature without any change of its
actuality.   —E-II

  All that specially concerns *Motion*, such as that it *has
been from all eternity, and to all eternity will remain immutable; that it is infinite in its kind; that it can neither be,
nor be understood through itself*, but only by means of
Extension.   —G I-IX

  A body in motion or at rest must be determined to motion or rest by another body, which other body has been
determined to motion or rest by a third body, and that third
again by a fourth, and so on to infinity.

  Hence it follows, that a body in motion keeps in motion,
until it is determined to a state of rest by some other body;
and a body at rest remains so, until it is determined to a
state of motion by some other body. This is indeed self-
evident. For when I suppose, for instance, that a given
body, A, is at rest, and do not take into consideration other
bodies in motion, I cannot affirm anything concerning the
body A, except that it is at rest. If it afterwards comes to
pass that A is in motion, this cannot have resulted from its

having been at rest, for no other consequence could have been involved than its remaining at rest. If, on the other hand, A be given in motion, we shall, so long as we only consider A, be unable to affirm anything concerning it, except that it is in motion. If A is subsequently found to be at rest, this rest cannot be the result of A's previous motion, for such motion can only have led to continued motion; the state of rest therefore must have resulted from something, which was not in A, namely, from an external cause determining A to a state of rest.

All modes, wherein one body is affected by another body, follow simultaneously from the nature of the body affected and the body affecting; so that one and the same body may be moved in different modes, according to the difference in the nature of the bodies moving it; on the other hand, different bodies may be moved in different modes by one and the same body.

When a body in motion impinges on another body at rest, which is unable to move, it recoils, in order to continue its motion, and the angle made by the line of motion in the recoil and the plane of the body at rest, whereon the moving body has impinged, will be equal to the angle formed by the line of motion of incidence and the same plane.

So far we have been speaking only of the most simple bodies, which are only distinguished one from the other by motion and rest, quickness and slowness. We now pass on to compound bodies.

When any given bodies of the same or different magnitude are compelled by other bodies to remain in contact, or if they are moved at the same or different rates of speed, so that their mutual movements should preserve among themselves a certain fixed relation, we say that such bodies are in union, and that together they compose one body or individual, which is distinguished from other bodies by this fact of union.   —E-II

N

NABI
See Prophecy

NATURA NATURATA
See Mode

NATURAL CONDITION OF MANKIND
See Tyranny

NATURAL HARMONY
See Social Life

NATURAL LAWS
See Democracy, Law, Law of Nature, Natural Right, Nature

NATURAL RIGHT
By natural right I understand the very laws or rules of nature, in accordance with which everything takes place, in other words, the power of nature itself. And so the natural right of universal nature, and consequently of every individual thing, extends as far as its power: and accordingly, whatever any man does after the laws of his nature, he does by the highest natural right, and he has as much right over nature as he has power. —P T-II

The good which every man, who follows after virtue, desires for himself he will also desire for other men, and so much the more, in proportion as he has a greater knowledge of God.

He who, guided by emotion only, endeavors to cause others to love what he loves himself, and to make the rest of the world live according to his own fancy, acts solely by impulse, and is, therefore, hateful, especially to those who take delight in something different, and accordingly study and, by similar impulse, endeavor, to make men live in accordance with what pleases themselves. Again, as the highest good sought by men under the guidance of emotion is often such, that it can only be possessed by a single individual, it follows that those who love it are not consistent in their intentions, but, while they delight to sing its praises, fear to be believed. But he, who endeavors to lead men by reason, does not act by impulse but courteously and kindly, and his intention is always consistent. Again, whatsoever we desire and do, whereof we are the cause in so far as we possess the idea of God, or know God, I set down to *Religion*. The desire of well-doing, which is engendered by a life according to reason, I call *piety*. Further, the desire, whereby a man living according to reason is bound to associate others with himself in friendship, I call *honor*; by *honorable* I mean that which is praised by men living according to reason, and by *base* I mean that which is repugnant to the gaining of friendship. I have also shown in addition what are the foundations of a state; and the difference between true virtue and infirmity may be readily gathered from what I have said; namely, that true virtue is nothing else but living in accordance with reason; while infirmity is nothing else but man's allowing himself to be led by things which are external to himself, and to be by them determined to act in a manner demanded by the general disposition of things rather than by his own nature considered solely in itself.

It is plain that the law against the slaughtering of animals is founded rather on vain superstition and womanish pity than on sound reason. The rational quest of what is useful to us further teaches us the necessity of associating ourselves with our fellowmen, but not with beasts, or things, whose nature is different from our own; we have the same rights in respect to them as they have in respect to us. Nay, as everyone's right is defined by his virtue, or power, men have far greater rights over beasts than beasts have over men. Still I do not deny that beasts feel: what I deny is, that we may not consult our own advantage and use them as we please, treating them in the way which best suits us; for their nature is not like ours, and their emotions are naturally different from human emotions. It remains for me to explain what I mean by just and unjust, sin and merit.

Every man exists by sovereign natural right, and, consequently, by sovereign natural right performs those actions which follow from the necessity of his own nature; therefore by sovereign natural right every man judges what is good and what is bad, takes care of his own advantage according to his own disposition, avenges the wrongs done to him, and endeavors to preserve that which he loves and to destroy that which he hates. Now, if men lived under the guidance of reason, everyone would remain in possession of this his right, without any injury being done to his neighbor. But seeing that they are a prey to their emotions, which far surpass human power or virtue, they are often drawn in different directions, and being at variance one with another, stand in need of mutual help. Wherefore, in order that men may live together in harmony, and may aid one another, it is necessary that they should forego their natural right, and, for the sake of security, refrain from all actions which can injure their fellow men. The way in which this end can be attained, so that men who are necessarily a prey to their emotions, inconstant, and diverse, should be able to render each other mutually secure, and feel mutual trust, is evident. It is shown, that an emotion can only be restrained by an emotion stronger than, and contrary to itself, and that men avoid inflicting injury through fear of incurring a greater injury themselves.

On this law society can be established, so long as it keeps in its own hand the right, possessed by everyone, of avenging injury, and pronouncing on good and evil; and provided it also possesses the power to lay down a general rule of conduct, and to pass laws sanctioned, not by reason, which is powerless in restraining emotion, but by threats. Such a society established with laws and the power of preserving itself is called a *State*, while those who live under its protection are called *citizens*. We may readily understand that there is in the state of nature nothing, which by universal consent is pronounced good or bad; for in the state of nature everyone thinks solely of his own advantage, and according to his disposition, with reference only to his individual advantage, decides what is good or bad, being bound by no law to anyone besides himself.

In the state of nature, therefore, sin is inconceivable; it can only exist in a state, where good and evil are pronounced on by common consent, and where everyone is bound to obey the State authority. *Sin*, then, is nothing else but disobedience, which is therefore punished by the right of the State only. Obedience, on the other hand, is set down as *merit*, inasmuch as a man is thought worthy of merit, if he takes delight in the advantages which a state provides.

Again, in the state of nature, no one is by common consent master of anything, nor is there anything in nature, which can be said to belong to one man rather than another: all things are common to all. Hence, in the state of nature, we can conceive no wish to render to every man his own, or to deprive a man of that which belongs to him; in other words, there is nothing in the state of nature answering to justice and injustice. Such ideas are only possible in a social state, when it is decreed by common consent what belongs to one man and what belongs to another.

From all these considerations it is evident, that justice and injustice, sin and merit, are extrinsic ideas, and not attributes which display the nature of the mind.   —E-IV

The power whereby natural things exist and operate is the very power of God itself. For as God has a right to everything, and, God's right is nothing else, but his very power, as far as the latter is considered to be absolutely free; it follows from this, that every natural thing has by nature as much right, as it has power to exist and operate; since the natural power of every natural thing, whereby it exists and operates, is nothing else but the power of God, which is absolutely free. —P T-II

See Democracy, Law

NATURE

By the help of God, I mean the fixed and unchangeable order of nature or the chain of natural events: for I have said before and shown elsewhere that the universal laws of nature, according to which all things exist and are determined, are only another name for the eternal decrees of God, which always involve eternal truth and necessity.

So that to say that everything happens according to natural laws, and to say that everything is ordained by the decree and ordinance of God, is the same thing. Now since the power in nature is identical with the power of God, by which alone all things happen and are determined, it follows that whatsoever man, as a part of nature, provides himself with to aid and preserve his existence, or whatsoever nature affords him without his help, is given to him solely by the Divine power, acting either through human nature or through external circumstance. So whatever human nature can furnish itself with by its own efforts to preserve its existence, may be fitly called the inward aid of God, whereas whatever else accrues to man's profit from outward causes may be called the external aid of God. —T P-III

Nothing, then, comes to pass in nature[1] in contravention to her universal laws, nay, everything agrees with them and follows from them, for whatsoever comes to pass, comes to pass by the will and eternal decree of God; that is, as we have just pointed out, whatever comes to pass, comes

[1] N.B. I do not mean here by "nature," merely matter and its modifications, but infinite other things besides matter.

to pass according to laws and rules which involve eternal necessity and truth; nature, therefore, always observes laws and rules which involve eternal necessity and truth, although they may not all be known to us, and therefore she keeps a fixed and immutable order. Nor is there any sound reason for limiting the power and efficacy of nature, and asserting that her laws are fit for certain purposes, but not for all; for as the efficacy and power of nature, are the very efficacy and power of God, and as the laws and rules of nature are the decrees of God, it is in every way to be believed that the power of nature is infinite, and that her laws are broad enough to embrace everything conceived by the Divine intellect; the only alternative is to assert that God has created nature so weak, and has ordained for her laws so barren, that He is repeatedly compelled to come afresh to her aid if He wishes that she should be preserved, and that things should happen as He desires: a conclusion, in my opinion, very far removed from reason.   —T P-VI

Everything takes place by the power of God. Nature herself is the power of God under another name, and our ignorance of the power of God is co-extensive with our ignorance of Nature. It is absolutely folly, therefore, to ascribe an event to the power of God when we know not its natural cause, which is the power of God.   —T P-I

See Miracles

NATURE OF KNOWLEDGE
See Ideas

NATURE'S ORDER
See Human Conduct

NECESSARY EXISTENCE
See Existence

NECESSITY
Whether we receive the good, which flows from virtue and the Divine love, as from God in the capacity of a judge,

SPINOZA DICTIONARY

or as from the necessity of the Divine nature, it will in either case be equally desirable; on the other hand, the evils following from wicked actions and passions are not less to be feared because they are necessary consequences. Lastly, in our actions, whether they be necessary or contingent, we are led by hope and fear.   —C-XXIII-O

If then human nature had been so constituted, that men should live according to the mere dictate of reason, and attempt nothing inconsistent therewith, in that case natural right, considered as special to mankind, would be determined by the power of reason only. But men are more led by blind desire, than by reason: and therefore the natural power or right of human beings should be limited, not only by reason, but by every desire, whereby they are determined to action, or seek their own preservation. I, for my part, admit, that those desires, which arise not from reason, are not so much actions as passive affections of man. But as we are treating here of the universal power or right of nature, we cannot here recognize any distinction between desires, which are engendered in us by reason, and those which are engendered by other causes; since the latter, as much as the former, are effects of nature, and display the natural impulse, by which man strives to continue in existence. For man, be he learned or ignorant, is part of nature, and everything, by which any man is determined to action, ought to be referred to the power of nature, that is, to that power, as it is limited by the nature of this or that man. For man, whether guided by reason or mere desire, does nothing save in accordance with the laws and rules of nature, that is, by natural right.   —P T-II

Most people believe, that the ignorant rather disturb than follow the course of nature, and conceive of mankind in nature as of one dominion within another. For they maintain, that the human mind is produced by no natural causes, but created directly by God, and is so independent of other

things, that it has an absolute power to determine itself, and make a right use of reason. Experience, however, teaches us but too well, that it is no more in our power to have a sound mind, than a sound body. Next, inasmuch as everything whatever, as far as in it lies, strives to preserve its own existence, we cannot at all doubt, that, were it as much in our power to live after the dictate of reason, as to be led by blind desire, all would be led by reason, and order their lives wisely; which is very far from being the case. For
"Each is attracted by his own delight."
—P T-II

It is not in the nature of reason to regard things as contingent, but as necessary. —E-II

Men are chiefly guided by desire, without reason; yet for all this they do not disturb the course of nature, but follow it of necessity. And, therefore, a man ignorant and weak of mind, is no more bound by natural law to order his life wisely, than a sick man is bound to be sound of body.
—P T-II

The mind has greater power over the emotions and is less subject thereto, in so far as it understands all things as necessary.

The more this knowledge, that things are necessary, is applied to particular things, which we conceive more distinctly and vividly, the greater is the power of the mind over the emotions, as experience also testifies. For we see, that the pain arising from the loss of any good is mitigated, as soon as the man who has lost it perceives, that it could not by any means have been preserved. So also we see that no one pities an infant, because it cannot speak, walk, reason, or lastly, because it passes so many years, as it were, in unconsciousness. Whereas, if most people were born full-grown and only one here and there as an infant, everyone would pity the infants; because infancy would not then be looked on as a state natural and necessary, but as a fault or

delinquency in Nature; and we may note several other instances of the same sort. —E-V

An emotion towards that which we conceive as necessary
is, when other conditions are equal, more intense than an
emotion towards which is possible, or contingent, or non-
necessary. —E-IV

For the nature of each thing is only competent to do that
which follows necessarily from its given cause. That every
man cannot be brave, and that we can no more command
for ourselves a healthy body than a healthy mind, nobody
can deny, without giving the lie to experience, as well as to
reason. "But," you urge, "if men sin by nature, they are
excusable;" but you do not state the conclusion you draw,
whether that God cannot be angry with them, or that they
are worthy of blessedness—that is, of the knowledge and
love of God. If you say the former, I fully admit that God
cannot be angry, and that all things are done in accordance
with His will; but I deny that all men ought, therefore, to
be blessed—men may be excusable, and, nevertheless, be
without blessedness and afflicted in many ways. A horse is
excusable, for being a horse and not a man; but, nevertheless, he must needs be a horse and not a man. He who goes
mad from the bite of a dog is excusable, yet he is rightly
suffocated. Lastly, he who cannot govern his desires, and
keep them in check with the fear of the laws, though his
weakness may be excusable, yet he cannot enjoy with contentment the knowledge and love of God, but necessarily
perishes. I do not think it necessary here to remind you,
that Scriptures, when it says that God is angry with sinners,
and that He is a Judge who takes cognizance of human actions, passes sentence on them, and judges them, is speaking
humanly, and in a way adapted to the received opinion of
the masses, inasmuch as its purpose is not to teach philosophy, nor to render men wise, but to make them obedient.
—C-XXV-O

See Conditioning, Eternity, Free Will, Human Conduct, Ideas, Law, Laws of Nature

NEGATION
See Ideas, Privation

NERO
See Essence

NEW IDEAS
See Novelty

NEW TESTAMENT
See Hebrew

NOVELTY
Be not astonished at new ideas; for it is very well known to you that a thing does not therefore cease to be true because it is not accepted by many. —G 2-XXVI

NUMBER
See Mode

O

OBEDIENCE

Obedience to God consists solely in love to our neighbor
—for whosoever loveth his neighbor, as a means of obeying God, hath, as St. Paul says (Rom. xiii. 8), fulfilled the
law.   —T P-XIII

Obedience does not consist so much in the outward act
as in the mental state of the person obeying; so that he is
most under the domination of another who with his whole
heart determines to obey another's commands; and consequently the firmest dominion belongs to the sovereign who
has most influence over the minds of his subjects; if those
who are most feared possessed the firmest dominion, the
firmest dominion would belong to the subjects of a tyrant,
for they are always greatly feared by their ruler. Furthermore, though it is impossible to govern the mind as completely as the tongue, nevertheless minds are, to a certain
extent, under the control of the sovereign, for he can in
many ways bring about that the greatest part of his subjects
should follow his wishes in their beliefs, their loves, and
their hates. Though such emotions do not arise at the express command of the sovereign they often result (as experience shows) from the authority of his power, and from
his direction; in other words, in virtue of his right; we may,
therefore, without doing violence to our understanding, conceive men who follow the instigation of their sovereign in
their beliefs, their loves, their hates, their contempt, and
all other emotions whatsoever.   ·   —T P-XVII

Therefore wrongdoing cannot be conceived of, but under government—that is, where, by the general right of the

whole dominion, it is decided what is good and what evil, and where no one does anything rightfully, save what he does in accordance with the general decree or consent. For that is wrongdoing, which cannot lawfully be committed, or is by law forbidden. But obedience is the constant will to execute that, which by law is good, and by the general decree ought to be done.   —P T-II

If a man, who is led by reason, has sometimes to do by the commonwealth's order what he knows to be repugnant to reason, that harm is far compensated by the good, which he derives from the existence of a civil state.   —P T-III

See Faith, Natural Right, Peace, Philosophy

OBEDIENCE TO REASON
See Social Life

OCCULT
It is no wonder that persons, who have invented occult qualities, intentional species, substantial forms, and a thousand other trifles, should have also devised spectres and ghosts, and given credence to old wives' tales, in order to take away the reputation of Democritus, whom they were so jealous of, that they burnt all the books which he had published amid so much eulogy. If you are inclined to believe such witnesses, what reason have you for denying the miracles of the Blessed Virgin, and all the Saints? These have been described by so many famous philosophers, theologians, and historians, that I could produce at least a hundred such authorities for every one of the former.   —C-LX-H B

OLD TESTAMENT
See Hebrew

OMENS
See Fear

OPINION
See Desire

OPINIONATED KNOWLEDGE
See Knowledge

ORESTES
See Essence

OVER-ESTEEM
See Esteem

OVID
See Books

OWN INTEREST
See Rational Life

P

PAIN

Pain is the transition of a man from a greater to a less perfection.

I say transition: for pleasure is not perfection itself. For, if man were born with the perfection to which he passes, he would possess the same, without the emotion of pleasure. This appears more clearly from the consideration of the contrary emotion, pain. No one can deny, that pain consists in the transition to a less perfection, and not in the less perfection itself: for a man cannot be pained, in so far as he partakes of perfection of any degree. Neither can we say, that pain consists in the absence of a greater perfection. For absence is nothing, whereas the emotion of pain is an activity; wherefore this activity can only be the activity of transition from a greater to a less perfection—in other words, it is an activity whereby a man's power of action is lessened or constrained. I pass over the definitions of merriment, stimulation, melancholy, and grief, because these terms are generally used in reference to the body, and are merely kinds of pleasure or pain.   —E-III

See Desire, Emotions, Hate, Humility, Self-Love

PARTIALITY

See Disparagement, Esteem, Pride

PARTICULAR THINGS

See Mind, Things

PASSIONS

I have labored carefully, not to mock, lament, or execrate, but to understand human actions; and to this end I have looked upon passions, such as love, hatred, anger, envy, ambition, pity, and the other perturbations of the mind, not in the light of vices of human nature, but as properties, just as pertinent to it, as are heat, cold, storm, thunder, and the like to the nature of the atmosphere, which phenomena, though inconvenient, are yet necessary, and have fixed causes, by means of which we endeavor to understand their nature, and the mind has just as much pleasure in viewing them aright, as in knowing such things as flatter the senses.

—P T-I

How the passions which are bad, should be banished: not as is commonly urged, namely, that these [passions] must first be subdued before we can attain to the knowledge, and consequently to the love, of God. That would be just like insisting that some one who is ignorant must first forsake his ignorance before he can attain to knowledge. But [the truth is] this, that only knowledge can cause the disappearance thereof—as is evident from all that we have said. Similarly, it may also be clearly gathered that without Virtue, or (to express it better) without the guidance of the intellect, all tends to ruin, so that we can enjoy no rest, and we live, as it were, outside our element. So that even if from the power of knowledge and divine love there accrued to the understanding not an eternal rest, such as we have shown, but only a temporary one, it is our duty to seek even this, since this also is such that if once we taste it we would exchange it for nothing else in the world.

This being so, we may, with reason, regard as a great absurdity what many, who are otherwise esteemed as great theologians, assert, namely, that if no eternal life resulted from the love of God, then they would seek what is best for themselves: as though they could discover anything better than God! This is just as silly as if a fish (for which, of course, it is impossible to live out of water) were to say: if no eternal life is to follow this life in the water, then I will leave the water for the land; what else, indeed, can they say to us those who do not know God?

Thus we see, therefore, that in order to arrive at the truth of what we assert for sure concerning our happiness and repose, we require no other principles except only this, namely, to take to heart our own interest, which is very natural in all things. And since we find that, when we pursue sensuousness, pleasures, and worldly things, we do not find our happiness in them, but, on the contrary, our ruin, we therefore choose the guidance of our understanding. As, however, this can make no progress, unless it has first attained to the knowledge and love of God, therefore it was highly necessary to seek this (God); and as we have discovered that He is the best good of all that is good, we are compelled to stop and to rest here. Outside Him, there is nothing that can give us any happiness. And it is a true freedom to be, and to remain, bound with the loving chains of His love.

We can see that reasoning is not the principal thing in us, but only like a staircase by which we can climb up to the desired place, or like a good genius which, without any falsity or deception, brings us tidings of the highest good in order thereby to stimulate us to pursue it, and to become united with it; which union is our supreme happiness and bliss. —G 2-XXVI

The force of any passion or emotion can overcome the rest of a màn's activities or power, so that the emotion becomes obstinately fixed to him. —E-IV

The power and increase of every passion, and its persistence in existing are not defined by the power, whereby we ourselves endeavor to persist in existing, but by the power of an external cause compared with our own. —E-IV

An emotion, which is a passion, ceases to be a passion, as soon as we form a clear and distinct idea thereof.

An emotion therefore becomes more under our control, and the mind is less passive in respect to it, in proportion as it is more known to us. —E-V

The mind is, only while the body endures, subject to those emotions which are attributable to passions.

Hence it follows that no love save intellectual love is eternal.

If we look to men's general opinion, we shall see that they are indeed conscious of the eternity of their mind, but that they confuse eternity with duration, and ascribe it to the imagination or the memory which they believe to remain after death. —E-V

In so far as men are assailed by emotions which are passions, they can be contrary one to another.

I said that Paul may hate Peter, because he conceives that Peter possesses something which he (Paul) also loves; from this it seems, at first sight, to follow, that these two men, through both loving the same thing, and, consequently, through agreement of their respective natures, stand in one another's way. But if we give the matter our unbiassed attention, we shall see that the discrepancy vanishes. For the two men are not in one another's way in virtue of the agreement of their natures, that is, through both loving the same thing, but in virtue of one differing from the other. For, in so far as each loves the same thing, the love of each is fostered thereby, that is the pleasure of each is fostered thereby. Wherefore it is far from being the case, that they are at variance through both loving the same thing, and through the agreement in their natures. The cause for their opposition lies, as I have said, solely in the fact that they are assumed to differ. For we assume that Peter has the idea of the loved object as already in his possession, while Paul has the idea of the loved object as lost. Hence the one man will be affected with pleasure, the other will be affected with pain, and thus they will be at variance one with another.

SPINOZA DICTIONARY

We can easily show in like manner, that all other causes of hatred depend solely on differences, and not on the agreement between men's natures.　　　　　—E-IV

Men can differ in nature, in so far as they are assailed by those emotions, which are passions, or passive states; and to this extent one and the same man is variable and inconstant.　　　　　—E-IV

Love, Hatred, Sorrow, and other passions are produced in the soul in various forms according to the kind of knowledge which, from time to time, it happens to have of the thing; and consequently, if once it can come to know the most glorious of all (God), it should be impossible for any of these passions to succeed in causing it the least perturbation.　　　　　—G 2-XIX

We must, however, note here as an excellent thing about the passions, that we see and find that all the passions which are good are of such kind and nature that we cannot be or exist without them, and that they belong, as it were, to our essence; such is the case with Love, Desire, and all that pertains to love.

But the case is altogether different with those which are bad and must be rejected by us; seeing that we cannot only exist very well without these, but even that only then, when we have freed ourselves from them, are we really what we ought to be.

To give still greater clearness to all this, it is useful to note that the foundation of all good and evil is *Love bestowed on a certain object*: for if we do not love that object which (*nota bene*) alone is worthy of being loved, namely, God, as we have said before, but things which through their very character and nature are transient, then (since the object is liable to so many accidents, ay, even to annihilation) there necessarily results hatred, sorrow, &c., according to the changes in the object loved. Hatred, when any

[219]

one deprives him of what he loves. Sorrow, when he happens to lose it. Glory, when he leans on self-love. Gratitude, when he does not love his fellow-man for the sake of God.

But, in contrast with all these, when man comes to love God who always is and remains immutable, then it is impossible for him to fall into this welter of passions. And for this reason we state it as a fixed and immovable principle that God is the first and only cause of all our good and delivers us from all our evil.

Hence it is also to be noted lastly, that only Love, &c., are limitless: namely, that as it increases more and more, so also it grows more excellent, because it is bestowed on an object which is infinite, and can therefore always go on increasing, which can happen in the case of no other thing except this alone. And, maybe, this will afterwards give us the material from which we shall prove the immortality of the soul, and how or in what way this is possible. —G 2-XIV

See Evil, Grief, Harmony, Hate, Knowledge, Man, Passive and Active, Race, Rational Life, Utopia, Women

PASSIVE

Passive states are not attributed to the mind, except in so far as it contains something involving negation, or in so far as it is regarded as a part of nature, which cannot be clearly and distinctly perceived through itself without other parts: I could thus show, that passive states are attributed to individual things in the same way that they are attributed to the mind, and that they cannot otherwise be perceived, but my purpose is solely to treat of the human mind.   —E-III

We are only passive, in so far as we are a part of Nature, which cannot be conceived by itself without other parts.
                                                        —E-IV

PASSIVE AND ACTIVE

To all the actions, whereto we are determined by emotion wherein the mind is passive, we can be determined without emotion by reason.

An example will put this point in a clearer light. The action of striking, in so far as it is considered physically, and in so far as we merely look to the fact that a man raises his arm, clenches his fist, and moves his whole arm violently downwards, is a virtue or excellence which is conceived as proper to the structure of the human body. If, then, a man, moved by anger or hatred, is led to clench his fist or to move his arm, this result takes place because one and the same action can be associated with various mental images of things; therefore we may be determined to the performance of one and the same action by confused ideas, or by clear and distinct ideas. Hence it is evident that every desire which springs from emotion, wherein the mind is passive, would become useless, if men could be guided by reason.   —E-IV

When the mind regards itself and its own power of activity, it feels pleasure: and that pleasure is greater in proportion to the distinctness wherewith it conceives itself and its own power of activity.   —E-III

When the mind conceives things which diminish or hinder the body's power of activity, it endeavors, as far as possible, to remember things which exclude the existence of the first-named things.   —E-III

I say that we *act* when anything takes place, either within us or externally to us, whereof we are the adequate cause; that is when through our nature something takes place within us or externally to us, which can through our nature alone be clearly and distinctly understood. On the other hand, I say that we are passive as regards something when that something takes place within us, or follows from our nature externally, we being only the partial cause.   —E-III

He, who possesses a body capable of the greatest number of activities, possesses a mind whereof the greatest part is eternal.

Since human bodies are capable of the greatest number of activities, there is no doubt but that they may be of such a nature, that they may be referred to minds possessing a great knowledge of themselves and of God, and whereof the greatest or chief part is eternal, and, therefore, that they should scarcely fear death. But, in order that this may be understood more clearly, we must here call to mind, that we live in a state of perpetual variation, and, according as we are changed for the better or the worse, we are called happy or unhappy.

For he, who, from being an infant or a child, becomes a corpse, is called unhappy; whereas it is set down to happiness, if we have been able to live through the whole period of life with a sound mind in a sound body. And, in reality, he, who, as in the case of an infant or a child, has a body capable of very few activities, and depending, for the most part, on external causes, has a mind which, considered in itself alone, is scarcely conscious of itself, or of God, or of things; whereas, he, who has a body capable of very many activities, has a mind which, considered in itself alone, is highly conscious of itself, of God, and of things. In this life, therefore, we primarily endeavor to bring it about, that the body of a child, in so far as its nature allows and conduces thereto, may be changed into something else capable of very many activities, and referable to a mind which is highly conscious of itself, of God, and of things; and we desire so to change it, that what is referred to its imagination and memory may become insignificant, in comparison with its intellect. —E-V

Whatsoever increases or diminishes, helps or hinders the power of activity in our body, the idea thereof increases or diminishes, helps or hinders the power of thought in our mind. —E-III

The mind, as far as it can, endeavors to conceive those things, which increase or help the power of activity in the body. —E-III

In proportion as each thing possesses more of perfection, so is it more active, and less passive; and, vice versâ, in proportion as it is more active, so is it more perfect.

Hence it follows that the part of the mind which endures, be it great or small, is more perfect than the rest. For the eternal part of the mind is the understanding, through which alone we are said to act; the part which we have shown to perish is the imagination, through which only we are said to be passive; therefore, the former, be it great or small, is more perfect than the latter.

Such are the doctrines which I had purposed to set forth concerning the mind, in so far as it is regarded without relation to the body; whence, it is plain that our mind, in so far as it understands, is an eternal mode of thinking, which is determined by another eternal mode of thinking, and this other by a third, and so on to infinity; so that all taken together at once constitute the eternal and infinite intellect of God. —E-V

By emotion I mean the modifications of the body, whereby the active power of the said body is increased or diminished, aided or constrained, and also the ideas of such modifications.

If we can be the adequate cause of any of these modifications, I then call the emotion an activity, otherwise I call it a passion, or state wherein the mind is passive. —E-III

PASSIVENESS
See Adequate Ideas, Emotions, Intellect

PASSIVITY
See Freedom, Human; Lust

PAUL
See Democracy, God, Law, Man, Theology

PEACE
Reason altogether teaches to seek peace, and peace cannot be maintained, unless the commonwealth's general laws be kept unbroken. —P T-III

Peace is not mere absence of war, but is a virtue that springs from force of character: for obedience is the constant will to execute what, by the general decree of the commonwealth, ought to be done. Besides that commonwealth, whose peace depends on the sluggishness of its subjects, that are led about like sheep, to learn but slavery, may more properly be called a desert than a commonwealth.
—P T-V

PERCEPTION

All the clear and distinct perceptions, which we form, can only arise from other clear and distinct perceptions, which are in us; nor do they acknowledge any cause external to us. Hence it follows that the clear and distinct perceptions, which we form, depend solely on our nature, and on its certain and fixed laws; in other words, on our absolute power, not on fortune—that is, not on causes which, although also acting by certain and fixed laws, are yet unknown to us, and alien to our nature and power. As regards other perceptions, I confess that they depend chiefly on fortune. Hence clearly appears, what the true method ought to be like, and what it ought chiefly to consist in—namely, solely in the knowledge of the pure understanding, and its nature and laws. In order that such knowledge may be acquired, it is before all things necessary to distinguish between the understanding and the imagination, or between ideas which are true and the rest, such as the fictitious, the false, the doubtful, and absolutely all which depend solely on the memory. For the understanding of these matters, as far as the method requires, there is no need to know the nature of the mind through its first cause; it is sufficient to put together a short history of the mind, or of perceptions, in the manner taught by Verulam.   —C-XLII-I B

See Ideas

PERFECT

The good worship God, that in continually serving Him
they become more perfect, and that they love God.

—C-XXXIV-B

PERFECT MAN
See Hate

PERFECTION

See Bondage, Desire, Emotions, God, Gratitude, Happiness, Hate, Ideas, Intellect, Intellectual Love, Knowledge,
Pain, Passive and Active, Pleasure, Reality, Sin, Universe

PERIPATETICS
See Mode

PERSEUS
See Books

PERSISTENCE

No one wishes to preserve his being for the sake of anything else.   —E-IV

Everything, in so far as it is in itself, endeavors to persist
in its own being.   —E-III

PERSUASION

If anyone wishes to persuade his fellows for or against
anything which is not self-evident, he must deduce his con-
tention from their admissions, and convince them either by
experience or by reasoning; either by appealing to facts of
natural experience, or to self-evident intellectual axioms.
Now unless the experience be of such a kind as to be clearly
and distinctly understood, though it may convince a man, it
will not have the same effect on his mind and disperse the
clouds of his doubt so completely as when the doctrine
taught is deduced entirely from intellectual axioms—that is,
by the mere power of the understanding and logical order,
and this is especially the case in spiritual matters which have
nothing to do with the senses.

[225]

But the deduction of conclusions from general truths *à priori*, usually requires a long chain of arguments, and, moreover, very great caution, acuteness, and self-restraint— qualities which are not often met with; therefore people prefer to be taught by experience rather than deduce their conclusion from a few axioms, and set them out in logical order. Whence it follows, that if anyone wishes to teach a doctrine to a whole nation (not to speak of the whole human race), and to be understood by all men in every particular, he will seek to support his teaching with experience, and will endeavor to suit his reasonings and the definitions of his doctrines as far as possible to the understanding of the common people, who form the majority of mankind, and he will not set them forth in logical sequence nor adduce the definitions which serve to establish them. Otherwise he writes only for the learned—that is, he will be understood by only a small proportion of the human race.

—T P-V

PHARAOH
See Prophecy

PHILOSOPHERS
See Ambition, Bible, Emotions, Essence, Evil, God, Ideas, Theology

PHILOSOPHY
Those who know not that philosophy and reason are distinct, dispute whether Scripture should be made subservient to reason, or reason to Scripture: that is, whether the meaning of Scripture should be made to agree with reason; or whether reason should be made to agree with Scripture: the latter position is assumed by the sceptics who deny the certitude of reason, the former by the dogmatists. Both parties are, as I have shown, utterly in the wrong, for either doctrine would require us to tamper with reason or with Scripture.

We have shown that Scripture does not teach philosophy, but merely obedience, and that all it contains has been adapted to the understanding and established opinions of the multitude. Those, therefore, who wish to adapt it to philosophy, must needs ascribe to the prophets many ideas which they never even dreamed of, and give an extremely forced interpretation to their words. —T P-XV

Between faith or theology, and philosophy, there is no connection, nor affinity. I think no one will dispute the fact who has knowledge of the aim and foundations of the two subjects, for they are as wide apart as the poles.

Philosophy has no end in view save truth: faith, as we have abundantly proved, looks for nothing but obedience and piety. —T P-XIV

See Essence, Faith, Happiness, Ideas

PIETY

We cannot think that opinions taken in themselves without respect to actions are either pious or impious, but must maintain that a man is pious or impious in his beliefs only in so far as he is thereby incited to helpfulness, or derives from them license to sin and rebel. If a man, by believing what is true, becomes antisocial, his creed is impious; if by believing what is false he becomes cooperative, his creed is pious; for the true knowledge of God comes not by commandment, but by Divine gift. God has required nothing from man but a knowledge of His Divine justice and charity, and that not as necessary to scientific accuracy, but to helpfulness. —T P-XIII

The precepts of true piety are expressed in very ordinary language, and are equally simple and easily understood. Further, as true salvation and blessedness consist in a true assent of the soul—and we truly assent only to what we clearly understand—it is most plain that we can follow with certainty the intention of Scripture in matters relating

to salvation and necessary to blessedness; therefore, we
need not be much troubled about what remains: such matters, inasmuch as we generally cannot grasp them with our
reason and understanding, are more curious than profitable.

—T P-VII

See Adequate Ideas, Natural Right, Wrongdoing

PINEAL GLAND
See Emotions

PITY
Pity, in a man who lives under the guidance of reason, is
in itself bad and useless.

He who rightly realizes, that all things follow from the
necessity of the divine nature, and come to pass in accordance with the eternal laws and rules of nature, will not
find anything worthy of hatred, derision, or contempt, nor
will he bestow pity on anything, but to the utmost extent of
human virtue he will endeavor to do well, as the saying is,
and to rejoice. We may add, that he, who is easily touched
with compassion, and is moved by another's sorrow or tears,
often does something which he afterwards regrets; partly
because we can never be sure that an action caused by emotion is good, partly because we are easily deceived by false
tears. I am in this place expressly speaking of a man living
under the guidance of reason. He who is moved to help
others neither by reason nor by compassion, is rightly styled
inhuman, for he seems unlike a man.   —E-IV

See Approval, Benevolence, Cruelty, Envy, Hate, Passions, Sympathy, Utopia

PLACE
See Eternity

PLATO
See Bible

PLATONISTS
See Superstition

PLEASURE

There are as many kinds of pleasure, of pain, of desire, and of every emotion compounded of these, such as vacillations of spirit, or derived from these, such as love, hatred, hope, fear, etc., as there are kinds of objects whereby we are affected. —E-III

We endeavor to affirm, concerning ourselves, and concerning what we love, everything that we conceive to affect pleasurably ourselves, or the loved object. Contrariwise, we endeavor to negative everything, which we conceive to affect painfully ourselves or the loved object. —E-III

Pleasure is the transition of a man from a less to a greater perfection. —E-III

Pleasure in itself is not bad but good: contrariwise, pain in itself is bad. —E-IV

Besides pleasure and desire, which are passivities or passions, there are other emotions derived from pleasure and desire, which are attributable to us in so far as we are active. —E-III

We endeavor to bring about whatsoever we conceive to conduce to pleasure; but we endeavor to remove or destroy whatsoever we conceive to be truly repugnant thereto, or to conduce to pain. —E-III

See Desire, Emotions, Fame, Happiness, Hate, Rational Life

PLEASURES OF SENSE
See Happiness

PLEDGES

Neither reason nor Scripture teaches one to keep one's word in every case. For if I have promised a man, for instance, to keep safe a sum of money he has secretly deposited with me, I am not bound to keep my word, from the time that I know or believe the deposit to have been stolen, but I shall act more rightly in endeavoring to restore it to its owners. So likewise, if the supreme authority has promised another to do something, which subsequently occasion or reason shows or seems to show is contrary to the welfare of its subjects, it is surely bound to break its word. As then Scripture only teaches us to keep our word in general, and leaves to every individual's judgment the special cases of exception, it teaches nothing repugnant to what we have just proved. —P T-III

The pledging of faith to any man, where one has but verbally promised to do this or that, which one might rightfully leave undone, or *vice versâ*, remains so long valid as the will of him that gave his word remains unchanged. For he that has authority to break faith has, in fact, bated nothing of his own right, but only made a present of words. If, then, he, being by natural right judge of his own case, comes to the conclusion, rightly or wrongly (for "to err is human"), that more harm than profit will come of his promise, by the judgment of his own mind he decides that the promise should be broken, and by natural right he will break the same. —P T-II

POLITICS
See Evil, Utopia

POSSIBILITY
See Things

POWER
By *virtue* and *power* I mean the same thing; that is, virtue, in so far as it is referred to man, is a man's nature or essence, in so far as it has the power of effecting what can only be understood by the laws of that nature. —E-IV

PRAISE
Furthermore I give the name of praise to the pleasure, with which we conceive the action of another, whereby he

has endeavored to please us; but of blame to the pain wherewith we feel aversion to his action.   —E-III

PRECONCEIVED OPINIONS
See History

PREJUDICES
I know how deeply rooted are the prejudices embraced under the name of religion; I am aware that in the mind of the masses superstition is no less deeply rooted than fear; I recognize that their constancy is mere obstinacy, and that they are led to praise or blame by impulse rather than reason.   —T P-PREFACE

PREJUDICES OF THE EMOTIONS
See Theology

PRIDE
The proud man delights in the company of flatterers and parasites, but hates the company of the high-minded.

It would be too long a task to enumerate here all the evil results of pride, inasmuch as the proud are a prey to all the emotions, though to none of them less than to love and pity. I cannot, however, pass over in silence the fact, that a man may be called proud from his underestimation of other people; and, therefore, pride in this sense may be defined as pleasure arising from the false opinion, whereby a man may consider himself superior to his fellows. The dejection, which is the opposite quality to this sort of pride, may be defined as pain arising from the false opinion, whereby a man may think himself inferior to his fellows. Such being the case, we can easily see that a proud man is necessarily envious, and only takes pleasure in the company, who fool his weak mind to the top of his bent, and makes him insane instead of merely foolish.

Though dejection is the emotion contrary to pride, yet is the dejected man very near akin to the proud man. For, inasmuch as his pain arises from a comparison between his own infirmity and other men's power or virtue, it will be removed, or, in other words, he will feel pleasure, if his imagination be occupied in contemplating other men's faults; whence arises the proverb, "The unhappy are comforted by finding fellow sufferers." Contrariwise, he will be the more pained in proportion as he thinks himself inferior to others; hence none are so prone to envy as the dejected, they are specially keen in observing men's actions, with a view to fault-finding rather than correction, in order to reserve their praises for dejection, and to glory therein, though all the time with a dejected air. These effects follow as necessarily from the said emotion, as it follows from the nature of a triangle, that the three angles are equal to two right angles. I have already said that I call these and similar emotions bad, solely in respect to what is useful to man. The laws of nature have regard to nature's general order, whereof man is but a part. I mention this, in passing, lest any should think that I have wished to set forth the faults and irrational deeds of men rather than the nature and properties of things. For, as I said, I regard human emotions and their properties as on the same footing with other natural phenomena. Assuredly human emotions indicate the power and ingenuity of nature, if not of human nature, quite as fully as other things which we admire, and which we delight to contemplate.　　　　　　　—E-IV

Extreme pride or dejection indicates extreme infirmity of spirit.

Hence it most clearly follows, that the proud and the dejected specially fall a prey to the emotions.

Yet dejection can be more easily corrected than pride; for the latter being a pleasurable emotion, and the former a painful emotion, the pleasurable is stronger than the painful.　　　　　　　—E-IV

Pride is thinking too highly of one's self from self-love. Thus pride is different from partiality, for the latter term is used in reference to an external object, but pride is used of a man thinking too highly of himself. However, as partiality is the effect of love, so is pride the effect or property of *self-love*, which may therefore be thus defined, *love of self or self-approval, in so far as it leads a man to think too highly of himself*. To this emotion there is no contrary. For no one thinks too meanly of himself because of self-hatred; I say that no one thinks too meanly of himself, in so far as he conceives that he is incapable of doing this or that. For whatsoever a man imagines that he is incapable of doing, he imagines this of necessity, and by that notion he is so disposed, that he really cannot do that which he conceives that he cannot do. For, so long as he conceives that he cannot do it, so long is he not determined to do it, and consequently so long is it impossible for him to do it. However, if we consider such matters as only depend on opinion, we shall find it conceivable that a man may think too meanly of himself; for it may happen, that a man, sorrowfully regarding his own weakness, should imagine that he is despised by all men, while the rest of the world are thinking of nothing less than of despising him. Again, a man may think too meanly of himself, if he deny of himself in the present something in relation to a future time of which he is uncertain. As, for instance, if he should say that he is unable to form any clear conceptions, or that he can desire and do nothing but what is wicked and base, &c. We may also say, that a man thinks too meanly of himself, when we see him from excessive fear of shame refusing to do things which others, his equals, venture. We can, therefore, set down as a contrary to pride an emotion which I will call self-abasement, for as from self-complacency springs pride, so from humility springs self-abasement.

—E-III

We endeavor to affirm, concerning that which we hate, everything which we conceive to affect it painfully; and, contrariwise, we endeavor to deny, concerning it, everything which we conceive to affect it pleasurably.

It may readily happen, that a man may easily think too highly of himself, or a loved object, and, contrariwise, too meanly of a hated object. This feeling is called *pride*, in reference to the man who thinks too highly of himself, and is a species of madness, wherein a man dreams with his eyes open, thinking that he can accomplish all things that fall within the scope of his conception, and thereupon accounting them real, and exulting in them, so long as he is unable to conceive anything which excludes their existence, and determines his own power of action. *Pride, therefore, is pleasure springing from a man thinking too highly of himself.*   —E-III

Extreme pride or dejection indicates extreme ignorance of self.   —E-IV
See Rational Life, Self-Abasement

PRIMARY CAUSES
See Memory, Race

PRIVATE ADVANTAGE
See State

PRIVATE PROPERTY
Nature offers nothing that can be called this man's rather than another's; but under nature everything belongs to all —that is, they have authority to claim it for themselves. But under government, where it is by common law determined what belongs to this man, and what to that, he is called just who has a constant will to render to every man his own, but he unjust who strives, on the contrary, to make his own that which belongs to another.   —P T-II

PRIVATION
I say then, first, that *privation* is not the act of depriving, but simply and merely a state of want, which is in itself nothing: it is a mere entity of the mind, a mode of

thought framed in comparing one thing with another. We say, for example, that a blind man is deprived of sight, because we readily imagine him as seeing, or else because we compare him with others who can see, or compare his present condition with his past condition when he could see; when we regard the man in this way, comparing his nature either with the nature of others or with his own past nature, we affirm that sight belongs to his nature, and therefore assert that he has been deprived of it. But when we are considering the nature and decree of God, we cannot affirm privation of sight in the case of the aforesaid man any more than in the case of a stone; for at the actual time sight lies no more within the scope of the man than of the stone; *since there belongs to man and forms part of his nature only that which is granted to him by the understanding and will of God.*

Hence it follows that God is no more the cause of a blind man not seeing, than he is of a stone not seeing. Not seeing is a pure negation. *So also, when we consider the case of a man who is led by lustful desires, we compare his present desires with those which exist in the good, or which existed in himself at some other time; we then assert that he is deprived of the better desires, because we conceive that virtuous desires lie within the scope of his nature. This we cannot do, if we consider the nature and decree of God. For, from this point of view, virtuous desires lie at that time no more within the scope of the nature of the lustful man, than within the scope of the nature of the devil or a stone.* Hence, from the latter standpoint the virtuous desire is not a privation but a negation.

Thus *privation* is nothing else than denying of a thing something, which we think belongs to its nature; *negation* is denying of a thing something, which we do not think belongs to its nature.

We may now see, how Adam's desire for earthly things was evil from our standpoint, but not from God's. Although

God knew both the present and the past state *of Adam,*
He did not, therefore, regard Adam as deprived of his past
state, that is, He did not regard Adam's past state as within
the scope of Adam's present nature. Otherwise God would
have apprehended something contrary to His own will, that
is, contrary to His own understanding.

Our freedom is not placed in a certain contingency nor
in a certain indifference, but in the method of affirmation
or denial; so that, in proportion as we are less indifferent
in affirmation or denial, so are we more free. For instance,
if the nature of God be known to us, it follows as necessarily from our nature to affirm that God exists, as from
the nature of a triangle it follows, that the three angles are
equal to two right angles; we are never more free, than
when we affirm a thing in this way. As this necessity is
nothing else but the decree of God, we may hence, after a
fashion, understand how we act freely and are the cause of
our action, though all the time we are acting necessarily
and according to the decree of God. This, I repeat, we may,
after a fashion, understand, whenever we affirm something,
which we clearly and distinctly perceive, but when we assert
something which we do not clearly and distinctly understand, in other words, when we allow our will to pass beyond the limits of our understanding, we no longer perceive
the necessity nor the decree of God, we can only see our
freedom, which is always involved in our will; in which
respect only our actions are called good or evil. If we then
try to reconcile our freedom with God's decree and continuous creation, we confuse that which we clearly and distinctly
understand with that which we do not perceive, and, therefore, our attempt is vain. It is, therefore, sufficient for us
to know that we are free, and that we can be so notwithstanding God's decree, and further that we are the cause
of evil, because an act can only be called evil in relation to
our freedom.

My understanding is too small to determine all the means,

whereby God leads men to the love of Himself, that is, to salvation. So far is my opinion from being hurtful, that it offers to those, who are not taken up with prejudices and childish superstitions, the only means for arriving at the highest stage of blessedness.

When one says that, by making men so dependent on God, I reduce them to the likeness of the elements, plants or stones, they sufficiently show that they have thoroughly misunderstood my meaning, and have confused things which impress the understanding with things which impress the imagination. If by their intellect only they had perceived what dependence on God means, they certainly would not think that things, in so far as they depend on God, are dead, corporeal, and imperfect (who ever dared to speak so meanly of the Supremely Perfect Being?); on the contrary, they would understand that for the very reason that they depend on God they are perfect; so that this dependence and necessary operation may best be understood as God's decree, by considering, not stocks and plants, but the most reasonable and perfect creatures.

I cannot refrain from expressing my extreme astonishment at remarks, that if God does not punish wrongdoing (that is, as a judge does, with a punishment not intrinsically connected with the offense), what reason prevents one from rushing headlong into every kind of wickedness? Assuredly he, who is only kept from vice by the fear of punishment, is in no wise acted on by love, and by no means embraces virtue. For my own part, I avoid or endeavor to avoid vice, because it is at direct variance with my proper nature and would lead me astray from the knowledge and love of God.

If we cannot extend our will beyond the bounds of our extremely limited understanding, we shall be most wretched —it will not be in our power to eat even a crust of bread, or to walk a step, or to go on living, for all things are uncertain and full of peril. —C-XXXIV-B

PROPHECY

The prophets were endowed with unusually vivid imaginations, and not with unusually perfect minds. This conclusion is amply sustained by Scripture, for we are told that Solomon was the wisest of men, but had no special faculty of prophecy. Heman, Calcol, and Dara, though men of great talent, were not prophets, whereas uneducated countrymen, nay, even women, such as Hagar, Abraham's handmaid, were thus gifted. Nor is this contrary to ordinary experience and reason. Men of great imaginative power are less fitted for abstract reasoning, whereas those who excel in intellect and its use keep their imagination more restrained and controlled, holding it in subjection, so to speak, lest it should usurp the place of reason.

Thus to suppose that knowledge of natural and spiritual phenomena can be gained from the prophetic books, is an utter mistake, which I shall endeavor to expose, as I think philosophy, the age, and the question itself demand. I care not for the girdings of superstition, for superstition is the bitter enemy of all true knowledge and true morality. Yes; it has come to this! Men who openly confess that they can form no idea of God, and only know Him through created things, of which they know not the causes, can unblushingly accuse philosophers of Atheism.   —T P-II

Treating the question methodically, I will show that prophecies varied, not only according to the imagination and physical temperament of the prophet, but also according to his particular opinions; and further that prophecy never rendered the prophet wiser than he was before.   —T P-II

God is equally gracious, merciful, and the rest, to all men; and as the function of the prophet was to teach men not so much the laws of their country, as true virtue, and to exhort them thereto, it is not to be doubted that all nations possessed prophets, and that the prophetic gift was not peculiar to the Jews. Indeed, history, both profane and sacred, bears witness to the fact. —T P-III

Prophetic knowledge is inferior to natural knowledge, which needs no sign and in itself implies certitude. —T P-II

Prophecy, or revelation, is sure knowledge revealed by God to man. A prophet is one who interprets the revelations of God to those who are unable to attain to sure knowledge of the matters revealed, and therefore can only apprehend them by simple faith.

The Hebrew word for prophet is *"nabi," i.e.* speaker or interpreter, but in Scripture its meaning is restricted to interpreter of God, as we may learn from Exodus vii 1, where God says to Moses, "See, I have made thee a god to Pharaoh, and Aaron thy brother shall be thy prophet;" implying that, since in interpreting Moses' words to Pharaoh, Aaron acted the part of a prophet, Moses would be to Pharaoh as a god, or in the attitude of a god. —T P-I

PROPHET
See Books, Faith

PROPOSITION
See Definition

PROVIDENCE
Providence is nothing else than the *striving* which we find in the whole of Nature and in individual things to maintain and preserve their own existence. For it is manifest that no thing could, through its own nature, seek its own annihilation, but, on the contrary, that every thing has in itself a striving to preserve its condition, and to impose itself. Following these definitions of ours we, therefore, posit a *general* and a *special providence. The general* [*providence*] is that through which all things are produced and sustained in so far as they are parts of the whole of Nature. The *special providence* is the striving of each thing sepa-

rately to preserve its existence [each thing, that is to say], considered not as a part of Nature, but as a whole [by itself]. This is explained by the following example: All the limbs of man are provided for, and cared for, in so far as they are parts of man, this is *general* providence; while *special* [*providence*] is the striving of each separate limb (as a whole in itself, and not as a part of man) to preserve and maintain its own well-being.   —G 1-V

See Miracles

PUBLIC AFFAIRS
See Evil

PUBLIC ENEMIES
See Democracy

PUBLIC RIGHT
See State

PUBLIC WELFARE
There can be no duty towards our neighbor which would not become an offense if it involved injury to the whole state, nor can there be any offense against our duty towards our neighbor, or anything but loyalty in what we do for the sake of preserving the state.

This being so, it follows that the public welfare is the sovereign law to which all others, Divine and human, should be made to conform.   —T P-XIX

If human nature were so constituted, that men most desired what is most useful, no art would be needed to produce unity and confidence. But, as it is admittedly far otherwise with human nature, a government must of necessity be so ordered, that all, governing and governed alike, whether they will or no, shall do what makes for the general welfare; that is, that all, whether of their own impulse, or by force or necessity, shall be compelled to live according to the dictate of reason. And this is the case, if the affairs of the dominion be so managed, that nothing which affects the general welfare is entirely entrusted to the good faith of any one. For no man is so watchful, that he never falls asleep; and no man ever had a character so vigorous and honest, but he sometimes, and that just when strength of character was most wanted, was diverted from his purpose and let himself be overcome. And it is surely folly to require of another what one can never obtain from one's self; I mean, that he should be more watchful for another's interest than his own, that he should be free from avarice, envy, and ambition, and so on; especially when he is one, who is subject daily to the strongest temptations of every passion.   —P T-VI

Contracts or laws, whereby the multitude transfers its right to one council or man, should without doubt be broken, when it is expedient for the general welfare to do so. But to decide this point, whether, that is, it be expedient for the general welfare to break them or not, is within the right of no private person, but of him only who holds government; therefore of these laws he who holds dominion remains sole interpreter.   —P T-IV

PUNISHMENT
See Indignation

PUSILLANIMITY
See Timidity

R

RACE

All objects of legitimate desire fall, generally speaking, under one of these three categories:—

1. The knowledge of things through their primary causes.

2. The government of the passions, or the acquirement of the habit of virtue.

3. Secure and healthy life.

The means which most directly conduce towards the first two of these ends, and which may be considered their proximate and efficient causes are contained in human nature itself, so that their acquisition hinges only on our own power, and on the laws of human nature. It may be concluded that these gifts are not peculiar to any nation, but have always been shared by the whole human race, unless, indeed, we would indulge the dream that nature formerly created men of different kinds. But the means which conduce to security and health are chiefly in external circumstance, and are called the gifts of fortune because they depend chiefly on objective causes of which we are ignorant; for a fool may be almost as liable to happiness or unhappiness as a wise man. Nevertheless, human management and watchfulness can greatly assist towards living in security and warding off the injuries of our fellow men, and even of beasts. Reason and experience show no more certain means of attaining this object than the formation of a society with fixed laws, the occupation of a strip of territory, and the concentration of all forces, as it were, into one body, that is the social body. Now for forming and preserving a society, no ordinary ability and care is required: that society will be most secure, most stable, and least liable to reverses, which is founded and directed by far-seeing and careful men; while, on the other hand, a society constituted by men without trained skill, depends in a great measure on fortune, and is less constant. If, in spite of all, such a society lasts a long time, it is owing to some other directing influence than its own; if it overcomes great perils and its affairs prosper, it will perforce marvel at and adore the guiding Spirit of God (in so far, that is, as God works through hidden means, and not through the nature and mind of man), for everything happens to it unexpectedly and contrary to anticipation, it may be said and thought to be by miracle. Nations, then, are distinguished from one another in respect to the social organization and the laws under which they live and are governed.　　　　　　　　　　—T P-III

RASHNESS
See Remorse

RATIONAL LIFE
I. All our endeavors or desires so follow from the necessity of our nature, that they can be understood either through it alone, as their proximate cause, or by virtue of our being a part of nature, which cannot be adequately conceived through itself without other individuals.

II. Desires, which follow from our nature in such a manner, that they can be understood through it alone, are those which are referred to the mind, in so far as the latter is conceived to consist of adequate ideas: the remaining desires are only referred to the mind, in so far as it conceives things inadequately, and their force and increase are generally defined not by the power of man, but by the power of things external to us: wherefore the former are rightly called actions, the latter passions, for the former always indicate our power, the latter, on the other hand, show our infirmity and fragmentary knowledge.

III. Our actions, that is, those desires which are defined by man's power or reason, are always good. The rest may be either good or bad.

IV. Thus in life it is before all things useful to perfect the understanding, or reason, as far as we can, and in this alone man's highest happiness or blessedness consists, indeed blessedness is nothing else but the contentment of spirit, which arises from the intuitive knowledge of God: now, to perfect the understanding is nothing else but to understand God, God's attributes, and the actions which follow from the necessity of His nature. Wherefore of a man, who is led by reason, the ultimate aim or highest desire, whereby he seeks to govern all his fellows, is that whereby he is brought to the adequate conception of himself and of all things within the scope of his intelligence.

V. Therefore, without intelligence there is not rational life: and things are only good, in so far as they aid man in his enjoyment of the intellectual life, which is defined by intelligence. Contrariwise, whatsoever things hinder man's perfecting of his reason, and capability to enjoy the rational life, are alone called evil.

VI. As all things whereof man is the efficient cause are necessarily good, no evil can befall man except through external causes; namely, by virtue of man being a part of universal nature, whose laws human nature is compelled to obey, and to conform to in almost infinite ways.

VII. It is impossible, that man should not be part of nature, or that he should not follow her general order; but if he be thrown among individuals whose nature is in harmony with his own, his power of action will thereby be aided and fostered, whereas, if he be thrown among such as are but very little in harmony with his nature, he will hardly be able to accommodate himself to them without undergoing a great change himself.

VIII. Whatsoever in nature we deem to be evil, or to be capable of injuring our faculty for existing and enjoying the rational life, we may endeavor to remove in whatever way seems safest to us; on the other hand, whatsoever we deem to be good or useful for preserving our being, and enabling us to enjoy the rational life, we may appropriate to our use and employ as we think best. Everyone without exception may, by sovereign right of nature, do whatsoever he thinks will advance his own interest.

IX. Nothing can be in more harmony with the nature of any given thing that other individuals of the same species; therefore for man in the preservation of his being and the enjoyment of the rational life there is nothing more useful than his fellow man who is led by reason. Further, as we know not anything among individual things which is more excellent than a man led by reason, no man can better display the power of his skill and disposition, than in so training men, that they come at last to live under the dominion of their own reason.

X. In so far as men are influenced by envy or any kind of hatred, one towards another, they are at variance, and are therefore to be feared in proportion, as they are more powerful than their fellows.

XI. Yet minds are not conquered by force, but by love and high-mindedness.

XII. It is before all things useful to men to associate their ways of life, to bind themselves together with such bonds as they think most fitted to gather them all into unity, and generally to do whatsoever serves to strengthen friendship.

XIII. But for this there is need of skill and watchfulness. For men are diverse (seeing that those who live under the guidance of reason are few), yet are they generally envious and more prone to revenge than to sympathy. No small force of character is therefore required to take everyone as he is, and to restrain one's self from imitating the emotions of others. But those who carp at mankind, and are more skilled in railing at vice than in instilling virtue, and who break rather than strengthen men's dispositions, are hurtful both to themselves and others. Thus many from too great impatience of spirit, or from misguided religious zeal, have preferred to live among brutes rather than among men; as boys or youths, who cannot peaceably endure the chidings of their parents, will enlist as soldiers and choose the hardships of war and the despotic discipline in preference to the comforts of home and the admonitions of their father: suffering any burden to be put upon them, so long as they may spite their parents.

XIV. Therefore, although men are generally governed in everything by their own lusts, yet their association in common brings many more advantages than drawbacks. Wherefore it is better to bear patiently the wrongs they may do us, and to strive to promote whatsoever serves to bring about harmony and friendship.

XV. Those things, which beget harmony, are such as are attributable to justice, equity, and honorable living. For men brook ill not only what is unjust or iniquitous, but also what is reckoned disgraceful, or that a man should slight the received customs of their society. For winning love those qualities are especially necessary which have regard to religion and piety.

XVI. Further, harmony is often the result of fear: but such harmony is insecure. Further, fear arises from infirmity of spirit, and moreover belongs not to the exercise of reason: the same is true of compassion, though this latter seems to bear a certain resemblance to piety.

XVII. Men are also gained over by liberality, especially such as have not the means to buy what is necessary to sustain life. However, to give aid to every poor man is far beyond the power and the advantage of any private person. For the riches of any private person are wholly inadequate to meet such a call. Again, an individual man's resources of character are too limited for him to be able to make all men his friends. Hence providing for the poor is a duty, which falls on the State as a whole, and has regard only to the general advantage.

XVIII. In accepting favors, and in returning gratitude our duty must be wholly different.

XIX. Again, meretricious love, that is, the lust of generation arising from bodily beauty, and generally every sort of love, which owns anything save freedom of soul as its cause, readily passes into hate; unless indeed, what is worse, it is a species of madness; and then it promotes discord rather than harmony.

XX. As concerning marriage, it is certain that this is in harmony with reason, if the desire for physical union be not engendered solely by bodily beauty, but also by the desire to beget children and to train them up wisely; and moreover, if the love of both, to wit, of the man and of the woman, is not caused by bodily beauty only, but also by freedom of the soul.

XXI. Furthermore, flattery begets harmony; but only by means of the vile offense of slavishness or treachery. None are more readily taken with flattery than the proud, who wish to be first, but are not.

XXII. There is in abasement a spurious appearance of piety and religion. Although abasement is the opposite to pride, yet is he that abases himself most akin to the proud.

XXIII. Shame also brings about harmony, but only in such matters as cannot be hid. Further, as shame is a species of pain, it does not concern the exercise of reason.

XXIV. The remaining emotions of pain towards men are directly opposed to justice, equity, honor, piety, and religion; and, although indignation seems to bear a certain resemblance to equity, yet is life but lawless, where every man may pass judgment on another's deeds, and vindicate his own or other men's rights.

XXV. Correctness of conduct, that is, the desire of pleasing men which is determined by reason, is attributable to piety. But, if it springs from emotion, it is ambition, or the desire whereby men, under the false cloak of piety, generally stir up discords and seditions. For he who desires to aid his fellows either in word or in deed, so that they may together enjoy the highest good, he, I say, will before all things strive to win them over with love: not to draw them into admiration, so that a system may be called after his name, nor to give any cause for envy. Further, in his conversation he will shrink from talking of men's faults, and will be careful to speak but sparingly of human infirmity: but he will dwell at length on human virtue or power, and the way whereby it may be perfected. Thus will men be stirred not by fear, nor by aversion, but only by the emotion of joy, to endeavor, so far as in them lies, to live in obedience to reason.

XXVI. Besides men, we know of no particular thing in nature in whose mind we may rejoice, and whom we can associate with ourselves in friendship or any sort of fellowship; therefore, whatsoever there be in nature besides man, a regard for our advantage does not call on us to preserve, but to preserve or destroy according to its various capabilities, and to adapt to our use as best we may.

XXVII. The advantage which we derive from things external to us, besides the experience and knowledge which we acquire from observing them, and from recombining their elements in different forms, is principally the preservation of the body; from this point of view, those things are most useful which can so feed and nourish the body, that all its parts may rightly fulfill their functions. For, in proportion as the body is capable of being affected in a greater variety of ways, and of affecting external bodies in a great number of ways, so much the more is the mind capable of thinking. But there seem to be very few things of this kind in nature; wherefore for the due nourishment of the body we must use many foods of diverse nature. For the human body is composed of very many parts of different nature, which stand in continual need of varied nourishment, so that the whole body may be equally capable of doing everything that can follow from its own nature, and consequently that the mind also may be equally capable of forming many perceptions.

XXVIII. Now for providing these nourishments the strength of each individual would hardly suffice, if men did not lend one another mutual aid. But money has furnished us with a token for everything; hence it is with the notion of money, that the mind of the multitude is chiefly engrossed: nay, it can hardly conceive any kind of pleasure, which is not accompanied with the idea of money as cause.

XXIX. This result is the fault only of those, who seek money, not from poverty or to supply their necessary wants, but because they have learned the arts of gain, wherewith they bring themselves to great splendor. Certainly they nourish their bodies, according to custom, but scantily, believing that they lose as much of their wealth as they spend on the preservation of their body. But they who know the true use of money, and who fix the measure of wealth solely with regard to their actual needs, live content with little.

XXX. As, therefore, those things are good which assist the various parts of the body, and enable them to perform their functions; and as pleasure consists in an increase of, or aid to, man's power, in so far as he is composed of mind and body; it follows that all those things which bring pleasure are good. But seeing that things do not work with the object of giving us pleasure, and that their power of action is not tempered to suit our advantage, and, lastly, that pleasure is generally referred to one part of the body more than to the other parts; therefore most emotions of pleasure (unless reason and watchfulness be at hand), and consequently the desires arising therefrom, may become excessive.

Moreover we may add that emotion leads us to pay most regard to what is agreeable in the present, nor can we estimate what is future with emotions equally vivid.

XXXI. Superstition, on the other hand, seems to account as good all that brings pain, and as bad all that brings pleasure. However, as we said above, none but the envious take delight in my infirmity and trouble. For the greater the pleasure whereby we are affected, the greater is the perfection whereto we pass, and consequently the more do we partake of the divine nature: no pleasure can ever be evil, which is regulated by a true regard for our advantage. But contrariwise he, who is led by fear and does good only to avoid evil, is not guided by reason.

XXXII. But human power is extremely limited, and is infinitely surpassed by the power of external causes; we have not, therefore, an absolute power of shaping to our use those things which are without us. Nevertheless, we shall bear with an equal mind all that happens to us in contravention to the claims of our own advantage, so long as we are conscious, that we have done our duty, and that the power which we possess is not sufficient to enable us to protect ourselves completely; remembering that we are a part of universal nature, and that we follow her order. If we have a clear and distinct understanding of this, that part of our nature which is defined by intelligence, in other words the better part of ourselves, will assuredly acquiesce in what befalls us, and in such acquiescence will endeavor to persist. For, in so far as we are intelligent beings, we cannot desire anything save that which is necessary, nor yield absolute acquiescence to anything save to that which is true: wherefore, in so far as we have a right understanding of these things, the endeavor of the better part of ourselves is in harmony with the order of nature as a whole. —E-IV

REALITY

Reality and *perfection* I use as synonymous terms. —E-II
See Bondage, Sin

[251]

REASON

Under the guidance of reason we should pursue the greater of two goods and the lesser of two evils.

We may, under the guidance of reason, pursue the lesser evil as though it were the greater good, and we may shun the lesser good, which would be the cause of the greater evil. For the evil, which is here called the lesser, is really good, and the lesser good is really evil, wherefore we may seek the former and shun the latter. —E-IV

In so far as the mind conceives a thing under the dictates of reason, it is affected equally, whether the idea be of a thing future, past, or present.

If we could possess an adequate knowledge of the duration of things, and could determine by reason their periods of existence, we should contemplate things future with the same emotion as things present; and the mind would desire as though it were present the good which it conceived as future; consequently it would necessarily neglect a lesser good in the present for the sake of a greater good in the future, and would in no wise desire that which is good in the present but a source of evil in the future, as we shall presently show. However, we can have but a very inadequate knowledge of the duration of things and the periods of their existence we can only determine by imagination, which is not so powerfully affected by the future as by the present. Hence such true knowledge of good and evil as we possess is merely abstract or general, and the judgment which we pass on the order of things and the connection of causes, with a view to determining what is good or bad for us in the present, is rather imaginary than real. Therefore it is nothing wonderful, if the desire arising from such knowledge of good and evil, in so far as it looks on into the future, be more readily checked than the desire of things which are agreeable at the present time. —E-IV

We may, under the guidance of reason, seek a greater good in the future in preference to a lesser good in the present, and we may seek a lesser evil in the present in preference to a greater evil in the future.

We may, under the guidance of reason, seek a lesser evil in the present, because it is the cause of a greater good in the future, and we may shun a lesser good in the present, because it is the cause of a greater evil in the future.

If these statements be compared with what we have pointed out concerning the strength of the emotions, we shall readily see the difference between a man, who is led solely by emotion or opinion, and a man, who is led by reason. The former, whether he will or no, performs actions whereof he is utterly ignorant; the latter is his own master and only performs such actions, as he knows are of primary importance in life, and therefore chiefly desires; wherefore I call the former a slave, and the latter a free man, concerning whose disposition and manner of life it will be well to make a few observations. —E-IV

See Adequate Ideas, Democracy, Desire, Emotions, Fame, Government, Hate, Intellectual Love, Kindness, Passive and Active, Rational Life, Utopia, Wisdom, Wrongdoing

REGRET

Regret is the desire or appetite to possess something, kept alive by the remembrance of the said thing, and at the same time constrained by the remembrance of other things which exclude the existence of it.

When we remember a thing, we are by that very fact, as I have already said more than once, disposed to contemplate it with the same emotion as if it were something present; but this disposition or endeavor, while we are awake, is generally checked by the images of things which exclude the existence of that which we remember. Thus when we remember something which affected us with a certain pleasure, we by that very fact endeavor to regard it with the same emotion of pleasure as though it were present, but this endeavor is at once checked by the remembrance of things which exclude the existence of the thing in question. Wherefore regret is, strictly speaking, a pain opposed to that pleasure, which arises from the absence of something we hate. But, as the name regret seems to refer to desire, I set this emotion down, among the emotions springing from desire. —E-III

He who remembers a thing, in which he has once taken delight, desires to possess it under the same circumstances as when he first took delight therein.

A lover will, therefore, feel pain if one of the aforesaid attendant circumstances be missing.

This pain, in so far as it has reference to the absence of the object of love, is called *Regret*. —E-III

RELIGION

The sovereign is the interpreter of religion, and further, that no one can obey God rightly, if the practices of his piety do not conform to the public welfare; or, consequently, if he does not implicitly obey all the commands of the sovereign. —T P-XIX

Religious quarrels do not arise so much from ardent zeal for religion, as from men's various dispositions and love of contradiction, which causes them to habitually distort and condemn everything, however rightly it may have been said. —C-LIV-F

Even if we did not know that our mind is eternal, we should still consider as of primary importance piety and religion, and generally all things which we showed to be attributable to courage and high-mindedness.

The general belief of the multitude seems to be different. Most people seem to believe that they are free, in so far as they may obey their lusts, and that they cede their rights, in so far as they are bound to live according to the commandments of the Divine law. They therefore believe that piety, religion, and, generally, all things attributable to firmness of mind, are burdens, which, after death, they hope to lay aside, and to receive the reward for their bondage, that is, for their piety and religion; it is not only by this hope, but also, and chiefly, by the fear of being horribly punished after death, that they are induced to live according to the Divine commandments, so far as their feeble and infirm spirit will carry them.

If men had not this hope and this fear, but believed that the mind perishes with the body, and that no hope of life hereafter remains for the wretches who are broken down with the burden of piety, they would return to their inclinations, controlling everything in accordance with their lusts, and desiring to obey fortune rather than themselves. Such a course appears to me not less absurd than if a man, because he does not believe that he can by wholesome food sustain his body forever, should wish to cram himself with poisons and deadly fare; or if, because he sees that the mind is not eternal or immortal, he should prefer to be out of his mind altogether, and to live without the use of reason; these ideas are so absurd as to be scarcely worth refuting. —E-V

As each man's faith must be judged pious or impious only in respect of its producing obedience or obstinacy, and not in respect of its truth; and as no one will dispute that men's dispositions are exceedingly varied, that all do not acquiesce in the same things, but are ruled some by one opinion some by another, so that what moves one to devotion moves another to laughter and contempt, it follows that there can be no doctrines in the Catholic, or universal, religion, which can give rise to controversy among good men. Such doctrines might be pious to some and impious to others, whereas they should be judged solely by their fruits.

To the universal religion, then, belong only such dogmas as are absolutely required in order to attain obedience to

SPINOZA DICTIONARY

God, and without which such obedience would be impossible; as for the rest, each man—seeing that he is the best judge of his own character—should adopt whatever he thinks best adapted to strengthen his love of justice.

—T P-XIV

I make this chief distinction between religion and superstition, that the latter is founded on ignorance, the former on knowledge; this, I take it, is the reason why Christians are distinguished from the rest of the world, not by faith, nor by charity, nor by the other fruits of the Holy Spirit, but solely by their opinions, inasmuch as they defend their cause, like everyone else, by miracles, that is by ignorance, which is the source of all malice; thus they turn a faith, which may be true, into superstition.   —C-XXI-O

See Natural Right, Superstition

REMORSE

Remorse comes only from this, that we do something about which we are then in doubt whether it is good, or whether it is bad; and *repentance*, from this, that we have done something which is bad. (Both are the result of rashness.)

Remorse and Repentance are not only not good, but they are, on the contrary, pernicious, and they are consequently bad. We are always succeeded better through Reason and the love of truth than through remorse and sorrow. These are, therefore, pernicious and bad, because they are a certain kind of sorrow, which [sorrow] we have already shown above to be injurious, and which, for that reason, we must try to avert as an evil, and consequently we must likewise shun and flee from these also, which are like it.

—G 2-X

REPENTANCE

Repentance is not a virtue, or does not arise from reason; but he who repents of an action is doubly wretched or infirm.

As men seldom live under the guidance of reason, these two emotions, namely, Humility and Repentance, as also Hope and Fear, bring more good than harm; hence, as we must sin, we had better sin in that direction. For, if all men who are prey to emotion were all equally proud, they would shrink from nothing, and would fear nothing; how then could they be joined and linked together in bonds of union? The crowd plays the tyrant, when it is not in fear; hence we need not wonder that the prophets, who consulted the good, not of a few, but of all, so strenuously commended Humility, Repentance, and Reverence. Indeed those who are a prey to these emotions may be led much more easily than others to live under the guidance of reason, that is, to become free and to enjoy the life of the blessed.   —E-IV

Repentance is pain accompanied by the idea of some action, which we believe we have performed by the free decision of our mind.

This is perhaps the place to call attention to the fact, that it is nothing wonderful that all those actions, which are commonly called *wrong*, are followed by pain, and all those, which are called *right*, are followed by pleasure. We can easily gather from what has been said, that this depends in great measure on education. Parents, by reprobating the former class of actions, and by frequently chiding their children because of them, and also by persuading to and praising the latter class, have brought it about, that the former should be associated with pain and the latter with pleasure. This is confirmed by experience. For custom and religion are not the same among all men, but that which some consider sacred others consider profane, and what some consider honorable others consider disgraceful. According as each man has been educated, he feels repentance for a given action or glories therein.   —E-III

Repentance is pain, accompanied by the idea of one's self as cause.   —E-III

Lastly, from this inconstancy in the nature of human judgment, inasmuch as a man often judges of things solely by his emotions, and inasmuch as the things which he believes cause pleasure or pain, and therefore endeavors to promote or prevent, are often purely imaginary; we may readily conceive that a man may be at one time affected with pleasure, and at another with pain, accompanied by the idea of himself as cause. Thus we can easily understand what are *Repentance* and *Self-complacency.*   —E-III

See Emotions, Fame, Humility, Remorse

REVELATION

See Prophecy

REVENGE

Revenge is the desire whereby we are induced, through mutual hatred, to injure one who, with similar feelings, has injured us.   —E-III

See Anger, Cruelty, Rational Life

REVERENCE

See Repentance

REWARD

See Religion

RICHES

See Happiness

RIDICULE

Derision and ridicule rest on a false opinion, and betray an imperfection in him who derides and jests.

The opinion on which they rest is false, because it is supposed that he who is derided is the first cause of the effects which he produces, and that they do not necessarily (like the other things in Nature) depend on God. They betray an imperfection in the Derider; because either that which is derided is such that it is derisible, or it is not such. If it is not such, then it shows bad manners, to deride that which is not to be derided; if it is such, then they [who deride it] show thereby that they recognize some imperfection in that which they deride, which they ought to remedy, not by derision, but much rather by good reasoning.　　—G 2-XI

RULES OF LIFE
　See Wisdom

S

ST. PAUL
See Obedience

SAMSON
See Books

SATISFACTION
See Understanding

SCEPTICS
See Philosophy

SCHOLASTICS
See Emotions

SCIENCE
Again, we cannot infer that because sciences of things Divine and human are full of controversies and quarrels, therefore their whole subject matter is uncertain.

—C-LX-H B

See Education, Happiness, Theology

SCORN
See Emotions

SCRIPTURE
I am far more careful than others not to ascribe to Scripture any childish and absurd doctrines, a precaution which demands either a thorough acquaintance with philosophy or the possession of divine revelations. Hence I pay very little attention to the glosses put upon Scripture by ordinary theologians, especially those of the kind who always interpret Scripture according to the literal and outward mean-

ing: I have never, except among the Socinians, found any
theologian stupid enough to ignore that Holy Scripture very
often speaks in human fashion of God and expresses its
meaning in parables. When Micaiah said to King Ahab,
that he had seen God sitting on a throne, with the armies
of heaven standing on the right hand and the left, and
that God asked His angels which of them would deceive
Ahab, this was assuredly a parable employed by the prophet
on that occasion (which was not fitted for the inculcation
of sublime theological doctrines), as sufficiently setting
forth the message he had to deliver in the name of God.
So also the other prophets of God made manifest God's
commands to the people in this fashion as being the best
adapted, though not expressly enjoined by God, for leading
the people to the primary object of Scripture, which, as
Christ Himself says, is to bid men love God above all
things, and their neighbor as themselves. Sublime speculations have, in my opinion, no bearing on Scripture. As far
as I am concerned I have never learnt or been able to learn
any of God's eternal attributes from Holy Scripture.

—C-XXXIV-B

Scripture is sacred, and its words divine so long as it
stirs mankind to devotion towards God.   —T P-XII

We may, then, be absolutely certain that every event
which is truly described in Scripture necessarily happened,
like everything else, according to natural laws; and if anything is there set down which can be proved in set terms
to contravene the order of nature, or not to be deducible
therefrom, we must believe it to have been foisted into
the sacred writings by irreligious hands; for whatsoever is
contrary to nature is also contrary to reason, and whatsoever
is contrary to reason is absurd, and, *ipso facto*, to be rejected.   —T P-VI

See Books, Bible, God, History, Philosophy, Prophecy,
Sin, Superstition

SECOND KIND OF KNOWLEDGE
See Knowledge

SECURITY
See State

SELF-ABASEMENT
Self-abasement is thinking too meanly of one's self by reason of pain.

We are nevertheless generally accustomed to oppose pride to humility, but in that case we pay more attention to the effect of either emotion than to its nature. We are wont to call *proud* the man who boasts too much, who talks of nothing but his own virtues and other people's faults, who wishes to be first; and lastly who goes through life with a style and pomp suitable to those far above him in station. On the other hand, we call *humble* the man who too often blushes, who confesses his faults, who sets forth other men's virtues, and who, lastly, walks with bent head and is negligent of his attire. However, these emotions, humility and self-abasement, are extremely rare. For human nature, considered in itself, strives against them as much as it can; hence those, who are believed to be most self-abased and humble, are generally in reality the most ambitious and envious.   —E-III
See Pride

SELF-APPROVAL
Self-approval is pleasure arising from a man's contemplation of himself and his own power of action.   —E-III

Self-approval may arise from reason, and that which arises from reason is the highest possible.

Self-approval is in reality the highest object for which we can hope. For no one endeavors to preserve his being for the sake of any ulterior object, and, as this approval is more and more fostered and strengthened by praise, and on the contrary is more and more disturbed by blame, fame becomes the most powerful of incitements to action, and life under disgrace is almost unendurable. —E-IV

SELF-COMPLACENCY

Self-complacency is pleasure accompanied by the idea of one's self as cause, and these emotions are most intense because men believe themselves to be free. —E-III

See Fame, Humility, Pride, Self-Love

SELF-CAUSED

By that which is *self-caused*, I mean that of which the essence involves existence, or that of which the nature is only conceivable as existent. —E-I

SELFISHNESS

Man, alike in the natural and in the civil state, acts according to the laws of his own nature, and consults his own interest. —P T-III

SELF-LOVE

Pain, accompanied by the idea of our own weakness, is called *humility*; the pleasure, which springs from the contemplation of ourselves, is called *self-love* or *self-complacency*. And inasmuch as this feeling is renewed as often as a man contemplates his own virtues, or his own power of activity, it follows that everyone is fond of narrating his own exploits, and displaying the force both of his body and mind, and also that, for this reason, men are troublesome one to another. —E-III

See Ingratitude

SELF-PRESERVATION

See Virtue

SELF-RESPECT

Self-respect does not extend [to anything] outside us, and is attributed to one who knows the real worth of his perfection, dispassionately and without seeking esteem for himself. —G 2-VIII

See Inferiority, Feeling of

SENECA
See Democracy, Society

SENSUAL PLEASURE
See Happiness, Intellectual Love

SEXUAL INTERCOURSE
See Lust

SHAME
Shame is pain accompanied by the idea of some action of our own, which we believe to be blamed by others.

We should here remark the difference which exists between shame and modesty. Shame is the pain following the deed whereof we are ashamed. Modesty is the fear or dread of shame, which restrains a man from committing a base action. Modesty is usually opposed to shamelessness, but the latter is not an emotion, as I will duly show; however, the names of the emotions (as I have remarked already) have regard rather to their exercise than to their nature.

—E-III

Shame is a certain kind of sorrow which arises in one when he happens to see that his conduct is despised by others, without regard to any other disadvantage or injury that they may have in view. —G 2-XII

See Emotions, Fame, Hate, Ingratitude, Rational Life, Timidity

SHAMELESSNESS
Shamelessness is nothing else than a want, or shaking off, of shame, not through Reason, but either from innocence of shame, as is the case with children, savage people, &c., or because, having been held in great contempt, one goes now to any length without regard for anything. —G 2-XII

SILENCE
See Mind

SIN

For my own part, I cannot admit that sin and evil have any positive existence, far less than anything can exist, or come to pass, contrary to the will of God. On the contrary, not only do I assert that sin has no positive existence, I also maintain that only in speaking improperly, or humanly, can we say that we sin against God, as in the expression that men offend God.

As to the first point, we know that whatsoever is, when considered in itself without regard to anything else, possesses perfection, extending in each thing as far as the limits of that thing's essence: for essence is nothing else. I take for an illustration the design or determined will of Adam to eat the forbidden fruit. This design or determined will, considered in itself alone, includes perfection in so far as it expresses reality; hence it may be inferred that we can only conceive imperfection in things, when they are viewed in relation to other things possessing more reality: thus in Adam's decision, so long as we view it by itself and do not compare it with other things more perfect or exhibiting a more perfect state, we can find no imperfection: nay it may be compared with an infinity of other things far less perfect in this respect than itself, such as stones, stocks, &c. This, as a matter of fact, everyone grants. For we all admire in animals qualities which we regard with dislike and aversion in men, such as the pugnacity of bees, the jealousy of doves, &c., these in human beings are despised, but are nevertheless considered to enhance the value of animals. This being so, it follows that sin, which indicates nothing save imperfection, cannot consist in anything that expresses reality, as we see in the case of Adam's decision and its execution.

Again, we cannot say that Adam's will is at variance with the law of God, and that it is evil because it is displeasing to God; for besides the fact that grave imperfection would be imputed to God, if we say that anything happens contrary to His will, or that He desires anything which He does not obtain, or that His nature resembled that of His creatures in having sympathy with some things more than others; such an occurrence would be at complete variance with the nature of the Divine will.

The will of God is identical with His intellect, hence the former can no more be contravened than the latter; in other words, anything which should come to pass against His will must be of a nature to be contrary to His intellect, such, for instance, as a round square. Hence the will or decision of Adam regarded in itself was neither evil nor, properly speaking, against the will of God: it follows that God must be its cause; not in so far as it was evil, for the evil in it consisted in the loss of the previous state of being which it entailed on Adam, and it is certain that loss has no positive existence, and is only so spoken of in respect to our and not God's understanding. The difficulty arises from the fact, that we give one and the same definition to all the individuals of a genus, as for instance all who have the outward appearance of men: we accordingly assume all things which are expressed by the same definition to be equally capable of attaining the highest perfection possible for the genus; when we find an individual whose actions are at variance with such perfection, we suppose him to be deprived of it, and to fall short of his nature. We should hardly act in this way, if we did not hark back to the definition and ascribe to the individual a nature in accordance with it. But as God does not know things through abstraction, or form general definitions of the kind above mentioned, and as things have no more reality than the Divine understanding and power have put into them and actually endowed them with, it clearly follows that a state of privation can only be spoken of in relation to our intellect, not in relation to God.

Thus, as it seems to me, the difficulty is completely solved. However, in order to make the way still plainer, and remove every doubt, I deem it necessary to answer the two following difficulties:—First, why Holy Scripture says that God wishes for the conversion of the wicked, and also why God forbade Adam to eat of the fruit when He had ordained the contrary? Secondly, that it seems to follow from what I have said, that the wicked by their pride, avarice, and deeds of desperation, worship God in no less degree than the good do by their nobleness, patience, love, &c., inasmuch as both execute God's will.

In answer to the first question, I observe that Scripture, being chiefly fitted for and beneficial to the multitude, speaks popularly after the fashion of men. For the multitude are incapable of grasping sublime conceptions. Hence I am persuaded that all matters, which God revealed to the prophets as necessary to salvation, are set down in the form of laws. With this understanding, the prophets invented whole parables, and represented God as a king and a law-giver, because He had revealed the means of salvation and perdition, and was their cause; the means which were simply causes they styled laws and wrote them down as such; salvation and perdition, which are simply effects necessarily resulting from the aforesaid means, they described as reward and punishment; framing their doctrines more in accordance with such parables than with actual truth. They constantly speak of God as resembling a man, as sometimes angry, sometimes merciful, now desiring what is future, now jealous and suspicious, even as deceived by the devil; so that philosophers and all who are above the law, that is, who follow after virtue, not in obedience to law, but through love, because it is the most excellent of all things, must not be hindered by such expressions.

Thus the command given to Adam consisted solely in this, that God revealed to Adam, that eating of the fruit brought about death; as He reveals to us, through our natural faculties, that poison is deadly. If you ask, for what object did He make this revelation, I answer, in order to render Adam to that extent more perfect in knowledge.

Hence, to ask God why He had not bestowed on Adam a more perfect will, is just as absurd as to ask, why the circle has not been endowed with all the properties of a sphere.

As to the second difficulty, it is true that the wicked execute after their manner the will of God: but they cannot, therefore, be in any respect compared with the good. The more perfection a thing has, the more does it participate in the Deity, and the more does it express perfection. Thus, as the good have incomparably more perfection than the bad, their virtue cannot be likened to the virtue of the wicked, inasmuch as the wicked lack the love of God, which proceeds from the knowledge of God, and by which alone we are, according to our human understanding, called the servants of God. The wicked, knowing not God, are but as instruments in the hand of the workman, serving unconsciously, and perishing in the using; the good, on the other hand, serve consciously, and in serving become more perfect. —C-XXXII-B

See Democracy; God, Nature and Properties of; Natural Right

SINGULAR
See Ideas

SLAUGHTERING OF ANIMALS
See Natural Right

SLAVE
See Democracy, Reason

SLAVERY
See Virtue

SLAVISHNESS
See Rational Life

SOBRIETY
See Emotions

SOCIAL LIFE

There is no individual thing in nature, which is more useful to man, than a man who lives in obedience to reason. For that thing is to man most useful, which is most in harmony with his nature; that is, obviously, man. But man acts absolutely according to the laws of his nature, when he lives in obedience to reason, and to this extent only is always necessarily in harmony with the nature of another man; wherefore among individual things nothing is more useful to man, than a man who lives in obedience to reason.

As every man seeks most that which is useful to him, so are men most useful one to another. For the more a man seeks what is useful to him and endeavors to preserve himself, the more is he endowed with virtue, or, what is the same thing, the more is he endowed with power to act according to the laws of his nature, that is to live in obedience to reason. But men are most in natural harmony, when they live in obedience to reason; therefore men will be most useful one to another, when each seeks most that which is useful to him.

What we have just shown is attested by experience so conspicuously, that it is in the mouth of nearly everyone: "Man is to man a God." Yet it rarely happens that men live in obedience to reason, for things are so ordered among them, that they are generally envious and troublesome one to another. Nevertheless they are scarcely able to lead a solitary life, so that the definition of man as a social animal has met with general assent; in fact, men do derive from social life much more convenience than injury. Let satirists then laugh their fill at human affairs, let theologians rail, and let misanthropes praise to their utmost the life of untutored rusticity, let them heap contempt on men and praises on beasts; when all is said, they will find that men can provide for their wants much more easily by mutual help, and that only by uniting their forces can they escape from the dangers that on every side beset them: not to say

SPINOZA DICTIONARY

how much more excellent and worthy of our knowledge it
is, to study the actions of men than the actions of beasts.

—E-IV

Whatsoever conduces to man's social life, or causes men
to live together in harmony, is useful, whereas whatsoever
brings discord into a state is bad.   —E-IV
See Ideas

SOCIAL ORDER
See Happiness

SOCIETY
The formation of society serves not only for defensive
purposes, but is also very useful, and, indeed, absolutely
necessary, as rendering possible the division of labor. If
men did not render mutual assistance to each other, no one
would have either the skill or the time to provide for his
own sustenance and preservation: for all men are not
equally apt for all work, and no one would be capable of
preparing all that he individually stood in need of. Strength
and time, I repeat, would fail, if every one had in person
to plough, to sow, to reap, to grind corn, to cook, to weave,
to stitch, and perform the other numerous functions required to keep life going; to say nothing of the arts and
sciences which are also entirely necessary to the perfection
and blessedness of human nature. We see that peoples living in uncivilized barbarism lead a wretched and almost
animal life, and even they would not be able to acquire
their few rude necessities without assisting one another to a
certain extent.

Now if men were so constituted by nature that they desired nothing but what is designated by true reason, society
would obviously have no need of laws: it would be sufficient to inculcate true moral doctrines; and men would
freely, without hesitation, act in accordance with their true
interests. But human nature is framed in a different fash-

ion: every one, indeed, seeks his own interest, but does not do so in accordance with the dictates of sound reason, for most men's ideas of desirability and usefulness are guided by their fleshly instincts and emotions, which take no thought beyond the present and their immediate object. Therefore, no society can exist without government, and force, and laws to restrain and repress men's desires and immoderate impulses. Still human nature will not submit to absolute repression. Violent governments, as Seneca says, never last long; the moderate governments endure.

So long as men act simply from fear they act contrary to their inclinations, taking no thought for the advantages or necessity of their actions, but simply endeavoring to escape punishment or loss of life. They must needs rejoice in any evil which befalls their ruler, even if it should involve themselves; and must long for and bring about such evil by every means in their power. Again, men are especially intolerant of serving and being ruled by their equals. Lastly, it is exceedingly difficult to revoke liberties once granted.

From these considerations it follows, firstly, that authority should either be vested in the hands of the whole state in common, so that everyone should be bound to serve, and yet not be in subjection to his equals; or else, if power be in the hands of a few, or one man, that one man should be something above average humanity, or should strive to get himself accepted as such. Secondly, laws should in every government be so arranged that people should be kept in bounds by the hope of some greatly-desired good, rather than by fear, for then everyone will do his duty willingly.

Lastly, as obedience consists in acting at the bidding of external authority, it would have no place in a state where the government is vested in the whole people, and where laws are made by common consent. In such a society the people would remain free, whether the laws were added to or diminished, inasmuch as it would not be done on external authority, but their own free consent. The reverse happens

when the sovereign power is vested in one man, for all act
at his bidding; and, therefore, unless they had been trained
from the first to depend on the words of their ruler, the
latter would find it difficult, in case of need, to abrogate
liberties once conceded, and impose new laws.   —T P-V
  See Natural Right, Rational Life

SOCINIANS
  See Scripture

SOCRATES
  See Hate

SOLITARY LIFE
  See Social Life

SOLITUDE
  Since fear of solitude exists in all men, because no one
in solitude is strong enough to defend himself, and procure
the necessaries of life, it follows that men naturally aspire
to the civil state; nor can it happen that men should ever
utterly dissolve it.   —P T-VI
  See State

SOLOMON
  See Definition, Law, Prophecy

SOMNAMBULISTS
  See Mind

SORROW
  Sorrow arises only from superficial opinion and imagination which follows therefrom: for it comes from the loss
of some good.
  Now we have already remarked above, that whatsoever
we do should tend towards progress and amelioration. But
it is certain that so long as we are sorrowing we render ourselves unfit to act thus; on this account it is necessary that
we should free ourselves from it. This we can do by thinking of the means whereby we may recover what we have

lost, if it is in our power to do so. If not, [we must reflect]
that it is just as necessary to make an end of it, lest we fall a
prey to all the miseries and disasters which sorrow necessarily brings in its train. And either course must be adopted
with joy; for it is foolish to try to restore and make good a
lost good by means of a self-sought and provoked evil.

—G 2-VII

See Communion with God, Confidence

SOUL
See Communion with God, Immortality of the Soul

SOVEREIGN RIGHT
See Democracy

SOVEREIGN RIGHT OF NATURE
See Rational Life

SPECULATION
See Knowledge, Grief

SPIRITUAL THINGS
See Free Will

STATE
A dominion then, whose well-being depends on any
man's good faith, and whose affairs cannot be properly
administered, unless those who are engaged in them will
act honestly, will be very unstable. On the contrary, to in-
sure its permanence, its public affairs should be so ordered,
that those who administer them, whether guided by reason
or passion, cannot be led to act treacherously or basely. Nor
does it matter to the security of a dominion, in what spirit
men are led to rightly administer its affairs. For liberality
of spirit, or courage, is a private virtue; but the virtue of a
state is its security. —P T-I
The man, who is guided by reason, is more free in a
state, where he lives under a general system of law, than in
solitude, where he is independent.

These and similar observations, which we have made on man's true freedom, may be referred to strength, that is, to courage and nobility of character. I do not think it worth while to prove separately all the properties of strength; much less need I show, that he that is strong hates no man, is angry with no man, envies no man, is indignant with no man, despises no man, and least of all things is proud. These propositions, and all that relate to the true way of life and religion, are easily proved, namely, that hatred should be overcome with love, and that every man should desire for others the good which he seeks for himself. We may also repeat that the strong man has ever first in his thoughts, that all things follow from the necessity of the Divine nature; so that whatsoever he deems to be hurtful and evil, and whatsoever, accordingly, seems to him impious, horrible, unjust, and base, assumes that appearance owing to his own disordered, fragmentary, and confused view of the universe. Wherefore he strives before all things to conceive things as they really are, and to remove the hindrance to true knowledge, such as are hatred, anger, envy, derision, pride, and similar emotions, which I have mentioned above. Thus he endeavors, as we said before, as far as in him lies, to do good, and to go on his way rejoicing.   —E-IV

That the preservation of a state chiefly depends on the subjects' fidelity and constancy in carrying out the orders they receive, is most clearly taught both by reason and experience; how subjects ought to be guided so as best to preserve their fidelity and virtue is not so obvious. All, both rulers and ruled, are men, and prone to follow after their lusts. The fickle disposition of the multitude almost reduces those who have experience of it to despair, for it is governed solely by emotions, not by reason: it rushes headlong into every enterprise, and is easily corrupted either by avarice or luxury: everyone thinks himself omniscient and

wishes to fashion all things to his liking, judging a thing
to be just or unjust, lawful or unlawful, according as he
thinks it will bring him profit or loss: vanity leads him
to despise his equals, and refuse their guidance: envy of
superior fame or fortune (for such gifts are never equally
distributed) leads him to desire and rejoice in his neighbor's downfall. I need not go through the whole list, everyone knows already how much crime results from disgust at
the present—desire for change, headlong anger, and contempt for poverty—and how men's minds are engrossed
and kept in turmoil thereby.

To guard against all these evils, and form a dominion
where no room is left for deceit; to frame our institutions
so that every man, whatever his disposition, may prefer
public right to private advantage, this is the task and this
the toil. Necessity is often the mother of invention, but she
has never succeeded in framing a dominion that was in less
danger from its own citizens than from open enemies, or
whose rulers did not fear the latter less than the former.

—T P-XVII

See Democracy, Natural Right, Rational Life, Social
Life, Society, Tyranny

STATE OF NATURE
See Government, Natural Right

STATESMEN
See Evil

STIMULATION
Stimulation may be excessive and bad; on the other hand,
grief may be good, in so far as stimulation or pleasure is
bad.   —E-IV
See Emotions, Primary

STOICS
See Emotions

SUBSTANCE

Existence belongs to the nature of substance.

Substance cannot be produced by anything external, it must, therefore, be its own cause—that is, its essence necessarily involves existence, or existence belongs to its nature.
—E-I

The being of substance does not appertain to the essence of man—in other words, substance does not constitute the actual being of man. —E-II

God, or substance, consisting of infinite attributes, of which each expresses eternal and infinite essentiality, necessarily exists. —E-I

Substance is necessarily infinite. —E-I

By *substance*, I mean that which is in itself, and is conceived through itself: in other words, that of which a concept can be formed independently of any other conception.
—E-I

There cannot exist in the universe two or more substances having the same nature or attribute. —E-I

The points to be noted concerning substance are these: First, that existence appertains to its essence; in other words, that solely from its essence and definition its existence follows. —C-XXIX-L M

By substance I mean that, which is in itself and is conceived through itself; that is, of which the conception does not involve the conception of anything else. By attribute I mean the same thing, except that it is called attribute with respect to the understanding, which attributes to substance the particular nature aforesaid. This definition, I repeat, explains with sufficient clearness what I wish to signify by substance or attribute. Should one desire, though there is no need, that I should illustrate by an example, how one and the same thing can be stamped with two names, in order not to seem miserly, I will give two. First, I say that by Israel is meant the third patriarch; I mean the same by Jacob, the name Jacob being given, because the patriarch in question had caught hold of the heel of his brother. Secondly, by a colorless surface I mean a surface, which reflects all rays of light without altering them. I mean the same by a white surface, with this difference, that a surface is called white in reference to a man looking at it, &c.

—C-XXVII-S DE V

See Attribute, Beauty, Definition, God, Mode, Universe

SUFFERING
See Emotions, Primary

SUICIDE
See Desire, Essence

SUPERSTITION
Men would never be superstitious, if they could govern all their circumstances by set rules, or if they were always favored by fortune: but being frequently driven into straits where rules are useless, and being often kept fluctuating pitiably between hope and fear by the uncertainty of fortune's greedily coveted favors, they are consequently, for the most part, very prone to credulity. The human mind is readily swayed this way or that in times of doubt, especially when hope and fear are struggling for the mastery, though usually it is boastful, over-confident, and vain.

This as a general fact I suppose everyone knows, though few, I believe, know their own nature; no one can have lived in the world without observing that most people, when in prosperity, are so overbrimming with wisdom (however inexperienced they may be), that they take every offer of advice as a personal insult, whereas in adversity they know not where to turn, but beg and pray for counsel from every passer-by. No plan is then too futile, too absurd, or too fatuous for their adoption; the most frivolous causes will raise them to hope, or plunge them into despair—if anything happens during their fright which reminds them of some past good or ill, they think it portends a happy or unhappy issue, and therefore (though it may have proved abortive a hundred times before) style it a lucky or unlucky omen. Anything which excites their astonishment they believe to be a portent signifying the anger of the gods or of the Supreme Being, and, mistaking superstition for religion, account it impious not to avert the evil with prayer and sacrifice. Signs and wonders of this sort they conjure up perpetually, till one might think Nature as mad as themselves, they interpret her so fantastically.

Thus it is brought prominently before us, that superstition's chief victims are those persons who greedily covet temporal advantages; they it is, who (especially when they are in danger, and cannot help themselves) are wont with prayers and womanish tears to implore help from God: upbraiding Reason as blind, because she cannot show a sure path to the shadows they pursue, and rejecting human wisdom as vain; but believing the phantoms of imagination, dreams, and other childish absurdities, to be the very oracles of Heaven. As though God had turned away from the wise, and written His decrees, not in the mind of man but in the entrails of beasts, or left them to be proclaimed by the inspiration and instinct of fools, madmen, and birds. Such is the unreason to which terror can drive mankind!

When the Scythians were provoking a battle, the Bactrians had deserted, and the Conqueror was lying sick of his wounds, "he once more turned to superstition, the mockery of human wisdom, and bade Aristander, to whom he confided his credulity, inquire the issue of affairs with sacrificed victims." Very numerous examples of a like nature might be cited, clearly showing the fact, that only while under the dominion of fear do men fall a prey to superstition; that all the portents ever invested with the reverence of misguided religion are mere phantoms of dejected and fearful minds; and lastly, that prophets have most power among the people, and are most formidable to rulers, precisely at those times when the state is in most peril. I think this is sufficiently plain to all, and will therefore say no more on the subject.

The origin of superstition above given affords us a clear reason for the fact, that it comes to all men naturally, though some refer its rise to a dim notion of God, universal to mankind, and also tends to show, that it is no less inconsistent and variable than other mental hallucinations and emotional impulses, and further that it can only be maintained by hope, hatred, anger, and deceit; since it springs not from reason, but solely from the more powerful phases of emotion. Furthermore, we may readily understand how difficult it is, to maintain in the same course men prone to every form of credulity. For, as the mass of mankind remains always at about the same pitch of misery, it never assents long to any one remedy, but is always best pleased by a novelty which has not yet proved illusive.

This element of inconsistency has been the cause of many terrible wars and revolutions; for, as Curtius has written so well: "The mob has no ruler more potent than superstition," and is easily led, on the plea of religion, at one moment to adore its kings as gods, and anon to execrate and abjure them as humanity's common bane.

But if, in despotic statecraft, the supreme and essential mystery be to hoodwink the subjects, and to mask the fear, which keeps them down, with the specious garb of religion, so that men may fight as bravely for slavery as for safety, and count it not shame but highest honor to risk their blood and their lives for the vainglory of a tyrant; yet in a free state no more mischievous expedient could be planned or attempted. Wholly repugnant to the general freedom are such devices as enthralling men's minds with prejudices, forcing their judgment, or employing any of the weapons of quasi-religious sedition; indeed, such seditions only spring up, when law enters the domain of speculative thought, and opinions are put on trial and condemned on the same footing as crimes, while those who defend and follow them are sacrificed, not to public safety, but to their opponents' hatred and cruelty: If deeds only could be made the grounds of criminal charges, and words were always allowed to pass free, such seditions would be divested of every semblance of justification, and would be separated from mere controversies by a hard and fast line.

Now, seeing that we have the rare happiness of living in a republic, where everyone's judgment is free and unshackled, where each may worship God as his conscience dictates, and where freedom is esteemed before all things dear and precious, I have believed that I should be undertaking no ungrateful or unprofitable task, in demonstrating that not only can such freedom be granted without prejudice to the public peace, but also, that without such freedom, piety cannot flourish nor the public peace be secure.

Such is the chief conclusion I seek to establish in this treatise; but, in order to reach it, I must first point out the misconceptions which, like scars of our former bondage, still disfigure our notion of religion, and must expose the false views about the civil authority which many have most impudently advocated, endeavoring to turn the mind of the people, still prone to heathen superstition, away from its legitimate rulers, and so bring us again into slavery.

I have often wondered, that persons who make a boast of professing the Christian religion, namely, love, joy, peace, temperance, and charity to all men, should quarrel with such rancorous animosity, and display daily towards one another such bitter hatred, that this, rather than the virtues they claim, is the readiest criterion of their faith. Matters have long since come to such a pass, that one can only pronounce a man Christian, Turk, Jew, or Heathen, by his general appearance and attire, by his frequenting this or that place of worship, or employing the phraseology of a particular sect—as for manner of life, it is in all cases the same. Inquiry into the cause of this anomaly leads me unhesitatingly to ascribe it to the fact, that the ministries of the Church are regarded by the masses merely as dignities, her offices as posts of emolument—in short, popular religion may be summed up as respect for ecclesiastics. The spread of this misconception inflamed every worthless fellow with an intense desire to enter holy orders, and thus the love of diffusing God's religion degenerated into sordid avarice and ambition. Every church became a theatre, where orators, instead of church teachers, harangued, caring not to instruct the people, but striving to attract admiration, to bring opponents to public scorn, and to preach only novelties and paradoxes, such as would tickle the ears of their congregation. This state of things necessarily stirred up an amount of controversy, envy, and hatred, which no lapse of time could appease; so that we can scarcely wonder that of the old religion nothing survives but its outward forms (even these, in the mouth of the multitude, seem rather adulation than adoration of the Deity), and that faith has become a mere compound of credulity and prejudices—aye, prejudices too, which degrade man from rational being to beast, which completely stifle the power of judgment between true and false, which seem, in fact, carefully fostered for the purpose of extinguishing the last spark of reason! Piety, great God! and religion are become a tissue of ridiculous mysteries; men, who flatly despise reason, who reject and turn away from understanding as naturally corrupt, these, I say, these of all men, are thought, O lie most horrible! to possess light from on High. Verily, if they had but one spark of light from on High, they would not insolently rave, but would learn to worship God more wisely, and would be as marked among their fellows for mercy as they now are for malice; if they were concerned for their opponents' souls, instead of for their own reputations, they would no longer fiercely persecute, but rather be filled with pity and compassion.

Furthermore, if any Divine light were in them, it would appear from their doctrine. I grant that they are never tired of professing their wonder at the profound mysteries of Holy Writ; still I cannot discover that they teach anything but speculations of Platonists and Aristotelians, to which (in order to save their credit for Christianity) they have made Holy Writ conform; not content to rave with the Greeks themselves, they want to make the prophets rave also; showing conclusively, that never even in sleep have they caught a glimpse of Scripture's Divine nature. The very vehemence of their admiration for the mysteries plainly attests, that their belief in the Bible is a formal assent rather than a living faith: and the fact is made still more apparent by their laying down beforehand, as a foundation for the study and true interpretation of Scripture, the principle that it is in every passage true and Divine. Such a doctrine should be reached only after strict scrutiny and thorough comprehension of the Sacred Books (which would teach it much better, for they stand in need of no human fictions), and not be set up on the threshold, as it were, of inquiry.　　　　　　　　　　　　　　　—T P-PREFACE

See Fear, History, Rational Life, Religion

SURPRISE

Surprise is found in one who knows a thing after the first superficial manner [of Knowledge]; for, since from a few particulars he draws a conclusion which is general, he stands surprised whenever he sees anything that goes against his conclusion; like one who, having never seen any sheep except with short tails, is surprised at the sheep from Morocco which have long ones. So it is related of a peasant that he had persuaded himself that beyond his fields there were no others, but when he happened to miss a cow, and was compelled to go and look for her far away, he was surprised at the great number of fields that there were beyond his few acres. And, to be sure, this must also be the case with many Philosophers who have persuaded themselves that beyond this field or little globe, on which they are, there are no more [worlds] (because they have seen no others). But surprise is never felt by him who draws true inferences.   —G 2-III

SYMBOLS
A matter is understood when it is perceived simply by the mind without words or symbols.   —T P-IV

SYMPATHY
Inclination is pleasure, accompanied by the idea of something which is accidentally a cause of pleasure.   —E-III

Pity is pain accompanied by the idea of evil, which has befallen someone else whom we conceive to be like ourselves.

Between pity and sympathy there seems to be no difference, unless perhaps that the former term is used in reference to a particular action, and the latter in reference to a disposition.   —E-III

Envy is hatred, in so far as it induces a man to be pained by another's good fortune, and to rejoice in another's evil fortune.
Envy is generally opposed to sympathy.   —E-III

Sympathy is love, in so far as it induces a man to feel pleasure at another's good fortune, and pain at another's evil fortune.   —E-III
See Antipathy, Rational Life

T

TEMPERANCE
See Emotions, Lust

THANKFULNESS
See Gratitude

THEOLOGIANS
See History

THEOLOGY

Who, unless he were desperate or mad, would wish to bid an incontinent farewell to reason, or to despise the arts and sciences, or to deny reason's certitude? But, in the meanwhile, we cannot wholly absolve them from blame, inasmuch as they invoke the aid of reason for her own defeat, and attempt infallibility to prove her fallible. While they are trying to prove mathematically the authority and truth of theology, and to take away the authority of natural reason, they are in reality only bringing theology under reason's dominion, and proving that her authority has no weight unless natural reason be at the back of it.

If they boast that they themselves assent because of the inward testimony of the Holy Spirit, and that they only invoke the aid of reason because of unbelievers, in order to convince them, not even so can this meet with our approval, for we can easily show that they have spoken either from emotion or vain-glory. It most clearly follows that the Holy Spirit only gives its testimony in favor of works, called by Paul (in Gal. v. 22) the fruits of the Spirit, and is in itself really nothing but the mental acquiescence which follows a good action in our souls. No spirit gives testimony concern-

ing the certitude of matters within the sphere of speculation, save only reason, who is mistress, as we have shown,
of the whole realm of truth. If then they assert that they
possess this Spirit which makes them certain of truth, they
speak falsely, and according to the prejudices of the emotions, or else they are in great dread lest they should be
vanquished by philosophers and exposed to public ridicule,
and therefore they flee, as it were, to the altar; but their
refuge is vain, for what altar will shelter a man who has
outraged reason?   —T P-XV
   See Essence

THEORY OF EDUCATION
   See Happiness

THEORY OF POLITICS
   See Evil

THING AS IT IS IN ITSELF, THE
   See Existence

THINGS
   The order and connection of ideas is the same as the order
and connection of things.   —E-II

   The mind can bring it about, that all bodily modifications
or images of things may be referred to the idea of God.
                                                      —E-V

   The more we understand particular things, the more do
we understand God.   —E-V

   By *particular things*, I mean things which are finite and
have a conditioned existence; but if several individual things
concur in one action, so as to be all simultaneously the effect of one cause, I consider them all, so far, as one particular thing.   —E-II

   Particular things I call *possible* in so far as, while regarding the causes whereby they must be produced, we

know not, whether such causes be determined for producing them.   —E-IV
See Eternity

THIRD KIND OF KNOWLEDGE
See Intellectual Love, Knowledge

THOUGHT
Thought is an attribute of God, or God is a thinking thing.   —E-II
See Grief

TIME
We can only distinctly conceive distance of space or time up to a certain definite limit; that is, all objects distant from us more than two hundred feet, or whose distance from the place where we are exceeds that which we can distinctly conceive, seem to be an equal distance from us, and all in the same plane; so also objects, whose time of existing is conceived as removed from the present by a longer interval than we can distinctly conceive, seem to be all equally distant from the present, and are set down, as it were, to the same moment of time.   —E-IV
See Immortality of the Soul, Mode

TIMIDITY
To an envious man nothing is more delightful than another's misfortune, and nothing more painful than another's success. So every man, according to his emotions, judges a thing to be good or bad, useful or useless. The emotion, which induces a man to turn from that which he wishes, or to wish for that which he turns from, is called *timidity,* which may accordingly be defined as *the fear whereby a man is induced to avoid an evil which he regards as future by encountering a lesser evil.* But if the evil which he fears be shame, timidity becomes *bashfulness.* Lastly, if the desire to avoid a future evil be checked by the fear of another evil, so that the man knows not which to choose,

fear becomes *consternation,* especially if both the evils feared be very great. —E-III

Timidity is the desire to avoid a greater evil, which we dread, by undergoing a lesser evil. —E-III

If any one knows what he must decide to do in order to advance a good thing, and to hinder a bad one, and yet does not do so, then we call it *pusillanimity;* and when the same is very great, we call it *timidity.* —G 2-IX

See Cowardice

TOLERANCE
See Tyranny

TRANSIENT
See Love

TREASON
See Democracy

TRUE GOOD
See Democracy, Happiness

TRUE HUMILITY
See Inferiority, Feeling of

TRUE IDEA
See Ideas

TRUE KNOWLEDGE
See Good and Bad

TRUTH
Truth is an affirmation (or a denial) made about a certain thing, which agrees with the same thing. —G 2-XV

See Blessedness, Falsity, Ideas, Knowledge, Love

TURKS
See Hate

TYRANNY
How much better would it be to restrain popular anger and fury, instead of passing useless laws, which can only be

broken by those who love virtue and the liberal arts, thus
paring down the state till it is too small to harbor men of
talent. What greater misfortune for a state can be conceived than that honorable men should be sent like criminals into exile, because they hold diverse opinions which
they cannot disguise? What, I say, can be more hurtful
than that men who have committed no crime or wickedness
should, simply because they are enlightened, be treated as
enemies and put to death, and that the scaffold, the terror
of evil-doers, should become the arena where the highest
examples of tolerance and virtue are displayed to the
people with all the marks of ignominy that authority can
devise?

He that knows himself to be upright does not fear the
death of a criminal, and shrinks from no punishment; his
mind is not wrung with remorse for any disgraceful deed:
he holds that death in a good cause is no punishment, but
an honor, and that death for freedom is glory.

What purpose then is served by the death of such men,
what example is proclaimed? the cause for which they die
is unknown to the idle and the foolish, hateful to the tur-
bulent, loved by the upright. The only lesson we can
draw from such scenes is to flatter the persecutor, or else
to imitate the victim.

If formal assent is not to be esteemed above conviction,
and if governments are to retain a firm hold of authority
and not be compelled to yield to agitators, it is imperative
that freedom of judgment should be granted, so that men
may live together in harmony, however diverse, or even
openly contradictory their opinions may be. We cannot
doubt that such is the best system of government and open
to the fewest objections, since it is the one most in harmony
with human nature. In a democracy (the most natural form
of government), everyone submits to the control of authority
over his actions, but not over his judgment and reason; that
is, seeing that all cannot think alike, the voice of the

majority has the force of law, subject to repeal if circumstances bring about a change of opinion. In proportion
as the power of free judgment is withheld we depart from
the natural condition of mankind, and consequently the
government becomes more tyrannical.   —T P-XX
   See Obedience

U

UNDERSTANDING

Whatsoever we endeavor in obedience to reason is nothing further than to understand; neither does the mind, in so far as it makes use of reason, judge anything to be useful to it, save such things as are conducive to understanding. —E-IV

We know nothing to be certainly good or evil, save such things as really conduce to understanding, or such as are able to hinder us from understanding. —E-IV

He who clearly and distinctly understands himself and his emotions loves God, and so much the more in proportion as he more understands himself and his emotions. —E-V

As regards the *Understanding* in the thinking thing, it has but one function, namely, to understand clearly and distinctly all things at all times; which produces invariably an infinite or most perfect satisfaction, which cannot omit to do what it does. —G 1-IX

UNION

See Love, Well-Being

UNION WITH GOD

See Freedom, Human

UNIVERSAL NATURE

See Rational Life

UNIVERSALS

See Ideas

UNIVERSE

In the universe there cannot exist two substances without their differing utterly in essence; substance cannot be produced or created—existence pertains to its actual es-

sence; all substance must be infinite or supremely perfect after its kind.   —C-II-O
See Beauty

UNJUSTNESS
See Hate, Natural Right

USEFULNESS
See Desire, Social Life, Virtue

UTOPIA
For this is certain, that men are of necessity liable to passions, and so constituted as to pity those who are ill, and envy those who are well off; and to be prone to vengeance more than to mercy and moreover, that every individual wishes the rest to live after his own mind, and to approve what he approves, and reject what he rejects. And so it comes to pass, that, as all are equally eager to be first, they fall to strife, and do their utmost mutually to oppress one another; and he who comes out conqueror is more proud of the harm he has done to the other, than of the good he has done to himself. And although all are persuaded, that religion, on the contrary, teaches every man to love his neighbor as himself, that is to defend another's right just as much as his own, yet we showed that this persuasion has too little power over the passions. It avails, indeed, in the hour of death, when disease has subdued the very passions, and man lies inert, or in temples, where men hold no traffic, but least of all, where it is most needed, in the law-court or the palace. We showed too, that reason can, indeed, do much to restrain and moderate the passions, but we saw at the same time, that the road, which reason herself points out, is very steep; so that such as persuade themselves, that the masses or men distracted by politics can ever be induced to live according to the bare dictate of reason, must be dreaming of the poetic golden age, or of a stage-play.   —P T-I
See Evil

V

VACILLATION

This disposition of the mind, which arises from two contrary emotions, is called *vacillation*; it stands to the emotions in the same relation as doubt does to the imagination; vacillation and doubt do not differ one from the other; except as greater differs from less. The human body is composed of a variety of individual parts of different nature, and may therefore be affected in a variety of different ways by one and the same body; and contrariwise, as one and the same thing can be affected in many ways, it can also in many different ways affect one and the same part of the body. Hence we can easily conceive, that one and the same object may be the cause of many and conflicting emotions.   —E-III

See Courage

VACILLATION OF THE SOUL

If we conceive that anyone loves, desires, or hates anything which we ourselves love, desire, or hate, we shall thereupon regard the thing in question with more steadfast love. On the contrary, if we think that anyone shrinks from something that we love, we shall undergo vacillation of soul.

From the foregoing, it follows that everyone endeavors, as far as possible, to cause others to love what he himself loves, and to hate what he himself hates: as the poet says: "As lovers let us share every hope and every fear: ironhearted were he who should love what the other leaves."

—E-III

If we remove a disturbance of the spirit, or emotion, from the thought of an external cause, and unite it to other thoughts, then will the love or hatred towards that external cause, and also the vacillations of spirit which arise from these emotions, be destroyed. —E-V

VAIN-GLORY
See Theology

VALOR
See Lust

VANITY
See Fame

VENERATION
If the object of wonder be a man's prudence, industry, or anything of that sort, inasmuch as the said man is thereby regarded as far surpassing ourselves, wonder is called *Veneration.* —E-III

VENGEANCE
See Gratitude

VERULAM
See Perception

VICE
See Evil, Fear, Liberty

VIRTUE
The highest good of those who follow virtue is common to all, and therefore all can equally rejoice therein.
Someone may ask how it would be, if the highest good of those who follow after virtue were not common to all? Would it not then follow, as above, that men living in obedience to reason, that is, men in so far as they agree in nature, would be at variance one with another? To such an inquiry I make answer, that it follows not accidentally but from the very nature of reason, that man's highest good

is common to all, inasmuch as it is deduced from the very essence of man, in so far as defined by reason; and that a man could neither be, nor be conceived without the power of taking pleasure in this highest good. For it belongs to the essence of the human mind to have an adequate knowledge of the eternal and infinite essence of God.   —E-IV

The mind's highest good is the knowledge of God, and the mind's highest virtue is to know God.   —E-IV

Humility is not a virtue, or does not arise from reason.
    —E-IV

Effigies, triumphs, and other incitements to virtue, are signs rather of slavery than liberty. For rewards of virtue are granted to slaves, not free men. I admit, indeed, that men are very much stimulated by these incitements; but, as in the first instance, they are awarded to great men, so afterwards, with the growth of envy, they are granted to cowards and men swollen from the extent of their wealth, to the great indignation of all good men. Secondly, those, who boast of their ancestors' effigies and triumphs, think they are wronged, if they are not preferred to others. Lastly, not to mention other objections, it is certain that equality, which once cast off the general liberty is lost, can by no means be maintained, from the time that peculiar honors are by public law decreed to any man renowned for his virtue.
    —P T-X

Man, in so far as he is determined to a particular action because he has inadequate ideas, cannot be absolutely said to act in obedience to virtue; he can only be so described, in so far as he is determined for the action because he understands.   —E-IV

The highest endeavor of the mind, and the highest virtue is to understand things by the third kind of knowledge.
    —E-V

The more every man endeavors, and is able to seek what is useful to him—in other words, to preserve his own being —the more is he endowed with virtue; on the contrary, in proportion as a man neglects to seek what is useful to him, that is, to preserve his own being, he is wanting in power.

No one, therefore, neglects seeking his own good, or preserving his own being, unless he be overcome by causes external and foreign to his nature. No one, I say, from the necessity of his own nature, or otherwise than under compulsion from external causes, shrinks from food, or kills himself: which latter may be done in a variety of ways. A man, for instance, kills himself under the compulsion of another man, who twists round his right hand, wherewith he happened to have taken up a sword, and forces him to turn the blade against his own heart; or again, he may open his own veins—that is, to escape a greater evil by incurring a lesser; or, lastly, latent external causes may so disorder his imagination, and so affect his body, that it may assume a nature contrary to its former one, and whereof the idea cannot exist in the mind. But that a man, from the necessity of his own nature, should endeavor to become non-existent, is as impossible as that something should be made out of nothing, as everyone will see for himself, after a little reflection.   —E-IV

No virtue can be conceived as prior to this endeavor to preserve one's own being.

The effort for self-preservation is the first and only foundation of virtue. For prior to this principle nothing can be conceived, and without it no virtue can be conceived.
                                                          —E-IV

To act absolutely in obedience to virtue is in us the same thing as to act, to live, or to preserve one's being (these three terms are identical in meaning) in accordance with the dictates of reason on the basis of seeking what is useful to one's self.   —E-IV

All are able to obey, whereas there are but very few, compared with the aggregate of humanity, who can acquire the habit of virtue under the unaided guidance of reason. Thus if we had not the testimony of Scripture, we should doubt of the salvation of nearly all men. —T P-XV

See Blessedness; Desire; Envy; Essence; Freedom, Human; Ideas; Liberty; Natural Right; Passions; Power; Race; Rational Life

W

WELL-BEING

We can attain well-being through knowledge. This kind of knowledge does not result from something else, but from a direct revelation of the object itself to the understanding. And if that object is glorious and good, then the soul becomes necessarily united with it. Hence it follows incontrovertibly that it is this knowledge which evokes love. So that when we get to know God after this manner then (as He cannot reveal Himself, nor become known to us otherwise than as the most glorious and best of all) we must necessarily become united with Him. And only in this union, as we have already remarked, does our blessedness consist.

I do not say that we must know Him just as He is, or adequately, for it is sufficient for us to know Him to some extent, in order to be united with Him. For even the knowledge that we have of the body is not such that we know it just as it is, or perfectly; and yet, what a union! what a love!

That this intelligence, which is the knowledge of God, is not the consequence of something else, but immediate, is evident from what we have proved before, (namely) that He is the cause of all knowledge that is acquired through itself alone, and through no other thing; moreover, also from this, that we are so united with Him by nature that without Him we can neither be, nor be known. And for this reason, since there is such a close union between God and us, it is evident that we cannot know Him except directly.

—G 2-XXII

See Law of Nature

WICKED
See Essence

WILL

Desire, we have said, is the inclination which the soul has towards something which it chooses as a good; whence it follows that before our desire inclines towards something outside, we have already inwardly decided that such a thing is good, and this affirmation, or, stated more generally, the power to affirm and to deny, is called the Will.

It thus turns on the question whether our Affirmations are made voluntarily or necessarily, that is, whether we can make any affirmation or denial about a thing without some external cause compelling us to do so. Now we have already shown that a thing which is not explained through itself, or whose *existence* does not pertain to its *essence*, must necessarily have an external cause; and that a cause which is to produce something must produce it necessarily; it must therefore, also follow that each separate act of willing this or that, each separate act of affirming or denying this or that of a thing, these, I say, must also result from some external cause: so also the definition which we have given of a cause is, that it cannot be free.

Possibly this will not satisfy some who are accustomed to keep their understanding busy with things of fancy more than with definite things which really exist in Nature; and, through doing so, they come to regard a thing of fancy not as such, but as a real thing. For, because man has now this, now that volition, he forms in his soul a general mode which he calls Will, just as from this man and that man he also forms the Idea of man; and because he does not adequately distinguish the real things from the things of fancy, he comes to regard the things of fancy as things which really exist in Nature, and so he regards himself as a cause of some things. This happens not infrequently in the treatment of the subject about which we are speaking.

For if any one is asked why people want this or that, the answer usually given is, because they have a will. But, since the Will, as we have said, is only an Idea of our willing this or that, and therefore only a mode of thought, a thing of fancy, and not a real thing, nothing can be caused by it; for out of nothing, nothing comes. And so, as we have shown that the will is not a thing in Nature, but only in fancy, I also think it unnecessary to ask whether the will is free or not free. —G 2-XVI

Will cannot be called a free cause, but only a necessary cause. —E-I

Will and understanding are one and the same. —E-II

The act of willing has been identified by some with affirmation and denial. Understanding (affirming or denying) is purely passive; it is an awareness, in the mind, of the essence and existence of things; so that it is never we who affirm or deny something of a thing, but it is the thing itself that affirms or denies, in us, something of itself.

Possibly some will not admit this, because it seems to them that they are well able to affirm or to deny of the thing something different from what they know about the thing. But this is only because they have no idea of the conception which the mind has of the thing apart from or without the words (in which it is expressed). It is quite true that (when there are reasons which prompt us to do so) we can, in words or by some other means, represent the thing to others differently from what we know it to be; but we can never bring it so far, either by words or by any other means, that we should feel about the things differently from what we feel about them; that is impossible, and clearly so to all who have for once attended to their understanding itself apart from the use of words or other significant signs.

Against this, however, some perchance may say: If it is not we, but the thing itself, that makes the affirmation and denial about itself in us, then nothing can be affirmed or denied except what is in agreement with the thing; and consequently there is no falsity. For we have said that falsity consists in affirming (or denying) aught of a thing which does not accord with that thing; that is, what the thing does not affirm or deny about itself. I think, however, that if only we consider well what we have already said about Truth and Falsity, then we shall see at once that these objections have already been sufficiently answered. For we have said that the object is the cause of what is affirmed or denied thereof, be it true or false: falsity arising thus, namely, because, when we happen to know something or a part of an object, we imagine that the object (although we only know very little of it) nevertheless affirms or denies that of itself as a whole; this takes place mostly in feeble minds, which receive very easily a mode or an idea through a slight action of the object, and make no further affirmation or denial apart from this.

Lastly, it might also be objected that there are many things which we sometimes want and [sometimes also] do not want, as, for example, to assert something about a thing or not to assert it, to speak the truth, and not to speak it, and so forth. But this results from the fact that Desire is not adequately distinguished from Will. For the Will, according to those who maintain that there is a Will, is only the activity of the understanding whereby we affirm or deny something about a thing, with regard to good or evil. Desire, however, is the disposition of the soul to obtain or to do something for the sake of the good or evil that is discerned therein; so that even after we have made an affirmation or denial about the thing, Desire still remains, namely, when we have ascertained or affirmed that the thing is good; such is the Will, according to their statements, while desire is the inclination, which we only subsequently feel, to advance it—so that, even according to their own statements, the Will may well exist without the

Desire, but not the Desire without the Will, which must
have preceded it.   —G 2-XVI

See Appetite, Desire, Emotions, Falsity, Free Will, Ideas,
Knowledge

WILL OF GOD
See Sin

WISDOM

So long as we are not assailed by emotions contrary to
our nature, we have the power of arranging and associating
the modifications of our body according to the intellectual
order.

By this power of rightly arranging and associating the
bodily modifications we can guard ourselves from being
easily affected by evil emotions. Greater force is needed
for controlling the emotions, when they are arranged and
associated according to the intellectual order, than when
they are uncertain and unsettled. The best we can do, therefore, so long as we do not possess a perfect knowledge of
our emotions, is to frame a system of right conduct, or fixed
practical precepts, to commit it to memory, and to apply
it forthwith to the particular circumstances which now and
again meet us in life, so that our imagination may become
fully imbued therewith, and that it may be always ready
to our hand.

For instance, we have laid down among the rules of
life, that hatred should be overcome with love or high-
mindedness, and not requited with hatred in return.
Now, that this precept of reason may be always ready to
our hand in time of need, we should often think over and
reflect upon the wrongs generally committed by men, and
in what manner and way they may be best warded off by
high-mindedness: we shall thus associate the idea of wrong
with the idea of this precept, which accordingly will always
be ready for use when a wrong is done to us. If we keep
also in readiness the notion of our true advantage, and of

the good which follows from mutual friendships, and common fellowships; further, if we remember that complete acquiescence is the result of the right way of life, and that men, no less than everything else, act by the necessity of their nature: in such case I say the wrong, or the hatred, which commonly arises therefrom, will engross a very small part of our imagination and will be easily overcome; or, if the anger which springs from a grievous wrong be not overcome easily, it will nevertheless be overcome, though not without a spiritual conflict, far sooner than if we had not thus reflected on the subject beforehand.

We should, in the same way, reflect on courage as a means of overcoming fear; the ordinary dangers of life should frequently be brought to mind and imagined, together with the means whereby through readiness of resource and strength of mind we can avoid and overcome them. But we must note, that in arranging our thoughts and conceptions we should always bear in mind that which is good in every individual thing, in order that we may always be determined to action by an emotion of pleasure. For instance, if a man sees that he is too keen in the pursuit of honor, let him think over its right use, the end for which it should be pursued, and the means whereby he may attain it. Let him not think of its misuse, and its emptiness, and the fickleness of mankind, and the like, whereof no man thinks except through a morbidness of disposition; with thoughts like these do the most ambitious most torment themselves, when they despair of gaining the distinctions they hanker after, and in thus giving vent to their anger would fain appear wise. Wherefore it is certain that those, who cry out the loudest against the misuse of honor and the vanity of the world, are those who most greedily covet it. This is not peculiar to the ambitious, but is common to all who are ill-used by fortune, and who are infirm in spirit. For a poor man also, who is miserly, will talk incessantly of the misuse of wealth and of the vices of the rich; whereby he merely torments himself, and shows the world that he is intolerant, not only of his own poverty, but also of other people's riches. So, again, those who have been ill received by a woman they love think of nothing but the inconstancy, treachery, and other stock faults of the fair sex; all of which they consign to oblivion, directly they are again taken into favor by their sweetheart. Thus he who would govern his emotions and appetite solely by the love of freedom strives, as far as he can, to gain a knowledge of the virtues and their causes, and to fill his spirit with the joy which arises from the true knowledge of them: he will in no wise desire to dwell on men's faults, or to carp at his fellows, or to revel in a false show of freedom. Whosoever will diligently observe and practice these precepts (which indeed are not difficult) will verily, in a short space of time, be able, for the most part, to direct his actions according to the commandments of reason.

—E-V

See Blessedness

WOMEN

Are women under men's authority by nature or institution? For if it has been by mere institution, then we had no reason compelling us to exclude women from government. But if we consult experience itself, we shall find that the origin of it is in their weakness. For there has never been a case of men and women reigning together, but wherever on the earth men are found, there we see that men rule, and women are ruled, and that on this plan, both sexes live in harmony. But on the other hand, the Amazons, who are reported to have held rule of old, did not suffer men to stop in their country, but reared only their female children, killing the males to whom they gave birth. But if by nature women were equal to men, and were equally distinguished by force of character and ability, in which human power and therefore human right chiefly consist; surely among nations so many and different some would be found, where both sexes rule alike, and others, where men are ruled by women, and so brought up, that they can make less use of their abilities.

And since this is nowhere the case, one may assert with perfect propriety, that women have not by nature equal right with men: but that they necessarily give way to men, and that thus it cannot happen, that both sexes should rule alike, much less that men should be ruled by women. But if we further reflect upon human passions, how men, in fact, generally love women merely from the passion of lust, and esteem their cleverness and wisdom in proportion to the excellence of their beauty, and also how very ill-disposed men are to suffer the women they love to show any sort of favor to others, and other facts of this kind, we shall easily see that men and women cannot rule alike without great hurt to peace.   —P T-XI

WONDER

Wonder is the conception of anything, wherein the mind comes to a stand, because the particular concept in question has no connection with other concepts.

The mind, from the contemplation of one thing, straightway falls to the contemplation of another thing, namely, because the images of the two things are so associated and arranged, that one follows the other. This state of association is impossible, if the image of the thing be new; the mind will then be at a stand in the contemplation thereof, until it is determined by other causes to think of something else.

Thus the conception of a new object, considered in itself, is of the same nature as other conceptions; hence, I do not include wonder among the emotions, nor do I see why I should so include it, inasmuch as this distraction of the mind arises from no positive cause drawing away the mind from other objects, but merely from the absence of a cause, which should determine the mind to pass from the contemplation of one object to the contemplation of another.

—E-III

Mental modification, or imagination of a particular thing, in so far as it is alone in the mind, is called *Wonder*; but if it be excited by an object of fear, it is called *Consternation*, because wonder at an evil keeps a man so engrossed in the simple contemplation thereof, that he has no power to think of anything else whereby he might avoid the evil.

—E-III

See Devotion

WORDS

A thing is called sacred and Divine when it is designed for promoting piety, and continues sacred so long as it is religiously used: if the users cease to be pious, the thing ceases to be sacred: if it be turned to base uses, that which was formerly sacred becomes unclean and profane. For instance, a certain spot was named by the patriarch Jacob the house of God, because he worshipped God there revealed to him: by the prophets the same spot was called the house of iniquity (see Amos v. 5, and Hosea x. 5), because the Israelites were wont, at the instigation of Jeroboam, to sacrifice there to idols. Another example puts the matter in the plainest light. Words gain their meaning solely from their usage, and if they are arranged according to their accepted signification so as to move those who read them to devotion, they will become sacred, and the book so written will be sacred also. But if their usage afterwards dies out so that the words have no meaning, or the book becomes utterly neglected, whether from unworthy motives, or because it is no longer needed, then the words and the book will lose both their use and their sanctity: lastly, if these same words be otherwise arranged, or if their customary meaning becomes perverted into its opposite, then

both the words and the book containing them become, instead of sacred, impure and profane.   —T P-XII
See Ideas

WORSHIP

Inward worship of God and piety in itself are within the sphere of everyone's private rights, and cannot be alienated. A man best fulfills God's law who worships Him, according to His command, through acts of justice and charity; it follows, therefore, that wherever justice and charity have the force of law and ordinance, there is God's kingdom.
      —T P-XIX

Man obeys God when he worships him in sincerity, and, on the contrary, does wrong when he is led by blind desire.
      —P T-II

WRITING
See Persuasion

WRONG
See Democracy

WRONGDOING

For all laws which can be broken without any injury to another, are counted but a laughing-stock, and are so far from bridling the desires and lusts of men, that on the contrary they stimulate them. For "we are ever eager for forbidden fruit, and desire what is denied."   —P T-X

Reason teaches one to practice piety, and be of a calm and gentle spirit, which cannot be done save under government; and, further, as it is impossible for a multitude to be guided, as it were, by one mind, as under dominion is required, unless it has laws ordained according to the dictate of reason; men who are accustomed to live under dominion are not, therefore, using words so improperly, when they call that wrongdoing which is done against the sentence of reason, because the laws of the best dominion ought to be framed according to that dictate.   —P T-II